D0843315

BETTY M. FLINT is with the Faculty of Education, Institute of Child Study, at the University of Toronto.

New Hope for Deprived Children is the carefully documented story of the development of a group of children from infancy through early adolescence. Exhibiting the effects of severe institutional deprivation in the early part of their lives, these children became the focus of a therapeutic programme within an institution designed to relieve their serious developmental deficiencies. The programme and its effects confirmed the faith of the researchers involved that recovery to a certain degree was possible, even within an institutional setting. Further recovery was effected by later placement in foster and adoptive homes.

The lives of twenty-eight of these children have been recorded and the data analysed. This book presents their stories in both human and scientific terms. The guidance procedures and therapeutic intervention were based on a personality theory of 'security,' which allowed the research and guidance team to provide a consistent frame of reference to all procedures designed to move the children increasingly closer to 'normal' behaviour. The range of adaptation to homes and community reflects the individual capacities of each child and the capabilities of each family to sponsor such individuality. Both the group analysis and the individual histories provide fascinating information and, additionally, pose many fundamental questions about human development.

BETTY M. FLINT

New hope for
deprived children

UNIVERSITY OF TORONTO PRESS
Toronto Buffalo London

© University of Toronto Press 1978
Toronto   Buffalo   London
Printed in Canada

Library of Congress Cataloging in Publication Data

Flint, Betty Margaret.
    New hope for deprived children.

    Bibliography: p.
    Includes index.
    1. Children – Institutional care – Canada – Longitudi-
nal studies. 2. Children, Adopted – Canada – Longitudinal studies. I. Title.
    HV887.C3F57   362.7'1   77-16287
    ISBN 0-8020-5394-7

To Mary Kilgour

Contents

Preface

This is a study of children reared during their earliest years in a severely depriving institution, and later placed in adoptive homes. It describes their growing up over a period of seventeen years; what was done with them; what was recorded about them; and what they have become, as young adults.

Those of us who in 1956–7 began the investigation reported here had only a glimmer of the difficulties which were to be involved in keeping it going for the following seventeen years. I think it is fair to say that we probably believed in the ultimate worth of each individual under study to find a place in the sun. This belief was supported by somewhat more scientific convictions that the human organism has within it the capacity to strive for its optimal developmental expression, given the support of a physically and emotionally nurturing environment. Willy-nilly, we have been able to convince a variety of funding groups, foundations, government officials, and university authorities that the outcome of our investigation would surely repay their yearly investment in our effort and knowledge.

The research team which has worked so well together over these years has become attached to the children and families who have allowed us to share their lives. The yearly agony of finding funds which was the lot of the chief investigator was mitigated by the human rewards of partaking in the drama of each child's life and by putting on a pair of two-way spectacles which has enabled us to act as a catalyst sharing the parent's vision of his child and the child's vision of the parent in his ultimate attainment of maturity.

It is not surprising that the thrust to carry out this study should come from the Institute of Child Study, University of Toronto. The fortunes of the Institute of Child Study have been identified with longitudinal research since its beginning in 1925. The founder, Dr W.E. Blatz, was convinced that only through longitudinal study would the key to human development be found. Those colleagues who worked with him over the years came to share his views and offered the necessary support and encouragement to the team on this project to carry them over the difficulties which are an inevitable part of any such long-term undertaking. The sophistication developed from two previous longitudinal studies in which families and children associated with the laboratory school of the Institute for almost fifty years had participated was useful in both data gathering procedures and analysis of our information. Two people in particular have been involved, both of whom have spent many years with the Institute. Miss Dorothy Millichamp, the assistant director of the Institute of Child Study, who shared her wisdom in setting up the rehabilitative programme described here and helped evaluate changes, write reports, and assess outcomes, has left her quiet mark on the quality of this venture. Dr Mary Northway, research coordinator of the Institute and an authority in her own field of sociometry, has helped both by finding money and insisting that results be published, thus putting her characteristic stamp on the study. Dr Bruce Quarrington and Mrs Carroll Davis have contributed their particular talents to this study and have enriched its outcome. The research team over the years has included Pearl Karal, Barbara Doidge, Ann Taylor, June Edmunds, and Mary Kilgour. Mary Kilgour's role was crucial to the study, which would never have taken place had she not been its central facilitator. Her dedication and stamina could not have been readily duplicated. Mrs Taylor's particular interest in the nature of a child's conceptualization of his world has enriched our understanding of the total rehabilitative process. Her clinical skills provided the data for guidance techniques when the children were in their homes. It was her responsibility to provide the analysis of the Rorschach data and the reporting of it. Mrs Edmonds ably carried out the final painstaking statistical work on the accumulated data.

Over the years the study was supported by grants from the following sources: the Laidlaw Foundation; the Ontario Mental Health Foundation; the Atkinson Charitable Foundation; the Neathern Foundation; the Blatz Memorial; National Health and Welfare, Canada; the B&B Hamilton Foundation; and the University of Toronto, which permitted the chief investigator time to involve herself.

This book has been published with the help of grants from the Social Science Research Council of Canada, using funds provided by the Canada Council, and from the Publications Fund of the University of Toronto Press and the University of Toronto.

NEW HOPE FOR DEPRIVED CHILDREN

Introduction

This study began in 1957[1] as the result of a search for a group of infants on whom to validate the Flint Infant Security Scale.[2] This test was a behaviour rating scale developed to measure the mental health of infants between the ages of three and twenty-four months. It was based on a modification of the security theory of Dr William Blatz.

Prior to 1957, several satisfactory studies had been carried out which measured the security of groups of infants reared at home. These had yielded a 'normal' range of security scores and appeared consistent from birth to twenty-four months of age. A contrasting group was needed to confirm that the Infant Security Scale would reflect significantly different scores in such a separate group.[3]

At this time child care agencies in Toronto responsible for the welfare of children whose families could not care for them were reacting to the Bowlby (1952) report on maternal deprivation.[4] Every effort was being made to remove infants from institutional care into foster homes in an attempt to prevent the recognized damage to the children's future development. Furthermore, the author's clinical experience had confirmed her belief that institutionally reared infants suffered immediate, if not long-term, impairment to intellectual function and to their capacity to relate to both adults and peers. In the past these deficiencies had served to preclude many of them from either foster or adoptive homes. Hence, by 1957, all but one institution for the care of infants had vanished from the city of Toronto. The single one remaining was the Neil McNeil Home administered by the Toronto Catholic Children's Aid Society. Because of a long-standing

1 Betty M. Flint, *The Security of Infants.* Toronto: University of Toronto Press, 1959.
2 The Flint Infant Security Scale. Guidance Centre, Faculty of Education, University of Toronto, 1974.
3 See Appendix.
4 John Bowlby, *Maternal Care and Mental Health.* W.H.O., Geneva, 1952.

shortage of Catholic foster homes the fifty-year-old institution was seriously overcrowded. Equipped to accommodate fifty infants under two years of age, it had become a residence of eighty-five children from birth to three and one-half years of age. A constant trickle of newborns was admitted and remained without foster homes until they reached approximately four years of age. These children suffered the classical syndromes of severly deprived institutionalized infants.

Accordingly, a group of sixteen of these infants were assessed on the Infant Security Scale and presented a frightening picture of declining mental health from the youngest to the oldest. The longer institutional care was prolonged the more serious was the deficiency.

Such a deviation in pattern from the normal groups of infants previously measured confirmed the validity of the Infant Security Scale. However, the researcher's feelings of elation regarding validity were superseded by the depression of observing the horrifying waste of human potential in these infants. Intervention was demanded. Our observations had led to the belief that the drastic decline observed in mental health from three to twenty-four months of age could be prevented or at least modified. Some rehabilitation was thought possible.

This conviction was reported to the Catholic Children's Aid and a partnership was eventually effected between the research staff of the Institute of Child Study, University of Toronto, and the Catholic Children's Aid Society.[5] The goal was to bring to a halt the recognized waste of human resources and the huge support system which had accompanied the effects of early institutional care. The agency was eager to see an end to the creation of consecutive generations of incompetent, non-functioning youngsters who grew to physical maturity and still remained a charge on the community.

A system had been developed over the years to maintain these bizarrely functioning children in a series of institutions. The Neil McNeil Home cared for them until they were about three and one-half to four years old, after which they were sent to a second institution where they remained until age seven. By this time they were so remote from the normal stream of home-reared peers that their capacity to adapt to home life was seriously damaged. This necessitated removal to another institutional arrangement from which the children were expected to attend a community school in preparation for the task of supporting themselves by age sixteen or eighteen. Such expectation was rarely borne out. Once they were launched in the community, the lack of competence in social, emotional, and intellectual spheres of life usually led to a breakdown of function and the

5 Betty M. Flint, *The Child and the Institution: A Study of Deprivation and Recovery.* Toronto: University of Toronto Press, 1966.

children became the delinquents, the drifters, the recipients of welfare, and eventually of a further form of institutional care such as training schools, mental hospitals, or penal institutions.

Through the joint efforts of the Institute of Child Study and the Catholic Children's Aid, money was obtained for the total rehabilitation of the institution reported here. From 1957 to 1974 these children, and ultimately their adoptive parents, shared part of their lives with the research staff of this study. The process of growing together was a deeply moving one which has opened our eyes to some facets of human development, freshened our awareness of the miracle of human individuality and resilience, and warmed our hearts to the children we helped to grow. The intensity of our relationship with the children allowed us to know their qualities very well, and we wanted to provide the best possible future for each child. We hoped for wisdom to predict future adjustments from our intimate knowledge of them after therapy. Predictions which were made in infancy and during the pre-school years have been surprisingly accurate in some instances. When our predictions were wrong, we sought evidence to indicate why they failed. When they were right we sought the early symptoms which provided the basis for our sound judgment. We have learned something, but not all. Some of what we have learned can be found herein.

1

The beginning

At the time the study of these institutionalized children began, they were housed in a beautiful, large, two-storey building. Originally a huge residence, it had been adapted to the care of young children. The centre hall plan lent itself to an arrangement of a series of rooms running off the halls, both upstairs and down. Within the rooms there was usually space for six or eight cribs. In one corner was a sink and a changing space for the youngest children. Between the cots, wooden partitions had been erected to half the height of the room, with glass from there to the ceiling. Around the cots sheets had been draped which prevented the children from seeing out. This arrangement had been adopted for the purpose of isolating the children to prevent the spread of infection which bedevils all young children in unstimulating institutional care.

The oldest children were cared for on the ground floor and the youngest on the second floor. Because of unsuccessful attempts at toilet training, no washrooms had been provided for the children for either toilet training purposes or to institute a programme of self-help in washing or grooming. Total reliance on potties was necessary for toilet training.

There was no provision for a play area within the building. The older children, some of whom were toddlers, were placed in the middle of the room in which they lived in order to have the freedom of the floor for a short period of time each day. No playthings were provided. The oldest group of children, approximately three to three-and-a-half years of age, had a room in which the cribs were pushed back to provide for a long bench from which they could eat. The space provided by this arrangement was also used as free play space for up to three hours a day. The only toys provided were cardboard cartons thrown randomly on the floor.

The younger children upstairs had no provision for play and were seldom taken from their cribs except for washing down and changing. A toy was sometimes tied to the side of the crib where it hung for months. Toys that inadvertently fell to the floor were never returned to the crib because of the danger of infection. Meal time was devoid of any pleasant ritual aspect. Food was prepared for children of all ages in approximately the same way and brought to each nursery on a tray. The oldest children had the same mushy mixture that was offered to the youngest. All foods were mixed together as a method of hurrying the procedure. This, of course, destroyed the colour and flavour of whatever separate foods might be present in the mix. The feeding was a hurried procedure with the attendants spooning it into the children as fast as possible. No child was allowed to help himself because it slowed down efficiency. No solids such as Zwieback, which the children could eat themselves, were given. The youngest babies were held for a bottle feeding but, as soon as each was capable of sucking without danger of choking, the bottle was propped on the pillow. The oldest children drank from a cup held by an adult. Some limited opportunity was provided for self-help in the feeding routine after twenty months of age.

Large cupboards were used to store clothing which was shared by all children and allowed for several changes a day. The caretakers were charged with responsibility for some of the laundry. No singular item of clothing was possessed by any one child. The nature of the care offered to the children was highly efficient. There was no time for cuddling, petting, chatting, or playing and this was reflected in the surprising silence of the children themselves. The dearth of interaction with the children was further exaggerated by the nature of their caretakers. With the exception of some nursing staff who had become the administrators, the major caretakers were nuns in transit from various European countries through Toronto. They were not child oriented and caretaking was not the focus of their lives. Very little communication took place between the nuns themselves, who spoke a variety of languages, and between the nuns and the children. No relationship could be built between infants and transient caretakers.

The house was surrounded by large, beautiful garden areas replete with fruit trees which blossomed profusely in the spring. Well-tended gardens reflected attentive caretaking. In one corner of the garden was a large, two-storey coach house, a remnant of earlier, more elegant life style. This had three separate rooms on the ground floor with washroom and small kitchen and two bedrooms upstairs. It was not used for the care of the children but, rather, served as a centre for some volunteer activity – sewing of clothing for the children and mending of sheets, etc., for the institution.

There was a marked similarity in the routine for all children, regardless of age. Uniformity of care for young infants allowed for interchangeability of staff on the first floor. Similarly, uniform care was considered desirable for the toddlers. Each child had almost identical experience from the time of his entrance to his discharge. They were placed in individual 'wards' according to age and moved from youngest to oldest through the intervening sequence of wards until they were three-and-a-half to four years of age. Such procedure prepared them for graduation to the next institution, one adapted to the status of four, five, and six year olds.

When the study was initiated the first systematic observation of these children was made over a period of six months. The Flint Infant Security Scale was used to measure the mental health of sixteen of the babies. Four children were observed at each of the following age levels (0-6 months), (6-12 months), (12-18 months), (18-24 months). By such selection we were able to demonstrate changes which might take place as institutional care was prolonged in the life of the children.

The outcome of the mental health measurement revealed that the mental health scores on these babies decreased significantly as age increased and institutional care was prolonged (see Appendix, Table 1). In the case of every child but one, the first score was significantly higher than the last. It was evident that the mental health of these babies had been adversely affected to a serious degree by their institutional experiences.

Furthermore, the more prolonged the experience, the more extreme was the effect. The most rapid decline was evident in the youngest children, an observation that seemed to reinforce the recognition of the vulnerability of the very young to adverse experience and, conversely, their capacity to respond resiliently to a 'salutory environment.'

The second most impressive finding was the extent of the individuality evident in the children. There were startling differences in security scores of children whose histories, physical well-being, length of time in the institution and quality of caretaking seemed identical. The most extreme example of this was demonstrated by two nine-month infants whose score differed by 43 points. Even the plotting of scores over five months demonstrated unique differences in the pattern of decline (see Appendix, Figures 2 and 3). It was evident that each child had a highly unique response to his institutional experience, a fact needing consideration when planning methods and quality of caretaking.

Although routine transfer from one nursery to the next seemed like a move from one barren surrounding to another, the babies, with three exceptions, showed a marked decrease in security scores immediately after the move. Such a decrease may have been the result of their need to become attached to the minute details of their surrounding in the absence of a human with whom they might form their primary attachment. It was speculated that this might indicate that the texture of one's crib, the bump in a particular spot in one's mattress, the spot on the wall that had been missed in the cleaning, the inevitable creak in the floor which resulted from someone passing by, became an essential part of the way in which a child defined himself in his world. Hence, removal from such seemingly trivial details of one barren environment to another equally devoid of unique characteristics created a vacuum within the child which left him without the trivial objects and events around which he had built his concept of self. In the absence of significant maternal figures and focused stimuli he had defined who he was by 'apparently' insignificant objects and events in his life.

When the security scores of these deprived infants were compared over a period of time with a group of home-reared infants, it was evident that the institutionalized infants scored consistently lower than the others (see Appendix, Table 2 and Figure 4). The fact that the difference between the two groups was relatively small up to six months of age and then became increasingly dramatic would indicate that something in the institutional environment was able to sustain the children within the early months of their lives at a level comparable in some instances with that of children reared at home. It was notable that after nine months of age the decline in mental health scores became accelerated when many of the deprived children showed little capacity to either respond to deliberate stimulation or to make any demands on their world. Increasing inhibition of motor activity and immobility of expressiveness either in body posturing or facial expression was manifest.

Observations of the children led us to speculate further that we were looking at two contradictory phenomena. One was the fact that each child living in closely similar surroundings was an individual in spite of it. The second fact was that a rating of the children along a continuum of sociability or non-sociability when defining characteristics of the group would find the children falling into three major categories. Such a conviction arose from analysis of the infant security record which enabled us to examine the strength and weakness of each child's adjustment to his circumstances.

Although a warm, continuous relationship with one or two persons was essential for all the children, there was apparently a difference in the way each child developed his own channel of communication with his meagre environment. The first way was that of the highly socially oriented infant who responded immediately to direct physical contact. Hence, when attempting therapy with this kind of child, intervention by means of picking up, cuddling, stroking, bouncing, and talking seemed the most directly effective. The second group of children rather than being oriented to people seemed to maintain contact through the materials and inanimate objects of their environment and through the opportunity to manipulate them. Children of this nature might remain apathetic towards a purely social game with adults but could allow themselves to respond to a game with play materials and indirectly permit a social relationship to be established with their own particular world. The children in the third group were neither highly socially oriented nor highly related to their material world. These were the children who might be described as WATCHERS. These children, less physically active than either of the other two groups of children would carefully observe the activity of anything within their view. This watching seemed to be an active process which kept them alive to a certain degree to the events of their environment.

In recognition of these differences the methods of therapeutic intervention which followed in the lives of these children made use of these qualities as the predominant means of establishing a relationship. It was recognized that some of the children did not clearly fall into any of the three categories and would be found on the continuum between classifications. Detailed analysis of their infant security tests was needed to establish the best possible process for therapy.

LORIE *

Lorie provides an example of the child who falls into the group most clearly oriented to social interaction – a little girl, seven months of age when first observed. She was one of the children whose progress was reported monthly by means of the Infant Security Scale. Her development was followed from her seventh to eleventh month, by which time the key to her treatment seemed evident.

Lorie's Monthly Infant Security Score

Age (months)	
7	+49
8	+40
9	+44
10	+29
11	+21

Lorie's steady decline in mental health was evident in her changed behaviour from an eager, interested, lovable baby at seven months, to a solemn, sad, inert youngster at eleven months. The circumstances of her environment dictated this rapid decline.

* *The Security of Infants* – 1959.

In her first nursery her bed was at the door where she could see out and be seen by the caretakers passing up and down the hall. She was accessible to patting and to being picked up briefly by the fleeting adults. Sometimes she was carried to morning chapel. Limited conversation was a part of her experience.

When moved to another ward she was placed in a cot removed from this stimulation and became merely one of a number of children, not singled out for attention. Her protest was expressed for about a month by screaming and crying. As no response was elicited she seemed to give up, withdrawing into apathy and responding meagrely to deliberate stimulation. She spent long periods of time rocking or standing with her eyes closed, her head resting dejectedly on the rail of her crib.

Analysis of her security profile over the five-month period indicated a highly secure infant at seven months of age, maintaining her security by a high level of both acceptance and dependence and a high expenditure of effort. Both these healthy assets started to dissipate by eight months of age and continued to do so until eleven months, when observation terminated. The lack of refusal on both dependence and effort categories indicate the encroachment of apathy regarding the people and events of her world.

It is evident that Lorie responds most directly to physical and social contact with adults. This seems to be her life-line. While her initial interest in toys and routine procedures faded, she still remained responsive to and sought out tactile contact such as cuddling. Her rapid decline reflecting this loss lends support to the supposition that she is particularly vulnerable to the loss of the human element in her environment. Such vulnerability suggests that she would recover her mental health by building a relationship with one or two people who would initiate the process by considerable physical contact and vocalization.

ERNEST

One of the children first observed in the institution was sixteen-months-old Ernest. Although fleetingly interested in people and playthings, he more typically demonstrated the characteristics of the 'watcher.' The maternal and stimulus deprivation had already made its impact to a serious degree by the time he was first observed. The tone of his behaviour was passive and his facial expression and communicative processes were extremely limited. His Infant Security rating indicated that he was a passively accepting child who shied away from physical contact either of a playful nature or in the nature of cuddling and patting. Rocking and thumb sucking were chronic tension releasers. His only active asset was his evidence of temper tantrums.

Ernest's Security scores

CA (months)	Security score
16.1	+.12
17	+.10
17.9	+.04
18.8	+.01
19.8	+.05

He was most content when sitting listlessly alone, a vantage point from which he would watch the activity of other children. This he seemed to enjoy. His acceptance of confinement was flavoured with his evident pleasure whenever the limited opportunity to observe was available.

Analysis of his security score indicated that he lacked to a serious degree a dependent relationship with caretakers and any motivation to exert effort. He seemed to be making minimal impact on his environment.

Any attempt to restore Ernest's mental health would need long-term work to establish a trusting relationship with adults in an attempt to develop feelings of self-worth and confidence. Such feelings would lead to a desire to put forth effort and to make demands on his world. Because Ernest was not immediately responsive to the attention of an adult, he would need to be approached indirectly. His enjoyment of watching the activity of other children could be used as a tool to build a communication bridge between his withdrawn self and his world.

Involvement in the limited activity of one or two of the other children for a short span of time each day would allow an adult to inadvertently become part of his world through the arrangement for and participation in such activity. Through time the role of the caretaker could be perceived by Ernest as a rewarding one.

By the time we had analysed our data and speculated about its outcome we concluded from it and other studies that the adults caring for young children in institutions engage in an interaction that shows amazing similarity wherever it is reported. The inevitable tango develops between the children who must be kept safe, clean, dry, and fed and the adults charged with a never-ending response to such need. The chronic problem of understaffed institutions moves the adults to ever-increasing constraints on the children's behaviour until regard for a child's well-being and healthy development is engulfed by the overwhelming need to nourish, to value conformity as an aid to efficiency, and to see the care of the children in terms of a group operation rather than as a sponsorship of each child's potential. The fact that the marked debilitating effects of infant group care became evident around six months of age indicates that once an infant reaches an age at which he should be sitting, reaching, seeking attention, and expecting opportunities for activity, such behaviour must be discouraged. The adult-child tango can be described in the following terms:

- a *child* is hungry and cries – the *adult* becomes irritated and does not respond – after all other children must be fed too!
- a *child* reaches for a toy and it drops – he cries and protests – the *adult* is too busy to retrieve it – eventually the protest stops – the *adult* has peace. Through time the child loses the desire to reach and to demand.
- a *child* babbles and seeks stimulation – no one is around to respond – eventually through lack of rewards the child stops seeking and babbling.
- a *child* attempts to pull himself to sit or stand – such activity needs supervision or it is unsafe. The *adult* puts him in his crib where safety prevails but motor activity is discouraged – rocking and thumb sucking replace healthful activity.
- a *child* reaches for a spoon or cup in an attempt to help himself. The *adult* in her hurry holds the hand away from the food and feeds the child herself.

The constant exigencies of institutional care quickly lead to the condition where the continuation of a smooth running operation embodied in the routine of the establishment, the needs of the hard-pressed adults, and the perpetuation of the system, take precedence over the individuality of the children and their developmental needs.

Descriptions of the adult caretakers' behaviour and that of the institutionalized children in their care have an amazing similarity from study to study wherever reported in various parts of the world.

2

Intervention and evaluation through play

The human problem of continued institutionalization for the children in this situation led to attempts to consider alternatives for their future. Past experience had clarified the fact that adjustment to a foster or adoptive home after any prolonged period of institutional living was enormously difficult and usually terminated in failure. Furthermore, foster and adoptive homes for very young infants who had not yet been damaged by such a depriving environment were scarce among Catholic families in Toronto and even throughout the Province of Ontario. Religious convictions would not permit rearing in Protestant homes. The much needed total reorganization of the institution was impossible for many reasons.

Although we recognized that the main deficiency in the lives of these children was the reliable presence of warm, loving caretakers to whom the children could relate, we had to accept a much more limited goal in an attempt to ameliorate their situation. It was anticipated that at least some of the children might be able to respond intellectually to the provision of play materials and a stimulating environment aside from the main stream of their routine existence within the institution. As a result we recommended the initiation of a playroom in the basement of the building which would be supervised by specialists in child care who were cognizant of the levels of development and the needs of young children.

Because play is a natural expression of childhood, it was anticipated that the children would quickly respond to materials and activities with a demonstration of curiosity and enjoyment. We hoped that eventually the use of toys might lead to feelings of self-confidence in this limited setting. The playroom was equipped with a wide range of articles including small furniture, records, household equipment, plants, animals, a piano, pictures, homemade books with single objects on each page, and a mirror. Could the provision of some normal environmental assets provide a medium for the emergence of 'normal' behaviour?

Nine children, between twenty-two months and three years of age, who seemed typical of the group, participated. The playroom was available for two hours each afternoon for a period of four and one-half months. Two supervisors (one of whom had carried out the original research) were in charge. In the initial stages one child at a time came with each adult. It was expected that a small play group similar to that of a nursery school playroom could eventually function.

How naive were our expectations! We did not realize that children need a backlog of experience in order to function effectively in a playroom. The children stood immobilized and disinterested or ran about the room erratically. The adults had to put the toys into the children's hands and manipulate them with the children. Imitation could not be elicited. The directions of the adults were not understood. Such words as 'choose' a toy were responded to with bewilderment and immobility. The children were incapable of interacting either with each other or with the adults. Two extremes of behaviour were demonstrated – either overly excited, frightened random behaviour or limpness and apathy.

Such a reaction necessitated the continuation of the programme on a highly individualized adult-child basis. After several weeks a few of the children could select a toy and play with it under the intense guidance of an accompanying adult. Gradually three children were enabled to play together in the playroom for periods of 15 minutes. After this time, behaviour became chaotic. By the end of the experimental period of four and one-half months, only five children under the supervision of two adults could play together for a short time. At no time did any group pattern similar to that of a nursery school become apparent.

Evaluation

Daily records kept by the supervisors enabled analysis of the children's reactions over the four-month period. This demonstrated that all the children displayed a meagre response. Six of the nine were finally able to select and follow a self-chosen interest for a very short time, occasionally being able to control themselves despite other children in the room. We judged these six to have made some slight gain from the programme as reflected in self-direction and control. The other aspect of their development where we sought for gains was their capacity to relate to the supervisors. The disregard observed for their usual caretakers seemed to reflect a lack of expectation that grown-ups could be rewarding in any way. They were no more interesting to the children than the sparse furniture in their rooms. Hence the first interactions with the playroom supervisors were of the same nature and it took several weeks before they responded in any way to adult direction. It was longer still before they recognized the supervisors as beneficent. The first healthy reaction of the six to their supervisors was to look for attention and to accept help in finding and choosing playthings. The children were finally responsive to the adult expectation to settle to play for a short period of time. Their trust was so fragile that any slight disturbance to the play-room caused them to return to their earlier behaviour, to withdraw from the play materials and to refuse to co-operate with adults. An unexpected reward that was noted was increased willingness on the children's part to communicate. In the initial stages, pushing, pulling, grunting, and gesturing had predominated. This was gradually replaced by attempts to communicate verbally with both adults and children.

The three children who showed no progress seemed unable to establish a relationship with adults. They either remained indifferent to, or refused any proffered help from the adults. Neither could they respond to any direction. They remained either apathetic or volatile, showing practically no gains in play habits and skills. Their only gains were in their willingness to attempt some form of speech. All the nine children's relationships with each other remained primitive and precluded any co-operative interaction with each other.

Evaluation of such results from this experiment indicated few long-term gains for the individual children. Rather it was used as a diagnostic indicator to confirm the fact that no short-term or peripheral treatment would be effective in changing the course of development to more normal levels. Essential mental health qualities were lacking and physical and psychological development were both seriously distorted.

We believed that the caution with which the children responded to adults on whom they should normally be depending indicated an absence of essential early relationships with caretakers. Their absence of speech but relative willingness to try to talk during the play sessions further indicated an early lack of human interactions which initiate and sponsor communication of a young child with his human world. The fact that despite living together for a long time in the institution these children saw each other as threatening and fear provoking indicated that social growth was uninitiated or seriously distorted. It was evident that any effective change in the mental health of these youngsters would take place only through a complete change of programme.

At this time, the academic and child care agencies were responding to John Bowlby's 1952 report from the World Health Organization. In this report, convincing evidence had demonstrated that children suffering such severe early deprivation as the ones in this study were probably permanently damaged intellectually and emotionally and hence were doomed to a bleak future. Contrary to this, the evidence of both our small investigations on security and play had pointed up such marked individual differences in the children's response to such deprivation that we believed some must be capable of a healthy response to a nurturing environment. It seemed clear that some children had much greater capacity than others to maintain some personal integrity despite environmental discouragement.

PLANNING FOR CHANGE

Our evidence that peripheral attempts to modify the children's behaviour in the direction of normalcy were doomed to failure led to the recommendation that only a total reorganization of the Home could provide a healthy environment for the children. The concern of the Catholic Children's Aid Society about the children's lack of potential for placement in homes and the prospect of unending, costly, debilitating institutional care for these children led to the provision of money to make such change possible. Mary Kilgour, now well-acquainted with the institution and aware of its problems as a result of her work on the security study and later on the play study was put in charge of the rehabilitative measures. Some of the staff of the Institute of Child Study, University of Toronto, continued their active involvement which had been initiated by their original contacts with the Institution and their human concerns about the welfare of its children.

The first step in rehabilitation was to assess the strengths and weaknesses of the total existing programme and the children within it. In this way, some realistic estimate of where to begin could be obtained. Furthermore, anticipation of the length of time required to make effective changes could be evaluated.

Summarizing the assets led to the belief that most of the children had *some* potential for maturing in abilities and personality. Hence, a change in their daily living habits should bring about development of a highly individualized nature. It appeared that some of the children would have potential for warm, human relationships, both with children and adult, despite the present serious disability in this aspect of development. A twofold therapeutic approach should be most effective, one for the institution programme and the second for individualized, therapeutic sessions. It was evident that the very young infants, who were the most healthy of the group, should be the most capable of immediate salutory response. Hence their treatment should be undertaken first with a view to finding homes for them fairly soon. On the other hand, treatment of the older children was likely to be long term, difficult, discouraging, and expensive. Probably a period of two years would be needed to modify their development to the point of acquiring a capacity to live in a family.

With these considerations in mind a general plan of re-organization was developed. The most crucial change was needed in the attitude of the caretakers.

Mechanical, routine care which focused on getting through the daily routine would have to be replaced by an attitude of caring about the children as persons capable of unique growth and development. Long-term development of each child must be the goal, not the maintenance of an adult-oriented programme. Recognition that the 'humanization' of the programme would create many difficulties for the staff as the children became more alert, curious, and demanding led to a consideration of either re-training the present staff or replacing it with new people, more open to such a changed point of view. It was evident that the staff was the really crucial element in the success of this project. Constant support would be needed over trying times. Sufficient numbers of staff would be required to allow for truly personalized care. Specialists such as psychiatrists, psychologists, medical doctors, and nutritionists, would be required to give advice on a variety of particular problems which posed dilemmas to the regular staff. Sufficient trained personnel should make up part of the regular staff to allow for a core of knowledgable persons to guide the others. In-service training in child development and techniques of management of young children would be needed, partly with a goal of providing some kind of consistency in the caretaking practices.

It became apparent that a twofold focus would have to be adopted for the rehabilitation programme. One focus would be on short-term goals where immediate changes could take place. The second had to be on long-term goals which would have to await the completion of the short term.

Immediate changes could be made in all routine aspects of care such as eating, sleeping, dressing, toileting, from purely mechanical hurried attention to friendly ministering with emphasis on child participation. Large unsupervised groups should be replaced by small, supervised groups. Upset children expressing emotion should be given concerned attention rather than be ignored. Rough, noisy control should be replaced by kindly direction. Each child should have some possessions of his own which would allow him some identity as a person. Each child should be assigned to a particular adult to whom he would be 'special.' The infants who are likely to respond most rapidly should be given priority in order to move them out of the institution as quickly as possible.

The long-term goals would be ultimately the achievement of some degree of mental health for each child. This would require individual assessment of strengths and weaknesses and some individualized programme for each. Records of the children's behaviour and changes through time should be kept in order to verify casual impressions and to help staff to evaluate accurately whatever progress is taking place, and ultimately be available for research. This should be the responsibility of one person to ensure that such records are consistently maintained.

SECURITY THEORY

Such a plan, although creating change, would obviously have been open to frag-
mented application should no consistent theoretical basis be used to direct its
consistency. Because our main interest was in the promotion of mental health
in young children and the work of the staff of the Institute of Child Study had
been with well children, the application of principles of normal development was
our focus. Recognition of the needs of normal children and provision of environmental support for the satisfaction of these needs became our goal. No child
would be diagnosed in terms of mental illness but rather his assets and liabilities
would be evaluated against the developmental expectations for his chronological
age. The nurturance of each child's strengths rather than a concentration on disabilities would be the aim of treatment. Consistent ongoing recording of the children's response should allow for the monitoring of his progress towards normal
developmental behaviour.

Available to initiate the recording were two behavioural assessments developed by some of the staff of the Institute of Child Study. The first was the Infant Security Scale, on which the infants up to two years of age could be evaluated. The second was a Pre-School Mental Health Assessment form appropriate
from ages two through five years. Both these behavioural check lists were developed from the Blatz concept of security which has been modified by some of
his colleagues,* to be appropriate to the infant and pre-school years. Dr W.E.
Blatz, founder of the Institute of Child Study and director from 1924–65, developed his personality theory largely at the adult level and called it the Security
Theory of Mental Health. Although making reference to its application through
childhood, he encouraged his staff and colleagues to elaborate more fully on
stages appropriate to early childhood. His final statement of Security theory before his death can be found in *Human Security.*[1]

Briefly, his theory stated: 'Mental Health is a serene state of mind arising
from the willingness to accept the consequences of one's own decisions and
actions.' Making decisions and accepting consequences were the crucial aspects
of this system. The way in which the decisions were made and accepted reflected
the degree of health of an individual. Insecurity could be relieved by a variety of
actions. One healthy method was to rely on a *mature dependent* agent who
shared the decisions which solved problems, and who was also willing to share
the consequences of the decisions. Another way was to rely totally on another
person who made the decisions and accepted the consequence of them. This

---

* D.A. Millichamp, Carroll Davis, and Betty M. Flint.
1 University of Toronto Press, 1966.

was the *infantile dependent* way, resembling the dependency of young children who must rely on caretakers who are responsible for their welfare. This method, healthy for infants, was unhealthy at maturity. Another potentially unhealthy way was by the use of *avoidance mechanisms (deputy agents)*. Such deputy agents as rationalization, compensation, and sublimation allowed one to experience *temporary* feelings of security. They provided immediate relief from anxiety, but to be continuously effective they must be either constantly reinforced or extended in scope. Although the limited use of such mechanisms is part of a healthy personality, such use could reach an unhealthy condition of being a predominant and permanent mechanism of adjustment. Should this happen, an individual would lose his capacity to criticize his own mental processes and thus become a poor mental health risk. The most healthy way to find resolutions of problems was by summoning effort to develop skills to solve them. In this way one relied on oneself to find solutions. Furthermore, one must accept the consequences of the decision made or the action taken which has been the response to an event. This was the *independently secure* method. Its healthy components were the person's capacity to make decisions, to act upon them, and to accept the consequences of them. In this way independent coping strategies were developed.

This theory applicable to adults, with its emphasis on independence, needed considerable adaptation to be appropriate to the activity and developmental level of infant and pre-school children. Such adaptation was made through research investigations on infants and by means of prolonged discussion with Dr Blatz and his colleagues. This revised statement appeared in the 1959 publication of the *Security of Infants*.* This theory was the basis of our first and second small studies in the Neil McNeil Home and later provided the frame of reference for the rehabilitation of the children.

---

* Betty M. Flint, *Security of Infants*, University of Toronto Press, 1959.

3

Rehabilitation

Fired with enthusiasm to 'save' this group of children, having obtained a grant to provide more staff and professional leadership, and armed with a workable personality theory, we initiated a rehabilitation programme. One of our greatest strengths was our knowledge of normal developmental behaviours from infancy through the pre-school years. Knowledge of the expectation for normal developmental levels allowed for evaluation of the extent of deviation from normal demonstrated by these children. As the children varied in age from three months to three years, adaptation to a variety of developmental levels had to be made. All but the youngest infants had some degree of developmental retardation.

As stated earlier, priorities in treatment were set so that the youngest, least damaged children might have an opportunity for quick recovery and hence early placement in homes. The attributes of a normal environment expected to sponsor healthy development were overly emphasized in an attempt to correct the results of the earlier deficiencies. For children up to one year old consistent physical care was given prime importance. This was accompanied by tactile stimulation through holding, patting, stroking, hugging, kissing, rocking, etc. The social aspect of this care took the form of chatter, tickling games, imitative games, singing, smiling, asking questions, and encouragement to respond at whatever level was possible for each individual child. Toys were provided for both indoor and outdoor activity. Demonstration and encouragement of their use accompanied their appearance. Motor skills were emphasized by constant encouragement of the children to sit up, to creep, to climb, to walk, to push and pull equipment.

As the children approached the chronological age of twelve months their retardation became increasingly evident. As a result, the idea of chronological age was disregarded in favour of the concept of developmental age. This was the basis on which they were evaluated and by which their steps towards healthy

development were judged. For the youngest of the group the sweeping programme changes which applied to all children were sufficient to initiate enthusiasm for living and increased alertness to their surroundings. On the other hand,
the older children ranging from approximately two and a half to three and a half
years of age needed more individualized therapy before they showed signs of
change.

As soon as any child demonstrated an interest in helping himself, every opportunity was given to allow for this in the routine of eating, dressing, toileting, and
washing. Play equipment and playrooms were adapted to developmental levels in
an effort to arouse curiosity and exploration. Finally an effort was made to extend the lives of the children beyond the confines of the institution by eventually taking them for excursions into the community.

The degree to which the children needed dependable, consistent adults in
their world who could respond to them in human terms made it evident that the
most critical aspect of the rehabilitation programme was the provision of sensitive, child-oriented caretakers. Hence money was made available to double the
original staff ratio of 38 adults to 85 children. Such a ratio of close to one to
one seems impressive, until it is remembered that this included both day and
night staff as well as caretaking and housekeeping.

Not only was a change in the number of caretakers required but a total reorganization had to take place as well. Earlier administrators, overwhelmed by the
need to find staff for twenty-four-hour care had organized the institution around
the needs of the staff rather than around those of the children. Preparation and
serving of meals, hours off and on duty, living accommodation, children's rest
periods and bed time had been arranged for the convenience of the staff. Efficiency and a healthy awareness of cleanliness were rated high on staff requirements. The permanent staff had been supplemented by nuns in transit through
Toronto from Europe to the United States. No child care requirements were part
of this arrangement. They were regarded merely as fleeting additions to the on-
going problem of providing care for the children.

The first requirement in the change of caretaking methods was to attempt
some change in the attitude of the existing staff members. Their familiarity with
the children and our reluctance to disrupt any salutory relationship that might
have existed made us reluctant to dismiss even the harsh, authoritarian caretakers
who were there. However, as changes in the institutional regime were imple-
mented and encouragement was given to the children to expect stimulating care,
the rift between the attitudes of old and new staff became impossible to bridge.
Eventually, all but a few of the original staff departed from the programme.

Formal staff training in methods of caretaking as well as attendance at lectures in child development were required of all staff. Monthly assessment of each

child by use of the Infant Security Records and the Pre-school Mental Health Assessment was required of each staff member. Since these were scaled behaviour check-lists they could be discussed regularly. The strengths and weaknesses of a child's adjustment could be demonstrated and goals for the following months' treatment could be set. Such discussions made staff members aware of the implications of children's behaviour and what it was telling about both developmental level and the children's feelings about themselves. As a result of these measures a core of trained caretakers became available who could act as resource people for the newer staff members. Community resources were used to diagnose and suggest treatment for children with puzzling problems. As well as the Research and Guidance Staff of the Institute of Child Study, the resources of the Hospital for Sick Children were used for diagnosis and direction for treatment of serious physical disabilities as well as for diagnosis of possible mental illnesses. The office administration of the institution was carried out by the Catholic Children's Aid, thus allowing the supervisor the opportunity to concentrate on the internal matters of children and staff.

In time, many of the children became capable of benefiting from a group play programme. A nursery school was begun in the garden coach house and four fully trained nursery school teachers were added to the staff. These specialists proved excellent source people for other less well trained staff.

Although such monumental improvement in relationship between adults and children was undoubtedly salutory, the children still seemed to lack a special person who might be interested in a single child only. The sense of belonging to one person and of possessing him to the exclusion of the rest of the group seemed a desirable goal for each child. To provide this situation for the children a volunteer programme was arranged. To guard against sporadic attendance, each woman who volunteered to become attached to one child was required to be committed to at least one half-day weekly. If this were not possible, her services were not used. Orientation sessions and a series of lectures on child development sensitized the volunteers to the particular need of these children for a dependable and trustworthy attachment to concerned adults in their world. This enabled each volunteer to recognize the degree of developmental immaturity in the physical, social, intellectual, and affectional aspects of her own particular charge. The work of the volunteer mother was to sponsor her particular child through a period of his life when he needed this opportunity for a unique attachment. She would also provide him with a trustworthy someone to extend his life beyond the institution into the community. Through contact with her he should become acquainted with family life and observe the interaction of various members of a family group. Such preparation was seen as a stepping stone to eventual foster home or adoptive placement. Record keeping also became one of the facets of the volunteer's work. Monthly progress reports on prepared record forms provided a way of evaluating the usefulness of the volunteer in the child's progression towards mental health. It further recorded a child's increasing capacity to respond in a healthy way to experiences in home and community which formerly had been completely foreign to him.

Having provided staff and volunteers to support the dependency needs of the children, the second aspect of planning for their recovery was to provide an opportunity to expend effort. Implicit in the security theory was the belief that once the children began to have feelings of self-worth their apathy and indifference to their environment would dissipate, to be replaced by a healthy curiosity and a desire to do things for themselves. Such provision could be made in two aspects of the children's lives. The first was through the encouragement of play activity, the second through encouragement to help themselves in the routine aspects of care such as eating, washing, dressing, and toileting.

To help in achieving the first purpose, a variety of play opportunities was provided. The direct emphasis on adult-child interaction was the most immediate change. Such tactile stimulation as tickling, patting, rubbing backs, as well as purely social interaction of a fun nature demonstrated the adult's interest in the children as playmates. Individual play sessions between one adult and one child were offered to each child to initiate interest in play material, to encourage manipulation of it, and to promote the use of language to describe it. To provide a more extensive experience, small playrooms with a variety of play equipment allowed small groups of children to come together under the supervision of trained play specialists. This was viewed as a second step in the progression from individual guidance to larger group activity which was to be provided eventually in the coach house nursery school at the extreme end of the large garden. Play was considered not only as an opportunity for constructive activity but also as an opportunity to confirm that there were warm, lovable, and supportive adults in their world. Emotional well-being would be encouraged by the sense of satisfaction achieved from the setting of goals and the attainment of them. The limits set on the use of toys and the behaviour of the children in the playrooms allowed the children to experience the fact that certain rules had to be obeyed if their activities were to be continued. Such outer controls imposed at first by the adults would gradually be replaced in part by the children's inner controls, thus allowing them to gain a capacity for self-directed activity. The provision of outdoor aids to activity in the garden – swings, slides, teeter totters, walking boards, wagons, bicycles, tricycles – encouraged the strengthening of weak, underdeveloped muscles and the gaining of control over gross musculature. Fine motor co-ordination was a by-product of the playroom equipment involving the use of scissors, paste, blocks, plasticene, for example. The mental discipline of making choices, which at first was completely baffling and bewildering, came under control and was eventually a matter of delicious lingering over alternatives.

The goals of the children's rehabilitation were always based on what would be normal expectations for development according to chronological age. Although the staff was trained to understand the limitations of deprived children, they always kept the expectation of normal behaviour as their long-term goal, while lowering their immediate expectations. Each child was assessed in terms of his own starting point in learning to play, and it terms of his own rate of progress. Records of his play were kept monthly. There was a constant setting of goals, evaluating change, and re-setting goals for children, not only for individuals, but also for particular play groups as they demonstrated developmental progress.

To overcome the ennui which had developed in the children as the result of the sameness of their past environment an orderly sorting out of routine times and play activity was imposed on the day. Clearly defined differences between bed-time and activity-time was the first distinction to be made, and within this, eating, washing, toilet training, dressing, and a variety of types of play activity were established. The order seldom varied so that the children could develop a comprehension of an orderly and meaningful day. One activity could be predicted from the preceding one. In this way the children could feel secure and less helpless in their surroundings. An 'anchor' was provided for activity by having 'getting-up time,' 'breakfast time,' 'play time,' 'toilet time,' 'lunch time,' 'sleep time,' and so on. This new orientation gave order and meaning to their lives. In order to challenge the children further, responsibility for helping themselves was urged wherever possible. The minutiae of self-care, such as wiping hands, brushing teeth, pulling on a sock, were within the scope of these small children and provided an opportunity to set up tasks with which they were capable of coping.

By establishing a logical sequence to activity, no matter how inconsequential, it was possible to arrange a plan of discipline whereby the children could understand that failure to carry out expected procedures brought about predictable consequences. Such consequences could be enforced by adults without rancour, hostility, or threat. The choice of carrying out the procedure was placed on the child's volition and allowed him a degree of self-discipline and control over his own behaviour. For example, should a child be dressing for outdoor play with the group and refuse to wear his mittens, the consequences would be failure to go outside with the other children. The choice to remain inside would usually be less inviting than going out, so choosing to join the group activity would likely be the result. Although such a child might be restrained as the result of an adult's insistence on carrying out expectations, the force used to hold or carry him through a situation was employed without anger.

The greatest change in routine procedures occurred in the aspect of eating. For those children old enough, small dining-room procedures were set up with one adult sitting beside and supervising four or five children at a small table and on small chairs. Eating utensils were provided and self-help was encouraged. Food was carefully prepared to be interesting to a variety of ages in terms of taste, texture, colour, and smell. Combinations of food were carefully chosen to encourage the eating of new food with already accepted, familiar foods. Definite procedures of standing behind chairs on entry to dining room, hands behind backs (this to avoid grabbing food), saying grace, sitting down, putting on serviettes, getting dinner, etc. allowed each child to master the detail and enjoy it. Such planning, accompanied by varied and interesting food was designed to prepare the children to become a part of the world outside the institution.

Such were the measures taken to overcome the deficits in personality observed in this group of institutionalized infants and pre-school children. We had anticipated the youngest, least damaged children would respond most rapidly to the changes. This proved to be so and permitted early transfer of these youngsters to adoptive and foster homes. We had expected the older, more severely damaged children who had experienced two and a half to four years of institutional life to take a depressingly long time to respond. Their lack of capacity to relate humanly, their inability to concentrate on anything, made them seem more like a pack of little animals than children. However, their unexpected capacity to respond to the therapeutic changes and their insatiable demand for adult contact and attention led us to recognize that the children were not so much 'damaged' as undeveloped. The dearth of normal experiences and opportunities in their environment had precluded the development of human qualities. Consequently, after a year of treatment many of the older children demonstrated trusting dependency on staff and volunteers and seemed to be developing feelings of self-trust. There was direction and purpose to much of their behaviour and demonstration of self-control within the limited structure of the treatment centre. Even these older children seemed to feel a sense of uniqueness about themselves, a feeling fostered by the fact that they had been supplied with toys, clothing, furniture, possessions, volunteers, and staff which were 'their own.'

As each child demonstrated sufficient evidence of normal behaviour to be acceptable in a home, one was carefully chosen wherein the families could accept children who were likely to present difficulties beyond usual expectations. Carefully pre-planned visits of the child to his new home might take as many as eight weeks before the transfer would be complete. The new parents were urged to allow their child to regress so that his dependency needs might be met in his new home. On-going guidance was available from the supervisor of the institution who knew the children best and from the social worker in charge of the placements.

Because of the dual nature of the project as a research and humanitarian effort, continuous records had been kept of all aspects of it. The pre-placement evaluations were made of the children themselves and records of the interactions between them and their prospective parents were kept. After a period of two and one-half years all the children had been removed from the institution to homes. On-going research was planned for the next twelve years until the children were through their pre-adolescence and in their fifteenth year. Because close contact with each family and child was projected ahead it was considered impossible to research every family and child. Hence, thirty-one were selected for future study. The selection was made on the basis of availability for interviewing, which meant within 40 or 50 miles of Toronto, and on the parents' willingness to share information with us through interviews with the research and guidance worker. Through good fortune the child care worker who had taken charge of the rehabilitation programme within the institution and who had also participated in the play and security studies, was able to continue as the guidance and research worker after the closing of the institution. Her vested interest in each child's welfare was demonstrated in her determination to participate in a final successful outcome as the children made a new adjustment to home and community, to mother, father, and siblings, as well as to peer groups outside their homes.

4

We plan ahead

Many of the senior staff of the Institute of Child Study had been interested in these children from the time of the first study. Hence, when an opportunity arose to plan ahead until the children were fifteen years of age, there was considerable enthusiasm in helping to map out the research strategy. With the active co-operation of the Catholic Children's Aid Society of Metro Toronto a plan of data collection and guidance was arranged to span the next decade or more of contact with the children and their families chosen for this purpose.

Mary Kilgour was appointed as the official case worker representing the Children's Aid to supervise the small number of children remaining in foster care. She was also appointed as the Research Data Collector and Guidance Worker representing the Institute of Child Study to keep contact with those who were in adoptive homes. She was to be the contact person who acted as the link between the children and families and the back-up research staff of the Institute of Child Study. The research team was to consist of a part-time psychologist to make regular assessments at six, nine, twelve, and fifteen years of age on the Binet Intelligence Test, the Rorschach Projective Test, and eventually the WISC Test at age fifteen. The psychologist was to analyse, record, and interpret her information and to act in consultation with Mary Kilgour, using the information for guidance purposes. In addition, any emergency which demanded extra attention would be brought to her for diagnosis and guidance. The Chief Investigator also became a member of the consulting team. Her participation was sometimes elicited in parent interviews when the 'going' between parents and children became rough. A secretary maintained the records, typed reports, and kept the files orderly and updated.

In order to obtain a record of systematic, every-day experiences in some form, Mary Kilgour was to collect information about the early life of the children and families on a 'Home Record Questionnaire.' This report was obtained through interviews each half year. The record form was constructed through the joint effort of the staff of the Institute of Child Study and covered many aspects of the daily life of the children. Routines, play, hobbies, social interaction, study habits, emotional expression and control, money management, relationship to siblings and parents were all recorded. Implicit in the questionnaire was the 'security theory.' By interview Miss Kilgour would solicit responses couched in terms of the children's behaviour rather than accept descriptive statements which might be highly slanted by a parent's interpretation. Similarly the worker would avoid making her own interpretations unless she indicated it in her records. A similar record was developed to elicit information from teachers or principals of schools which the children would be attending. Once more behavioural statements would be recorded rather than interpretative ones.

Thirty-one children were selected for the follow-up study because of the difficulty of collecting intensive data on a larger group. These children and their families lived close enough to the research team to be readily accessible. Very few of the children lived outside of Metropolitan Toronto. The parents made a commitment to share information about themselves and their children with the research team. That this arrangement was not a one-way street is evidenced by the fact that the research team and the clinicians associated with it were available on request for guidance and support of these families in the process of rearing their children.

So successful was the outcome of this planning that by the official termination of data collection, twenty-five of the children and families were still actively involved. As the research team continued to work as a group completing analysis of data and remaining accessible for consultation, contact was maintained with many of the children through ages seventeen, eighteen, and nineteen. Complete life records were available on all 25.

The hypothesis put forward at the beginning of the follow-up study was that *most* of these children could be expected to make a satisfactory adjustment to their homes and their communities despite their early severe and prolonged institutional deprivation. This expectation was held in view of three known factors: (1) the enormous diversity among the infants in their vulnerability to adverse institutional conditions observed at the beginning of the study which showed that some children had some innate capacity to sustain a state of wellbeing much longer than others; (2) the high degree of success of the therapeutic programme within the institution which had prepared these then unplaceable children for placement in homes; (3) the consistent guidance afforded by the Child Care Worker after the children's placement in their homes. The status of the Institute of Child Study staff as part of this support system was undoubtedly also a factor in maintaining the interest of the parents.

DATA COLLECTION

The collection of data had three major facets:

1 The *Home Life Questionnaire* was collected twice yearly by Mary Kilgour from the time of each child's placement in his home to the termination date of the study.

The following format provided the guidelines by which objective descriptions were elicited about the children's behaviour. These data were collected from the mother on interview. Should additional guidance be indicated from the routine interviews, further time was arranged and data from all these additional sessions was recorded. Telephone conversations with the worker, medical records, parent consultations with counsellors, psychiatric interviews, and additional information which had any reference to the children's adjustment were all added to the continuous files.

The nature of the routine home interview was to collect information about every aspect of the children's lives as they grew towards maturity. The following format outlined tentative questions around which the worker conducted her interview. Such a procedure allowed for considerable flexibility in adapting to a variety of family life styles and to a range of ages.

Name of child	Age	Grade	Date

Household
    Mother   Father
    Names and ages of brothers and sisters
    Others living with family

ACTIVITIES AND INTERESTS
Sports:
    What sports does he enjoy?
    Where does he play and how did he come to take it up?
    Why do you think he enjoys it?
    Does he feel that he is good at sports?
    How does he take it when he loses, or does not do so well?
    If he dislikes sports could you say why?

Special interests:
    Describe things he likes to do (for example – carpentry, sewing, crafts, pets,
        records, nature, collections, snooping, tinkering, clubs).
    With whom does he like to do these things?
    Would he rather work alone or does he like you to help?
    How long have his various interests lasted?
    List any lessons or classes he attends.

31 We plan ahead

TV

How much time does he watch TV?
Is it a favourite occupation?

Reading:

Is reading a favourite occupation?
To what extent? What does he read?

Family life:

What kinds of responsibilities does he have around the house? (e.g. looking
 after his belongings, chores, errands, sees things that need doing).
How do you get him to do the things he is supposed to do?
How does he respond? (or how does this work out?)
What kinds of things does he like to do with the whole family?
What kinds of things does he like to do with his mother?
With his father?
Describe how he gets along with each of his brothers and sisters (fun together,
 fights, etc.)
Which brothers and sisters often play together?
What do you do when the children fight?
Then what happens?
How do they settle their own disputes?

Money:

Does he get an allowance? How much?
Does he earn any money? How?
What does he do with his money?
Is his allowance ever docked?

School:

How do you think he is getting along at school? Does he object to going?
If so what do you do about it?
Does he do homework? If so how much help does he need with it?
How often do you talk to his teacher?

Other children:

Does he prefer company or to play alone?
Would you say he tends to have one friend, several, or a whole gang?
Does he go looking for his friends or do they call for him?
Does he seem to be a leader or a follower?
What kinds of trouble does he run into with his friends?
What do you do about it?
How does he get along with adults other than parents and teachers?

Personal:
>   What is his general mood around the house?
>   How does he feel about being oldest, middle, youngest?
>   If he is adopted, or foster child, how does he feel about this?
>   What things *frustrate* him?
>   Then what happens?
>   Does he like to be helped?
>   What makes him really *angry*?
>   How does he show his anger?
>   What do you do about it?
>   Then what happens?

In the following statements check the ones that apply to him

Happy go lucky	Worries and stews and fusses
Feels he can do anything	Complains and objects
Heedless, foolhardy	Timid about new, cautious
Likes to do something new	Likes to be told exactly what is going
Likes to go places alone	to happen
Jumps into things	Thinks before he acts
Worries and keeps it to himself	Hates to be dirty or untidy

SUMMARY

How would you describe him? (Chatty, withdrawn, trustworthy, sociable, over-
    friendly, never satisfied, a 'real boy' – a typical girl, etc.)
How does he go about getting his own way?
What does he do that specially pleases you?
What does he do that worries or annoys you?

SCHOOL QUESTIONNAIRE

(2) Information about the children's behaviour at school was collected in a similar way, but only once a year. The following record form indicates the scope of
the questions. This form was more specific in its questions than the Home Life
Questionnaire because the information was not always solicited in interview by
the worker. Should a child's adjustment be proceeding comfortably, the record
form was mailed for the teacher or principal to complete and return. Should particular difficulties be evident, the worker would go to the school on appointment
and interview the teacher. During these interviews an attempt would be made to
interpret the child's disabilities in terms of his earlier prolonged deprivation. If
difficulties continued, a second or even a third teacher interview might be held.
This information was included in the on-going records.

33 We plan ahead

SCHOOL QUESTIONNAIRE

School: *Name of child:*   *Grade:*

Note: One or more alternatives under each heading may be checked.

1 When a child can't cope or grasp instructions, does he?
    (a) daydream – or drift away 'freeze up'?
    (b) talk and disturb others?
    (c) seek adult help by asking pertinent or irrelevant questions?
    (d) get back to the task if given individual explanation (praise and encourage-
    ment to continue)?

Comments: What do you find is the best way to help him?

2 When does he direct his efforts?
    (a) Tasks he can pursue alone
    (b) Activities where a group is involved
    (c) Does he like to take his work home?

What type of school work does he do best? (make the most effort)
Comments:

3 How does he seek attention and approval?
    (a) By interrupting other children
    (b) Trying very hard to do everything to please
    (c) Does he seem worried about disapproval?

What does he do when he makes mistakes?
Comments:

4 What about his ability to concentrate?
    (a) Can he stick at a task without continuous adult re-direction?
    (b) Gives up – day dreams or dawdles?
    (c) Does he give up if a task is too long for him?
    (d) Does he try to do better if he gets a poor mark or is he discouraged?
    (e) Is it difficult for him to listen?

Comments:

Speech: His ability to express his thoughts
    (a) Can he make clear to you what he wants to say?
    (b) Do you find his vocabulary adequate?

Comments:

Social: How does he get along with other children?
    Does he make approaches or wait for them?
    Do you think he sometimes feels inadequate?
    Does he use bragging, teasing, bullying, 'tall tales' to get attention?

Comments:

Co-ordination – How is his ability to handle a pencil, cut out?
General Question – Assets Liabilities

(3) Regular appointments were made for each child to come to the Institute of
Child Study for an interview with the psychologist on the project. These appointments were arranged at a time close to each child's sixth, ninth, twelfth, and fifteenth birthday. Binet intelligence tests and the Rorschach Ink Blot test were
administered at six, nine, and twelve years of age. At age fifteen the Wechsler Intelligence Test for Children (WISC) was substituted for the Binet. The rationale
for this substitution was that the second test demonstrated most clearly the
quality of the child's intellectual function at age fifteen.

Three different psychologists participated in data collection over a span of
twelve years. One psychologist remained with the team for the last eight years of
the study and provided a consistency to the role, both in assessments of the children and in consultation to the now familiar families. She too became immersed
in 'the security theory' so that consistency would be maintained in the approach
of the whole team to the guidance of families. Part of her role in the research
was to analyse and report on her aspect of the data as they accumulated. Her interest was in the quality and characteristics of intellectual function and resulted
in her analysis of Rorschach responses according to the way a child organized his
conceptual world. The sequences demonstrated by the children on this study
were compared with the norms established by Ames, Métraux, and Walker
(1971).

ANALYSIS OF DATA

The sequential records taken from home and school reports held information
which could be examined in several different ways.

(1) The first method of analysis to be adopted was an exploration of the
security of the children as reflected in the statements on the records which described their behaviours. These could be taken from the records and allocated to
categories congruent with the security theory of mental health.

(2) The second method of analysis made possible by the presence of behavioural statements describing the children's activities was that of examining these
as indicators of social maturity. Doll's definition of social maturity as described
on the Vineland Social Maturity Scale provided a ready means of categorizing
the behaviours at nine, twelve, and fifteen years of age. Such identification and
tabulation would provide a validated outside criterion for our security measures.

(3) Further outside criteria to be considered in conjunction with the security
data was the analysis of the Rorschach Ink Blot data. These data had been used

clinically throughout the study to provide confirmation of guidance procedures to the families. For this purpose it was used as an adjunct to the results of the children's performance on the Binet and WISC tests. Beyond yielding this kind of information there was an available method of analysing these data according to a conceptual framework developed by Ames, Métraux, and Walker (1971) *Adolescent Rorschach Responses*. This permitted an examination of their developing thought processes and a comparison of our subjects with norms developed from a larger general population. It was possible to evaluate this at each of the testing age levels (six, nine, twelve, and fifteen years) as well as through time.

(4) The children's performance on both Binet and WISC tests was examined in order to compare their performance with expected norms. Further examination of subtest performance within the group and also range of performance could identify characteristics unique to the function of the group itself.

The focus of analysis was twofold: first an examination of all the above aspects of the children's adaptation at age fifteen, and secondly an examination of the data longitudinally from six through fifteen years of age to identify changes and continuities through time.

Following is a chart which indicates the data analysis and age levels on which it focused.

	Ages 6	7	8	9	10	11	12	13	14	15
Home records	√	√	√	√	√	√	√	√	√	√
School records	√	√	√	√	√	√	√	√	√	√
Security measures	√			√			√			√
Social maturity				√			√			√
Intelligence ratings	√			√			√			√
Rorschach ink blot	√			√			√			√

5

The concept of security

The belief of the researchers involved first in the therapeutic programme within the institution and second in the guidance of parent practices after the children's placement in homes was that a mentally healthy person could function adequately in both his home and community. Hence the purpose of our practices with the children was to sponsor mentally healthy development as a basis for successful adjustment in both cognitive and emotional dimensions of living. In order to do this, the security theory of mental health provided the guidelines and the goals over the 15-year period of the study.

The Blatz earlier formulation defined mental health as a 'serene state of mind arising from the willingness to accept the consequences of one's own decisions and actions.' Such serenity was achieved by a conscious process of decision-making to resolve the constant stream of daily problems with which a person is confronted. The solution to problems can be found in many ways, some of which are decidedly healthier than others. One way is reliance on a *mature dependent agent* who shares the decisions which solve the problems, and who also shares the consequences of the decisions. This is a healthy method. Another way is total reliance on another person to make the decisions and to accept the consequences. This is called the *infantile dependent* solution which resembles the dependency of a very young child. Although an acceptable method by which a young child maintains mental health, this is an unhealthy way in adult life as it is a form of regression which is potentially hazardous. Another way of solving problems is the use of *avoidance mechanisms* (*deputy agents*). Such deputy agents as rationalization, compensation, and sublimation permit the individual a temporary feeling of security but must be reinforced or increased in number to maintain security. Although providing immediate relief from anxiety, these are potentially undependable because they might become predominant and permanent mechanisms of adjustment. In such an event the individual loses his capacity to criticize his own mental processes and thus becomes a poor mental health risk.

The most healthy way to solve problems is the independently secure way of putting forth effort to learn a skill, thereby relying on oneself for the solution. In addition, one must accept the consequences of whatever decision is made. Independent security rests on a person's capacity to make, and act upon, his own decisions. While doing this, he necessarily learns to accept insecurity, because through learning he discovers adequate ways of overcoming the anxiety of facing a problem and gradually develops a habit of thinking (and feeling) that he is capable of solving his problems through his own efforts.

The above security theory, largely appropriate for adults, underwent modification by Flint and colleagues when applied to infants and young children. The Blatz concept of reliance on decision-making and the acceptance of consequences as the basis for mental health was not totally appropriate when applied to infants and young children. Hence a restatement indicated the basis of an infant's mental health to be an *immature dependent* relationship on a mother's dependent, consistent attention to his needs. This relationship develops in the following manner:

MENTAL HEALTH

Mental health* begins in infancy and can be defined as a serene state of mind arising from a feeling of self-worth and a conviction that the world is benign. It is developed in a child, from birth on, through a compatible relationship with his mother.† This relationship gradually reduces and finally overcomes the newborn infant's insecurity on being thrust into a world requiring considerably more adaptation than that experienced *in utero*. His totally helpless state requires constant care from his mother in order to reduce his recurrent discomfort arising from cold, wetness, and hunger. During the neo-natal period this care is almost totally physical because the immaturity of the child arbitrates against his responding to care in any other way than by falling asleep after it is received. However, as he matures and becomes more wakeful and more aware of his environment, the child must recognize some relationship between the action which relieves his discomfort and the person who makes him comfortable. His reliance on parental care is the first step in the arousal of feelings of comfort and security and reflects his *immature dependency*.

As he continues to gain comfort from his *immature dependency*, gradually he becomes aware that he can expect care when he needs it and that there is a dependable 'someone' on whom he can rely to replace his discomfort with comfort. He soon associates a 'warm' feeling with the sight, sounds, smells, and adminis-

---

* From *The Security of Infants*, Toronto: University of Toronto Press, 1959.
† This term means his primary caretaker – not necessarily his biological mother.

trations of this person because she consistently has relieved his anxiety and he can rest easy in the belief that she will always do so. He begins to recognize too not only that she cares for him when he cries, thus responding to his demand for care, but also that he can expect her to anticipate his needs. This anticipation in turn reduces his incidences of discomfort while prolonging his periods of comfort. As his awareness of this situation grows, an infant develops an expectation that the world will be benign in the future as it has been in the past.

Once a child experiences the association between his mother's consistent relieving of discomfort and has an expectation that the world is benign, he is experiencing the *dependent trust feelings*. This is reflected in his behaviour as he accepts happily the care his mother gives to his eating, bathing, dressing, and sleeping activities as well as to his need for playthings and social contacts. His anticipation of her attention is obvious in such behaviour as quietening when he hears her approach, a reduction of activity when being changed, and a show of excitement on seeing his bottle.

These early acts of caring for a child, although predominantly physical in nature and designed to relieve discomfort, have an important psychological aspect also. They usually are accompanied by affectionate interplay between a mother and child and would seem to be an expression of the mother's feeling of love and tenderness towards her baby. While changing, dressing, feeding, and bathing him, she will tickle, talk to, coo at, cuddle, pat, scold, and rock her child. This, in turn, elicits a response of chuckles, gurgles, kicking, hand-waving, and general delight from the baby as he slowly grasps the thought that he is a person of value to his mother. This gradually becomes established in his mind as a feeling of *self-worth*.

It is this feeling of self-worth which lends the child sufficient confidence to put forth self-initiated effort towards limited goals in his world. He now wants to demand attention even when it is not really needed; he is energetic, socially outgoing, and interested in learning. He can also enjoy paying attention to play equipment because his feelings of self-worth naturally find expression in a joyful release of energy. The rewarding consequences of such self-initiated effort further enhance the child's feeling of self-worth as he begins to be capable of satisfying some of his own needs (that is, for change of activity, or for food) and achieving some of his goals.

As *self-confidence* pervades his activity, the infant experiences feelings of *self-trust*, the second essential quality of mental health in a young child. This self-trust is reflected in an infant's behaviour when he begins to show signs of what his mother will call 'personality.' Now he not only accepts her care but energetically demands it as well. He anticipates his mother's appearance when he hears her footsteps, and protests if they do not come towards him as he expected.

He calls for attention if he feels ignored, indicates his desire for food, toys, change of activity, and more people, according to his own self-centred goals. He is no longer satisfied that his mother should anticipate all his needs. If his feelings of dependent trust and self-trust are becoming well established, he now believes that his self-initiated effort is rewarding not only because it is fun for himself alone, but also because it is acceptable to and appreciated by his mother. This acceptance becomes a reinforcement to the child's *self-confidence*, expressed in his enjoyment of activity. Now he is quick to express his wishes and vehement in his protest when thwarted. He will want to play in the bedroom drawers, take the pots and pans out of the kitchen, feed himself before he is capable, and climb on the table to see what's there. His enjoyment of life reflects an underlying *'good' feeling*.

If he is to continue to grow in mental health it is essential that the adults around him support his effort, although frequently it brings conflict between his mother and himself. This is a crucial time when he is ready to enjoy the satisfaction of completing a self-initiated activity, but must necessarily be limited to ensure his own safety and the convenience of the total family. Should he be thwarted constantly in his efforts to project himself into his environment, he may lose some of his feeling of self-trust and eventually even lose his desire to be effortful. Such a condition will not arise, however, if opportunity is provided for him to direct his energy and outgoingness towards acceptable and safe goals. By providing substitute activities for those which are unacceptable, a parent continues to promote an increasingly deep sense of self-trust which can be seen in an infant's exuberant expressions of 'good' feeling.

Inevitably a parent will be unable to divert all a child's self-initiated activity into substitute channels, and the necessary thwarting of his goals will precipitate an angry protest and temporary emotional turmoil. This emotional outburst, in all its vehemence, sometimes shakes the faith of a parent in the wiseness of her decision. She should, rather, feel comforted by the fact that this is merely an expression of frustration from a self-directed, mentally healthy youngster who feels free to express himself, confident in the expectation that his rebellion will precipitate no denial of his mother's love although she may disapprove of his behaviour. It is only a less mentally healthy child who dares not chance such a strong display of feeling. He is full of doubts that it would be tolerated, hence he must inhibit much of his effort whether in emotional expression or effortful behaviour.

Thus, to summarize, a child who has developed *self-trust* will demand care and attention, will anticipate rewarding consequences to his self-initiated effort in play, social contacts, and routine aspects of his life, and will enjoy the satisfaction of achieving his goals, with the expectation that most of them will be acceptable to his parent. Such a child is developing a core of security, and the stronger the core, the more sure and confident will the child feel in his world.

As a baby develops a core of security most of his experiences will be well taken care of by himself and his mother. However, he will be faced inevitably with some situations of stress which will temporarily dispel his serenity and shake his conviction that the world is benign. At these times he will feel vulnerable and will resort to one of two modes of behaviour to relieve his feeling of uneasiness and momentarily resolve his difficulties. He may either regress to a less mature stage of development in which he depends on his mother to relieve his stress by making a decision and accepting the consequences of it, or employ a deputy agent which will permit him temporarily to delay making a decision, to delay putting forth effort, or to delay accepting the consequences of his action.

Should he resort to a *regressive formula*, he will demand care, comfort, and attention in situations where he is capable of resolving the problem through his own efforts. This regression will be seen in his relationships with other people, both adults and children, in his play with play equipment and toys, and in his attitude towards his routine care of eating, sleeping, bathing, toileting, and dressing. For example, he may steadfastly refuse to accept some new food introduced to his diet, refuse to permit himself to be put to bed or bathed by anyone other than his mother, or be thoroughly uninterested in actively co-operating when being dressed – he may, for instance, refuse to hold his arm out for his coat sleeve. He may remain inattentive, or perseverate with toys, and cling desperately to his mother when he is expected to warm to a visitor.

Should he resort to a *deputy agent formula*, he will use a variety of behaviours to avoid either putting forth effort to solve a problem or facing the consequences inherent in a threatening situation. These deputy agents generally take the form of crying, withdrawing from, over-reacting to, and being compulsive about situations which a child perceives as threatening. Each child will employ his own variety, kind. and frequency depending on his degree of mental health. Thus deputy agents may appear in a few or in all of the behavioural areas of an infant's life – eating, sleeping, bathing, toileting, play with play materials, social situations involving both adults and children, and physical experiences. They are likely to be evident particularly in new and strange situations which naturally hold more insecurity for an infant than those with which he is familiar. Some deputy agents which might appear in an infant's behaviour would be spitting out food, refusing to lie down in bed, screaming when toilet training is initiated, being tense and fearful when bathed, crying at loud or sudden noises, withdrawing from other children, resenting an adult's paying attention to another child, and being erratic and inattentive when playing with materials.

Some deputy agents can be expected to appear in all children as temporary mechanisms which tide them over times of stress. Some may be used for a while but disappear when an infant grows more secure. Then again, they may be replaced by others more appropriate to the next stage of development or to a change in the demands of his culture. They can be reduced or increased in intensity according to the degree of stress in which a child finds himself. They operate to relieve temporarily the distress arising from a situation with which an infant feels unable to cope either by putting forth effort or through seeking assistance from a dependable agent, his mother.

POOR MENTAL HEALTH

In contrast to well children are babies who do not develop a core of security, and who, remaining in a constant state of uneasiness or anxiety, show symptoms that indicate mental ill health. Such infants employ regressive and deputy agent actions as permanent and predominating aspects of personality. Their ill health can be described as an uneasy state of mind arising from a lack of feeling of self-worth and a suspicion that their world is untrustworthy.

Why do some babies get into this state? It would appear that they are questioning the dependent trust which should be firmly established with their mother. They seem to be doubting the reliability of the parental agent. They experience feelings of apprehension that care may not be forthcoming when needed and feel uncertainty that the world is benign. Such apprehension and uncertainty can be the result of an unpredictable mother whose physical care is based on her own whims and goals rather than on her baby's needs. In this case, the child cannot predict that his mother will either accurately anticipate his needs or respond to the demands he makes. In order to achieve even temporary serenity, the infant will over-demand care and attention at unpredictable times. His mother's assurance of comfort though minimal, has nevertheless been the main source of comfort that he has known. Therefore, he will cling to his mother in every way possible. He will whine in her absence, cling to her when she is near, and become frenzied if he anticipates a removal of her attention. Although he lacks dependent trust, he cannot risk ever refusing her ministrations because he fears refusal will bring a further withdrawal of the comfort he so intently seeks. More seriously, should he consistently be denied necessary care when it is needed, he will gradually reduce his expectations to an apathetic acceptance of care and attention when offered and will make no demands on his mother at all.

The mentally ill child, lacking dependent trust, will most likely be deficient in self-trust also. The inadequate attention of his mother, which has probably provided little, or at best inconsistent, affectionate interplay, has mitigated against the development of any strong feeling of self-worth, and thus has robbed him of any motivation to be effortful and outgoing in his world. His underlying feeling seems to be one of chronic anxiety, apparent in his cautiousness, timidity, and, in the most extreme cases, apathy. He seems either uncertain or unaware that self-initiated effort is rewarding. Hence he is uninterested in food or in feeding himself, accepts in an apathetic way the procedures necessary for bedtime, bath, and dressing, lacks interest in play materials, and can muster little excitement in anticipation of response to a social contact. He may demonstrate many tics such as sucking his thumb, rocking, and shaking his bed. His apathetic state is further deepened should he fail to receive either encouragement for or approval of any self-initiated effort he may make.

It is this state of serious withdrawal which is observed in babies reared in those institutions which give little attention to their emotional needs. In the absence of consistent warmth and loving attention from one adult, such institutional babies show a picture of apathy. Mealtime, bath and bedtime are drab routine chores, experienced without interest or enthusiasm. No sparkle of anticipation appears when an adult approaches; toys fall from cribs to be left unsought; language and motor skills are grossly retarded. Such babies appear to remain psychologically immature, while operating mainly at the physiological level of life. They accept food and rest at appropriate times, but beyond this seem to have withdrawn from life's experiences as if operating behind one enormous deputy agent. They appear to have no self-trust and very little dependent trust.

Less seriously disturbed children who are burdened with erratic feelings of self-trust, probably as a reflection of a questionable dependent trust, show behaviour which is frequently unpredictable. At one time they may appear effortful and bouncy, only to withdraw their energies at another time, becoming apprehensive and perhaps even sullen. They may demand affection, only to turn away when it is given. They may want to play or to help themselves in routines, but be unable to take the initiative without first referring to an adult for approval or waiting to be urged. At one time they may seem to enjoy being with people, both adults and children, while again they may scream to be taken away.

Treatment of mentally ill babies necessarily consists of rearranging their environment and evaluating the efficacy of the new arrangement by observing behaviour. Usually, the solution seems to be to establish or re-establish a dependent trust in a young child. Where little trust in a dependable adult has been built, the procedure is uncomplicated. Providing a dependable adult to care for a child gives sufficient opportunity for establishing this 'first' relationship. Treatment of an older infant, who may have had a dependent trust and some self-trust feelings which have been shattered or at least threatened, is somewhat more complicated and requires more time. It will be necessary to break through the child's defences (obvious in his deputy agent behaviour) before an adult can gradually reassure him of her trustworthiness. Until this is accomplished, no trust relationship can exist between the two, and the child will continue to rely on his deputy agents, refusing either to put forth effort in an acceptable direction or to comply with the requests and administrations of the adult.

THE MATURING CHILD

As a child moves from infancy through the pre-school and elementary school years a consolidation of feelings of dependent trust and self-trust would be the manifestation of continuing mental health. How this comes about is reflected in the shift in the balance of the interaction between the child and his caretakers. Whereas in early childhood the healthy child has been largely dependent on the adult who organizes his world, and accepts the consequences of this organization, as the child grows older he finds that he is increasingly able to rely on himself to reduce his needs in order to relieve his insecurity. This is brought about by his increasing competence to deal with his own world and to accept the consequences of his own actions as he matures. This characteristic is reinforced by the parent's increasing inability to anticipate all the child's needs and hence reduce insecurity in what was formerly a satisfactory way.

For these reasons, self-initiated effort increasingly becomes one of the manifestations of the older, healthy child. Furthermore, the attainment of security through self-effort is self-reinforcing and leads not only to further effort but also to increasingly enhanced feelings of self-confidence. Gradually a child can move from the attainment of very limited goals (e.g., self-feeding) to more challenging attainments (putting on one's clothes to go outside) to quite responsible activities (going to the store to do the shopping or driving the family car). Hence, through time, self-worth becomes a pervasive attitude which reflects a child's confidence that he can overcome future problems as successfully as he has done in the past. Hence, feelings of insecurity do not become overwhelming but can be regarded as transient. Furthermore, a healthy sense of self-worth allows a child the opportunity to accept the consequences of his behaviour; hence he is increasingly able to set his goals, admit mistakes, and tolerate criticism.

The maturing child carries with him vestiges of earlier mechanisms of adjustment as he adapts his coping strategies to the changing challenges of his world. He remains a mixture of three psychological states of Immature Dependence, Dependent Trust, and Self-Worth. As a healthy child matures from infancy through adolescence there is a shift in balance of these three states from an early preponderance of immature dependency through dependent trust to self-trust which is finally reflected in behaviour as a preponderance of self-directed activity. It is evident that this shift in balance can be identified by changing behaviours as a child interacts with the persons and objects in his world. Furthermore, his reliance has moved from his dependence on one primary caretaker to several persons in his life (father, mother, teacher, peers).

As a child matures, changes in status take place between himself and his caretakers. We know that a certain degree of immature dependency of a child on his caretakers persists from infancy through to maturity. We also know that this reliance, the nature of which is for specific care and direction, decreases through time. We do not know at what point the nature of this reliance changes from that which reflects a predominance of immature dependent feelings to dependent trust. Immature dependency is marked by a child's leaning on the physical care and parental directives regarding his behaviour. The more (trusting) mature form of reliance emerges as a child demonstrates that he is increasingly internalizing the values of his parents. This has come about by his living with reliable, trustworthy, and dependable people whose directives he can predict and whose opinions he has come to respect. This enhancing quality of dependent trust replaces, in large part, the necessity for immature dependence, while allowing a child to perpetuate a comfortable relationship with his caretakers.

This maturing dependent trust relationship implies decreasing support from the directives of one's parents which is compensated by increased self-direction in independent activities. Such activity will be accompanied by the comfort of believing that much of his activity will be approved by his parents. Such feelings cannot be attained until sufficient of the parents' *values* have been internalized to permit the child freedom to act on the assumption that his behaviours will likely be congenial with that of his family.

When the state of mind is achieved which is largely characterized by dependent trust, the child finds support for his mental health in three ways; one through feelings of compatibility with his parents and their goals for him, secondly by relying on those internalized values which he has accepted during a lifetime with them, and third, by self-chosen activity outside the jurisdiction of his home and beyond the direct supervision of his family. Such a state of mind does not preclude the fact that some of this activity, particularly in peer relationships, will be in conflict with the directives and values of his parents. Hence we find children moving through the predominantly dependent trust phase, carrying sufficient feelings of self-confidence that they can both accept and question the nature of parental controls.

The dependent trust relationship allows a child to feel that his efforts will largely be supported by his caretakers, and gives him the 'go ahead' to become increasingly self-directed. Should a child fail to negotiate this phase successfully then his defences will appear either in over-compliance or rebellious hostility to his family's wishes and values. He may be overwhelmed by conflict and his ongoing psychological development brought to a halt. On the other hand, insistent feelings of rebellion may be expressed in his removing himself from his family. Such behaviours are evidence of a failure to develop security and reflect the need for compensatory activities of a regressive or deputy agent nature. These behaviours can be expressed with varying intensity along a continuum from severe withdrawal to intense acts of aggression. The yardstick whereby security feelings are measured behaviourally must therefore be reflected in the nature and degree of effort manifest by the maturing person. Self-initiated and self-directed effort is the expression of the secure individual within the accepted framework of his culture.

SECURITY ANALYSIS

Method of Defining Developmental Stages of Security
Making use of our home records it was possible to impose the security theory concept upon them from ages six through fifteen years. The developmental sequence of immature dependent behaviours preceding the presence of dependent trust behaviours and eventually being eclipsed at maturity by behaviours reflecting self-directed effort and self-worth was evident. Furthermore, regressive and deputy agent behaviours were readily identified.

On the basis of this perusal, agreement was reached by the research team about the following definitions:
Immature dependence was thought to be expressed by the presence of indicators of
- reliance on parental encouragement and intervention for achievement
- acquiescence to parental expectations and demands
- reliance on parents for physical care and for communication to others
- reliance on parents for help, advice, and affection
- finding satisfaction in close, warm relations with parents
Dependent trust was thought to be expressed by the presence of indicators of
- sharing feelings
- belief in parents' acceptance of his/her activities
- expectation of approval of his activities
- internalized acceptance of family values
- viewing adults as comfortably supportive
- enjoying being with his family
- a belief that one's parents will support a child when in stress (not necessarily approve his behaviour)

A lack of dependence – *immature and dependent trust would be expressed by indicators*
- that the child was rejecting parental direction, rules, expectations, values and affection
- of the child acting overly independent
- of withdrawal and avoidance of parent and parental expectations
- of rejection of family activities (picnics, holidays)
- of seeking inappropriate physical contact (reassurance)
- of fear of parents

Self-worth and effort would be expressed by the presence of
- actions involving self-motivated activities: (a) chores or jobs done spontaneously as part of duties or for money; (b) sports or hobbies carried out as an expression of his own interest; (c) successful school activity appropriate to his level of ability; (d) expressions of ... liking, loving, accepting with enjoyment, accepting the inevitable, tolerating criticism
- identifying with family activities and values
- identifying with peers' activities and values
- identifying with a team and groups
- carrying out family expectations and goals *without urging*

A lack of self-worth and effort would be expressed by – Deputy agent and regressive behaviour
- Hostile expressions of resentment re parental practices and expectations
- Fear of effort which might result in criticism
- sour grapes
- denial
- rationalization
- alibis
- blaming others
- bossing
- controlling
- crying
- temper tantrums
- yelling

} re achievement, friends or effort

Analysis of Home Records according to Security Categories
Having agreed to the characteristics to be expected in each of the categories, it remained to select the exact behavioural descriptions from the records and reach some common agreement between raters as to their placement.

The behavioural statements on the Home Records resulted from interviews with parents (and sometimes children) on a minimum of twice yearly visits.

These statements, although not all vebatim, reported on the children's activity in all aspects of their daily lives. Because our records had been collected with a view to objective data, few of the statements were of an interpretative nature, i.e., the child care worker refrained from imposing *her* interpretations of the mother's reporting. Occasionally a summarizing statement might have been made by her which summed up several statements, e.g., 'Greg likes hockey, swimming, and baseball' might be reported as 'Greg likes sports.' Statements were not made which would not have been confirmed by a child's mother.

The first necessity was to arrive at rater agreement as to the placement of the behaviour descriptions under the selected categories. Using a master sheet of definitions as a guideline, three separate raters assigned behavioural statements from the home records. On examination it appeared that a major difficulty in achieving reliability was not assignment of a statement to a category but rather the matter of agreement about the number of categories chosen to be assigned. For example, many statements could be regarded as one, two, or even three separate items. 'Enjoys hockey, baseball, track' could be listed as three items or as one item, 'Enjoys sports.' Hence substantial agreement appeared on assignment of items to appropriate categories and disagreement appeared in the *number* of items assigned. It was assumed then that each rater was in agreement regarding the *clinical implications* of the statements selected despite the number selected to support the clinical judgment.

To overcome this difficulty and to focus on the clinical *implications* of the statements according to the Security Theory, a method of arriving at a balance of factors which considered the proportion of one kind of statement (dependent trust) against the proportion of another kind of statement (self-worth) was adopted. This allowed the critical aspect of the data to be manifest (the implications of the statements) and further permitted comparison of the scores of one child against another regardless of the unequal number of items appearing on each record.

A further difficulty in the assignment of items to categories arose over the differentiation of items reflecting a lack of immature dependence and dependent trust. Unlike the positive aspect of these categories, differentiation on the negative aspect was impossible. Hence it was decided that on the negative side of the immature dependence – dependent trust categories, each item would be listed under a common heading, Lack of Dependence.

Rater Agreement
Rater agreement was arrived at by the following method:
(1) Raters A and B jointly analysed and discussed the placement of items from four records hence achieving 100% agreement.

(2) Raters A, B, and C separately analysed several records, calculated agreement, and discussed discrepancies.

(3) Rater C completed analysis of six records which had been jointly done by Raters A and B and achieved a high level of agreement with these.

(4) Raters A and C completed the analysis of the remaining records independently of each other. Inter-rater reliability was calculated by Spearman rank order correlations. Level of agreement on effort categories, raters A and C, was .99. Level of agreement on dependence categories was .96.

Scoring
Items under the category headings of immature dependence, dependent trust, and lack of dependence, were summed separately and computed as a percentage of the total number of items listed under all three categories. Each percentage derived was considered a Percentage Score for that category.

Example

Immature dependence	Dependent trust	Lack of dependence	Total no. items
1 Has to be pushed into things 2 Must have TV supervised and rationed 3 Has to be told to take a bath 4 Has to be urged to read 5 Will come for help before trying anything	1 Will listen to reason 2 Enjoys doing things with the family 3 Shares feelings and opinions with family 4 Confides in mother 5 Is matter of fact about responsibilities	1 Loses money – doesn't care 2 Stubborn 3 Rejects help 4 Defiant 5 Refuses to do what Dad says 6 Never tells us about his friends	
No. of items 5	5	6	16
Calculation 5/16 X 100	5/16 X 100	6/16 X 100	
Percentage score 31	31	38	100

A similar method was employed to arrive at self-worth and effort and lack of self-worth, and effort percentage scores.

A total security rating was calculated by taking dependence percentage scores (immature dependence plus dependent trust), and adding self-worth and effort percentage score. This sum was then divided by two.

Security rating − (D% + E%) / 2.

RESULTS

Distribution of Items between Security Categories
Home records for each child were analysed according to the above method for the years six, nine, twelve, and fifteen and percentage scores arrived at for all five categories. (See Appendix, Table 8, Security categories in percentage scores.)

Means were then drawn for the five categories (see Table 1 below).

TABLE 1
Percentage means of the distribution of items according to security categories

	6 years	9 years	12 years	15 years
Immature dependence	43	46	19	24
Dependent trust	29	27	46	40
Lack of dependence	28	27	35	36
	100%	100%	100%	100%
Effort	53	55	62	62
Lack of effort	47	45	38	38
	100%	100%	100%	100%

An *Analysis of Variance* was carried out on the percentage figures of dependent trust across the years six, nine, twelve, and fifteen with the results in Table 2.

TABLE 2
Analysis of Variance: dependent trust at 6, 9, 12, and 15 years

	S.S.	D.F.	Variance
Between groups	5473.71	3	1824.57
Within group	25732.66	82	313.81
Total	31205.37	85	F − 5.8132 significant at .01 level

T-tests were calculated for the significance of the difference between the means at the years 9 and 12 for categories immature dependence, dependent trust, and effort.

TABLE 3
Levels of significance of the difference between
means at 9 and 12 years for security categories

	Mean 9 years	12 years	D.F.	Level of significance	
Immature dependence	46.00	18.86	41	7.67	.001
Dependent trust	26.90	46.33	41	3.28	.01
Effort	54.64	62.14	41	1.49	.20

RESULTS

1 There was a reduction in the proportion of immature dependent behaviour from age six through fifteen years, with a marked shift occurring between the ages of nine and twelve (significant at .001 level).

2 Conversely there was a significant increase in the proportion of dependent trust from ages six through twelve years.

3 A *t*-test indicates the significant shift to take place between nine and twelve years of age.

4 There is an increase in the proportion of lack of dependence from nine through fifteen years of age.

5 The proportion of effort remains relatively stable from six years through fifteen, with a slight but non-significant increase apparent after nine years.

Interpretation
It is apparent that from age six through fifteen these children are dependent on their families. In the early years this dependence is flavoured with immaturity; as the children grow older, dependent trust predominates. This is the expected healthy direction to development of trust in family and a growing awareness of self-worth. Between the ages of nine and twelve years a significant change takes place in the maturing relationship between the children and their parents.

The proportion of effortful behaviour is consistent from six through fifteen years and indicates that these are effortful children developing a sense of self-worth. Such results confirm the expected model of the Security Theory when applied through time.

Examination of the *group* means of the *security ratings* indicate that the scores remain consistent from six years through fifteen years of age. Hence, although the quality of the children's relationship with parents shifts from an immature to a more mature type of security, the overall security ratings reflected in their behaviours over the years shows little change.

Group mean security ratings (by age)

6 years	9 years	12 years	15 years
66.4	64.2	62.3	62.3

Examination of *individual* security scores for each child from six years through nine, showed variable stability through time (Appendix, Table 3). The mean differences between high and low security ratings for the group was 19, but the range was from 3 to 41. The median is 15. Hence it appears that within the group almost half the individuals showed wide fluctuations in Security Scores from six through fifteen years.

6

Social maturity

Our interest in the adaptation of these children to their life situations was not limited to an examination of their security. That dimension of their lives involving peer relationships might well have been seriously undermined by their early experiences. The early lack of interest in others while in the institution had been prolonged for two to three years. Consequent records of peer relationships frequently hinted at difficulties with contemporaries and led to the suspicion that there might be a common deficit in the social capabilities of many of these children. Furthermore, their considerable dependency on parents, which had been encouraged, could have acted as a constraint on their reaching out for successful interactions with members of their peer group. Their capacity, or desire, to take care of themselves and others could also have been slow in developing as a result of early deficit and later immature dependency on the parent.

Much of the literature on deprivation told us that early deprived children were frequently 'loners.' Even more serious, some of them related so poorly to family and community expectations that they were described as 'psychopaths.' We believed that none of our children deserved this description. As a result we sought objective ways to measure degree of socialization. Both home and school questionnaires included sections on the children's social development. This information, in conjunction with what we knew about their hobbies, sports activities, and other interests gave us a frequent account of their social performance within their peer groups, as well as other compensatory activities which were expressions of overall adjustment. As well as providing information on social adjustment each year, the data which accumulated until this operation was terminated was available for final group analysis which could be carried out by means of the Vineland Social Maturity Scale.

The fact that it had been possible to partial out the various components of security and examine them in conjunction with each other and against the full scores provided an internal validation of the theoretical construct. Validation of our hypothesis against an outside criterion would enhance our study even more and provide a means of critically examining our conclusions.

The Vineland Scale of Social Maturity developed by Doll seemed to provide a means by which this would be possible. The data gathering procedures on the Vineland Scale were the same as those of our parent interview forms, involving a sophisticated interviewer and descriptions of behaviours which could be assigned to categories within the author's frame of reference regarding social maturity.

The Vineland Scale was validated and standardized according to age levels from birth though 20 years of age and on both male and female populations. The items of the scale, arranged in normal average life age progression, fit comfortably into the developmental concepts of security. The central purpose of the items of the scale is to represent some particular aspect of the ability to look after one's own practical needs.

In the author's estimate of social maturity, two aspects are considered: the ontogenetic evaluation of an individual as (1) an independent social unit with emphasis on his subjective self-sustaining social adequacies, and (2) the individual as a co-operating member of the social group. The author of the scale believes that, as each person relates to another in the social milieu, personal and subjective experiences acquire social significance through sharing. This can be observed in behaviour which is an expression of social competence. Therefore, in measurement, the concern is with human behaviour as ultimately expressed in some situation which demonstrates its relevance through social competence. This competence can be thought of in terms of personal independence and social responsibility. Social competence is not static. It varies according to both phylogenetic and ontogenetic evolution and varies also with physical and cultural conditions according to the time, place, and circumstance. Therefore, social competence can be expressed in relation to age, status, opportunity, talent, health, degree of freedom, and so on. Hence it is possible to think of social competence in terms of social usefulness, self-sufficiency, and service to others and as such it can be measured and related to life age.

Thinking developmentally, social maturation has at least three major dimensions: (1) from dependence to independence, i.e., from the early reliance of the infant on subsistence and personal care through the self-help type of behaviour of early childhood to the emancipation of the youth and adult; (2) from irresponsibility to responsibility whereby he shares group and family responsibility in early childhood to become a contributing member of society in adulthood; and (3) from incompetence to competence which is a synthesis of both progressive independence and responsibility.

In application, the scale describes behaviour on a continuum from infancy through adulthood. Each of a series of behaviours is related to progressive chronological age and is assigned item numbers which express the level of development or life age. An overall score can be obtained by summing passed items, thus enabling a comparison between life age and chronological age. Furthermore, this can be reduced, as in the calculation of IQ, to a social quotient which is a reflection of a corrected score. It is then possible to compare IQ with SQ, with 100 as the base.

Used clinically, the Vineland Social Maturity Scale has been accepted in relationship to IQ as an indicator of maladjustment of two types. When the social quotient is considerably higher than the intelligence quotient, the individual is considered to be over-striving in the social aspect of his life and hence is anxious (IQ < SQ). On the other hand where the intelligence quotient is considerably higher than the social quotient, the individual is considered to be under-achieving socially and probably is carrying feelings of social inadequacy (SQ < IQ).

In our present study social quotients were calculated on the basis of the behavioural statements taken from the home records. The behaviours at ages fifteen, twelve, and nine were readily identified according to this schema. However, at age six this treatment of the data was not successful as the behavioural statements did not so clearly fit the Vineland frame of reference. Hence, no social maturity scores were calculated at age six (see Appendix, Table 4).

When social ages were calculated and averaged for ages nine, twelve, and fifteen, it became apparent that the group as a whole scored lower than age expectancy (CA) at each of these testing points. In addition, the discrepancy apparent at nine years increased through twelve to fifteen years as if once a certain level of maturity had been attained further social advances were acquired at a decreasing pace. This was demonstrated by the fact that the group mean at nine years of age was eight (SQ89), at twelve years of age it was ten (SQ83.5), and at fifteen years of age it was 12.5 (SQ83).

An analysis of variance of the change which took place from ages nine through fifteen indicated that this shift was not statistically significant.

Group means of social quotients on the Vineland Social Maturity Scale

	9.0 years	12.0 years	15.0 years
Mean SQ	89.16	83.56	83.20
Mean social age	8.0	10.2	12.5

Analysis of Variance – SQ's at 9, 12, and 15 years of age

	S.S.	D.F.	Variance
Between groups	558.43	2	279.21
Within groups	8527.52	72	118.44
Total	9085.95	74	F – 2.3573 NS

Pringle's study of English children confirmed Doll's finding that IQ and social maturity are related. Although the general tenor of Pringle's study focused on a lack of social competence as a reflection of emotional maladjustment, she states: 'In general a marked positive discrepancy (between IQ and SQ) is accompanied by problem behaviour but a marked negative discrepancy may merely indicate an over protected child although he could possibly become a problem later is not one at the present time' (p. 37). It is important to notice that only the extremes of discrepancy between IQ and SQ are considered to reflect maladjustment.

Investigation of the histories of three of the children who had large discrepancies between SQ and IQ scores at age fifteen would confirm that some degree of emotional turbulence had been part of their growing up but declined at the approach of maturity. One child (#15) had considerable friction with his family and benefited from family therapy after such disturbing anti-social behaviour as stealing (SQ 93, IQ 128). Subsequent follow-up indicates that this boy, now twenty-one years old, is a healthily functioning young man working in a financial institution, who lives at home and contributes to the support of his family. He continues to save money for the purpose of future academic training. Child #20, at age fifteen had an SQ of 88, and an IQ of 121. Prior to this time he had a record of under-achieving at school, demonstrated considerable 'lippiness' and resentfulness at home and was being alternately tolerated and rebuked by his frustrated family. Present follow-up of this boy, now nineteen years of age, indicates that after dropping out of school he returned to complete his grade 13 as a preliminary to further training. He has successful peer relationships and life with his family has become much more congenial. Child #1, who at age fifteen had an SQ of 94 and an IQ of 115, had a quieter history of family interaction, although he was under-achieving at school. Goal-directed in his hobbies and rather solitary in pursuit of his activities he functioned more remotely from his peers than many children. A later report at age eighteen indicated improved school performance and an arrangement with a 'rock' group whereby he acted as their business manager. Family relations continued in a satisfactory manner.

It is interesting to note that there were three children in the study (8,11,6) who could be described as emotionally vulnerable at age fifteen and who had shown recurrent disturbance over the years prior to and following its official termination. They had sQs and IQs which were less discrepant and had lower IQs than the group discussed above. Therefore, it seems fair to assume that the general picture for our children who all show consistent inferiority in sQ in contrast to IQ is not one of emotional disturbance. Rather their early environmental austerity and subsequent encouragement to become immaturely dependent on their families has created a developmental disability in social maturity.

The consistent degree of social immaturity of these children at fifteen years of age leads to the speculation that this might be a permanent deficit impossible to change completely in the course of growing up. The lack of social awareness apparent in the lives of these children when first observed in the institution may have spelled out a deficit which was critical to future adjustment. Although it has been demonstrated that these children were able to invest themselves deeply in family life, many of them have had some difficulty making congenial adjustments to contemporaries. Furthermore, their lack of involvement in group activities may be indicative of a lack of interest in or feeling of responsibility for community or group activities – one quality measured on the Vineland Scale (for Social Maturity Scores and Intelligence Quotients, see Appendix, Table 4).

Gary Jones is an example of a boy with marked social immaturities when first placed with his family. Through time there were remarkable advances in his adjustment to his new environment and a blossoming of healthy intellectual curiosity. Despite these advances, his social deficiencies were remarkably persistent from the time of his placement at two years of age until the time of this writing when he is now twenty years old.

During his initial placement with his family he was supported through a frightening period of anxiety about losing his new parents through death. On entrance to school his social inadequacies led to his isolation from his peers. He seemed to gain few social skills and his teasing, irritating behaviour discouraged fruitful social interaction instead of attracting children to him. In his first couple of years in school he was isolated both in the classroom and on the playground. Teachers and parents both welcomed guidance from the child care worker about this disability but none of the forms of intervention appreciably improved his social skills. Characteristically a social group was disrupted by his clumsy attempts to intrude himself into it.

Fortunately, healthy compensatory lone activity made its early appearance and this was encouraged by his highly accepting family. Carpentry, plumbing, electrical problems, all proved a challenge to him. Cupboards were wired for lights and buzzers, radios and television sets were brought to his workshop for repairs; an intercom system was hooked up from the garage to the basement; the library was explored for more sophisticated information. Conversations with radio and electrical repair men were a delight to Gary who could discuss matters at a surprisingly sophisticated level.

As he moved into high school his advanced knowledge led to a proficiency in electronics. His self-directed activity and his capacity to complete his own goals although an asset academically did nothing to encourage his development of social skills. He went through high school with very few friends and these were of a casual nature. His parents, through acceptance of his interests as well as his social immaturity, acted as a support through some lonely times. Despite his unusual motivation in the pursuit of his own goals, his marks in high school were relatively low. His present status seems to reflect a consolidation of his personality as one who has learned to live comfortably without an extended social life. His capabilities are being used profitably and future prognosis would indicate that he will likely become a productive, self-supporting and contributing member of his community.

His resistance to intervention designed to overcome the disabilities created by his social immaturities is reflected in the following two letters. Letter A was sent to the principal of his elementary school as the result of one of our regular psychological interviews when Gary was eleven years, ten months of age. The information from the Home and School Questionnaire was used as additional information on which to base the recommendations of this report. Letter B was sent to the Child Care worker in response to her request to bring us up to date about the events of his life.

LETTER A

April 3, 1969

Dear Sister:

Mr. and Mrs. Jones accompanied their son Gary to this Institute for a routine assessment. Their child is one of a group of youngsters whose mental health development is being recorded in a longitudinal study for research purposes.

The following is a summary of this assessment including suggestions that I am sure will be beneficial to Gary's teacher, in handling him and understanding his specific needs.

Gary is a shy, friendly youngster who functions in the upper end of normal range intelligence.

His vocabulary is average for his age. He expresses himself logically but it is difficult for him to express ideas unless a format *is presented to him.*

Gary is still a dependent child, slightly impulsive and tense. He was adopted at 2 years of age after an infancy of extreme deprivation in an institution. With understanding parents, he has made tremendous strides intellectually and emo-

tionally. The boy's mother and father are very sensitive to his needs and have worked closely with us in using the suggestions given them. Because of their constant awareness of his behaviour in his growing years and the help they have given him, Gary has developed well in his home environment. He is now fairly content and much less tense or impulsive in his secure home.

However, socially in the school and community there is still evidence of his early history of deprivation. Because of these inadequate, immature social skills he tends to be bossy and silly, and literally does not know how to behave and get along with his peers. He needs to be told what is expected of him. He has not confidence in himself and he must have adult support by 'spelling it out,' for him, each step of the way.

His teacher needs to help him express himself and not leave him to flounder – or he will give up. In the structured curriculum material he should perform adequately, but she will find her effort rewarding if she could organize his work and encourage him to respond towards a stated goal.

He still needs help and training in judgment situations. He should be helped to grasp alternatives rather than left on his own to make decisions.

The boy needs guidance and encouragement before he commences tasks rather than criticism for not completing what he was not sure of in the beginning.

When in a group of his peers he also needs help from an adult, so that his silly immature behaviour does not cause disruption. An eye should be kept on him for any trouble, and if possible try to keep him in the group. This is the only way he is going to gain adequate social skills.

LETTER B

August 18, 1976,
General Delivery,

Dear Miss Kilgour:

I am sorry I took so long to answer, but your letter arrived just before we were ready to leave on holidays.

You seem very interested in my future plans. I will start off by telling you that I plan to attend college in Peterborough this fall, to take an Electronics Technician course. After this I plan to get a job in this field. You know what it is like to have familiar surroundings, so I would like to work in the area if I can.

Last Monday we left for Peterborough to find a place to stay, and tour the college; an orientation day. We visited friends in Weston and Bowmanville. On Friday we went to see Ontario Place. For the beginning and end of last week we camped at Beavermead Park in Peterborough.

The college was quite a sight to see. The main entrance is on the fourth floor. The floor in this area is covered with shiny rubber mats with holes in the floor to attach display cases. This is very similar to a lobby in a shopping mall. All the latest designs are used in this building. The stairwells are outlined with numerous lights like around a billboard.

The colour scheme is quite different with purple classroom doors and lockers. The classroom doors measure about 2 1/2 × 8 feet with burnished brass hardware. The ceilings in the halls and classrooms are sloped at an angle to reflect the light. This building is a split level located on the side of a hill. The outside is covered in burnished brass shaped in boxes. It looks different, but nice.

You knew that I was interested in antiques with a small collection of my own in the basement. I will have to put my hobby aside for a while even though (although?) I am in close contact with the Champlain Trail Museum in Pembroke and The Archives in Ottawa.

Now its time to ask about yourself. What have you been doing since you left the Institute? How did they make out with the book they were writing, based on their studies. When do you go to your cottage and how often are you there? You know I have an aunt living at 24 Jane St. She works at a Flower Shop.

I would enjoy seeing and hearing from you soon. Tell me where your cottage is, and is there a phone?

Here are two school graduation pictures. I thought you might like to give the other to some one else or something.

Well I must go; because, as you say 'time goes too quickly' and I have many things to do.

Sincerely
Garry
(sgd.) Garry (CA, 19 years)

7

Emancipation

Our search for qualities in the environment which modify the constitutional characteristics of the growing individual leads us quickly to the relationship that exists between parent and child in the course of his growing up from infancy through adolescence. The quality of a parent-child relationship is a critical one in establishing a child's attitude towards the world in which he lives and the people with whom he is in direct interaction. How he sees his parents in terms of their support of his development and recognition of his individuality undoubtedly will have much to do with his own attitude towards others in his world. We have stated that a parent's attitude of acceptance of his child's uniqueness and fostering of his individuality can lead the child to feel that the world is benignly disposed towards him. On the other hand, a relationship between mother and child from infancy onward can be crucial in cultivating the idea that the world is unpredictable, lacking in support, and destructive of his needs and ambitions.

It has become evident that some children, from birth, have constitutional dispositions that are uncongenial to the parents with whom he is fated to live. A child with an irritable disposition, restless and quick to react, can prove to be a misery if born to a rather contemplative, slow-moving parent who feels comfortable in an orderly, systematic, and predictable world. The multitude of transactions which take place between mother and child is first developed to serve the dependency needs of the infant. Once these have been met and the child begins to feel that he is a person, some of his effort in growing up is directed to the process of differentiating himself from his mother and towards setting up his unique interactions and activities in his environment which are expressions of his singular experiences and self-direction. This process has been called 'emancipation' by Carroll Davis in her book *Room to Grow*. She has developed a method to assess parent-child relationships which can be applied from the early pre-school years through adolescence. By such means patterns of healthy and unhealthy emancipation of a child from his mother can be described.

Davis's study of a group of children from pre-school years through adolescence had led her to believe that the essential striving of each individual is to become a unique person. She has arrived at this position by examining the quality of the interactions which takes place between parent and child in the numerous situations they share as the child grows with his family. The process of the child's emergence from almost complete dependency on parents during infancy to almost total emancipation from them at maturity is a highly individual phenomenon.

To accomplish healthy emancipation, co-operation is needed between parent and child. The matter of where the goals of the growing process are placed for both the parent and child are the crucial ones in the emancipation process. Should the child and parent share somewhat similar goals, the parent is able to facilitate the development of individuality and foster competencies, and the course of emancipation tends to run smoothly. Should parent and child have divergent goals, the course of emancipation is distorted and becomes conflicted and eventually unhealthy. Since the child's strivings are towards expression of individuality, he will either develop ways of circumventing the parent's attempts to produce conformity or react with open conflict.

The multitude of continuing interactions between parent and child can reflect different expectations on the part of the parent from situation to situation; for example, high expectations for independent action in dressing and eating situations but an enormous degree of dependency on the choice of friends. To examine each life situation in detail might lead to the suspicion that parents are wildly inconsistent in their practice with their children. However, when all situations are lumped together over a period of time, the overall pattern of interaction between parent and child can be characterized by an attitude which predominates the total relationship through time. This is characteristically an attitude which establishes reciprocal trust between them or is a reflection of uncertainty and irritability in their relationship. If a parent is able to facilitate the development of individuality and foster competencies in his child, then he is likely to be rewarded by a large degree of co-operation. Such an emancipation process provides the child with enough room to grow into an independent and competent person.

To examine parent-child interactions one must consider it as a fourfold relationship. From *a parent's* point of view, the parent wants his child to lean on him and welcome his protection while at the same time wanting him to emerge and to act independently in those aspects of his life in which he is acquiring competence.

From *the child's* point of view, the child desires to be liberated from his parents, to be allowed to take independent action, and to become an individual, while at the same time knowing that he has the support of a helpful, guiding parent when needed. This fourfold relationship can become one of mutual trust and can be identified by Davis's emancipation analysis.

This *trust in action* has been described as a fourfold interaction which contains both *reliance* and *emergence* on the child's part and *care* and *respect* on the part of the parent. The child, as he relies, leans comfortably on others for help and guidance which is needed, and as he emerges, he steps out as a self-reliant individual. Reliance on and emergence from the care and guidance of a parent are not mutually exclusive but rather walk together, hand in hand. They combine mutually creating their own alchemy of growth. The adult contribution to this relationship is to provide opportunity for his child to rely on him when it is needed and at the same time to respect the room required for the child to express his emerging self. These four components of a parent-child relationship are defined as trust. They can be depicted in a diagram on which the parent role is indicated on the left side of a quadrant and the child is represented on the right.

parent	child
Gives care	Relies on care and accepts help
Has respect for emergence	Emerges as an individual

When the four aspects of this interaction are in a productive relationship which sponsors the child's ongoing development, they are said to be *in balance*. When this happens, the process of emancipation is proceeding comfortably. On the other hand, this comfortable state of affairs cannot remain static as a child's development is always accompanied by a necessary shift in relationship with parents as new events call upon modifications in the amount and quality of care and guidance offered by the parent and the degree to which the child perceives that he needs it. Hence imbalances in the interaction are bound to appear throughout the multitude of interactions which accompany the changing experiences of daily living. Such imbalances, although expected, should not predominate a healthy parent-child interaction.

There are particular qualities which can be detected in interaction where they are out of balance. These can be expressed on the diagram in the same fashion as the balanced relationship. There are four main patterns of imbalance, as follows:

(1) When a parent offers too much help which the child accepts. This is an *over-dependent* relationship and can be depicted.

parent	child
Too much care offered	Too much care accepted

p	c
√	√

(2) When a parent offers so little care and guidance that the child must keep asking for it or seeking it. This is *lack of care.*

parent	child
	child seeks care
parent gives too little care	

p	c
	√
√	

(3) When a parent gives too much care and control and his child evades or fights it. This is defined as *over-care* and can be depicted

parent	child
parent gives too much control	
	child avoids or fights it

p	c
√	
	√

(4) When a parent offers too little care and guidance which the child no longer seeks. The child manages himself with consequent arousal of anxiety. This can be depicted by

parent	child
Parent gives too little care and control	Child manages tasks by himself. No longer seeks help

p	c
√	√

The outcomes of these various relationships are predictable. *Mutual trust* sponsors ongoing, healthy development on the child's part.

(1) *Over-dependence* allows a child to rest too comfortably in dependence, hence curtailing his capacity for independent action.

(2) *Lack of care* on the parent's part is sensed by the child as lack of support, so the child keeps seeking help beyond the normal expectations and appears clinging, uncertain, and over-dependent.

(3) *Over-care* on the part of the parent who offers too much care and control results in the child becoming rebellious and often hostile.

(4) *Too little care* on the parent's part which is accepted by his child results in the child becoming overly independent while carrying feelings of anxiety about his ability to cope.

The application of this concept to the data contained in the home records offered an opportunity to explore the children's adjustment according to the reported parent-child interactions. The longitudinal nature of the data would allow investigation of the stability through time of the quality of these interactions. It would allow also for an examination of what its nature might be at age fifteen and how it might be related to the other measures of adjustment taken at that time.

Method
The data from the home records were analysed according to the emancipation schema, taking the information at least once yearly after the children's placement in homes.

Subjects
Only those subjects (19 in all) who remained in the same home from first placement were selected; of these, only 16 had complete records from placement to age fifteen.

Nature of Data
The categories selected for analysis were taken from the records if the information was appropriate for the following situations:
Social – Peer and adult relationships, other than family
Activities – Interests and hobbies
Family chores – Household duties
Fun – Those activities planned for pure enjoyment
Siblings – The parental intervention in sibling relationships
Money – Attitudes towards the acquisition and spending of money
Personal care – Looking after such functions as dressing, cleaning teeth, buying clothing
Meals – The parent's attitude towards eating activities
School – Attitudes about the child's school activities
Personal responsiveness – Attitudes around the child's spontaneous response to events of an interpersonal nature
Sports – Attitudes regarding sports activities

Balances and imbalances were coded for each situation and totalled for each record once yearly. Assuming that a preponderance of balances indicated the most healthy adaptation between parent and child, these were examined. In order to have some basis of comparing one child with another, the balance scores were considered in relation to the total number of imbalances also present and this was expressed as a percentage of the total number of interactions. Hence a balance score was a portion of 100%.

In a search for any common pattern of emancipation, or for any characteristically high or low scores at particular ages, each child's balance score was graphed

Figure 1
Emancipation graphs: Percentage balances through four to fifteen years of age.

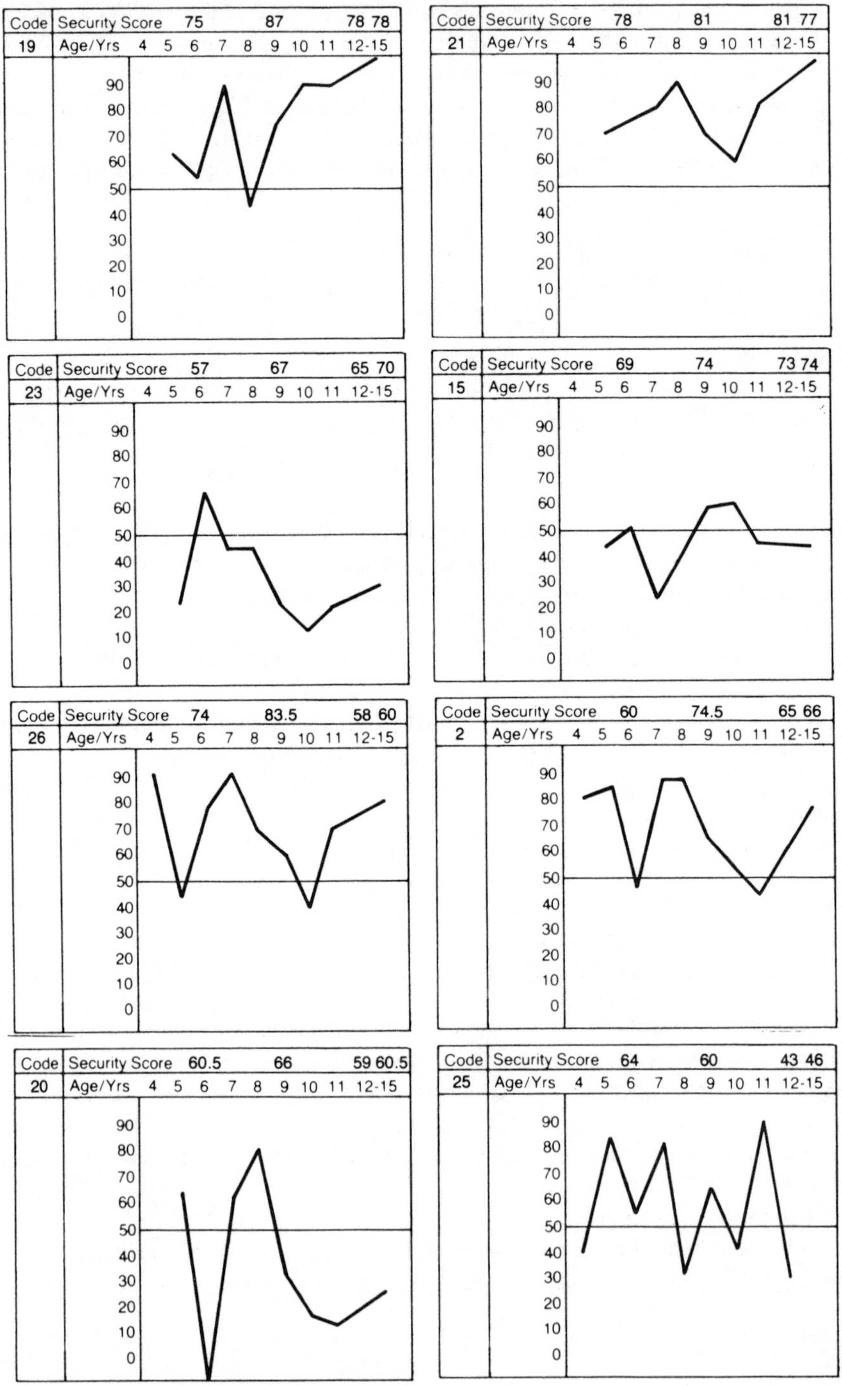

Code	Security Score	75		87			78 78
19	Age/Yrs 4 5 6 7 8 9 10 11 12-15						

Code	Security Score	78		81			81 77
21	Age/Yrs 4 5 6 7 8 9 10 11 12-15						

Code	Security Score	57		67			65 70
23	Age/Yrs 4 5 6 7 8 9 10 11 12-15						

Code	Security Score	69		74			73 74
15	Age/Yrs 4 5 6 7 8 9 10 11 12-15						

Code	Security Score	74		83.5			58 60
26	Age/Yrs 4 5 6 7 8 9 10 11 12-15						

Code	Security Score	60		74.5			65 66
2	Age/Yrs 4 5 6 7 8 9 10 11 12-15						

Code	Security Score	60.5		66			59 60.5
20	Age/Yrs 4 5 6 7 8 9 10 11 12-15						

Code	Security Score	64		60			43 46
25	Age/Yrs 4 5 6 7 8 9 10 11 12-15						

Code 17

Code	Security Score		54		48			53	55
17	Age/Yrs	4	5	6	7	8	9 10 11	12-15	

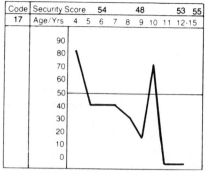

Code 3

Code	Security Score		69.5		83.5		76.5 68.5
3	Age/Yrs	4 5 6 7 8 9 10 11 12-15					

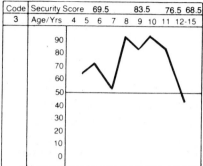

Code 7

Code	Security Score			72		76 78
7	Age/Yrs	4 5 6 7 8 9 10 11 12-15				

Code 1

Code	Security Score	71		62		67 71
1	Age/Yrs	4 5 6 7 8 9 10 11 12-15				

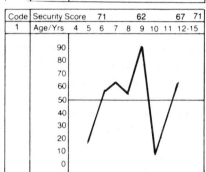

Code 6

Code	Security Score	59		54		44.5 18.5
6	Age/Yrs	4 5 6 7 8 9 10 11 12-15				

Code 5

Code	Security Score	
5	Age/Yrs	4 5 6 7 8 9 10 11 12-15

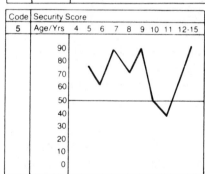

Code 11

Code	Security Score	60		57		50 57.5
11	Age/Yrs	4 5 6 7 8 9 10 11 12-15				

Code 27

Code	Security Score	62		74		73 79
27	Age/Yrs	4 5 6 7 8 9 10 11 12-15				

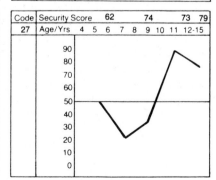

using 50% balances as a reference point to see how many times balances exceeded or fell below *this point.*

RESULTS (see Emancipation graphs, Figure 1)

Figure 1 clearly demonstrates that such highly individualized patterns were present that identification of any common pattern would be impossible. Each mother-child interaction is unique from time of placement through fifteen years.

Only one child's emancipation scores are above the 50% base line for the total time (child 21), demonstrating a very comfortable mother-child relationship during this emancipation period. Two other children are consistently above the 50% base line (child 19 and child 3) with the exception of one year. These also had a smooth course of emancipation. Of the 16 children, 8 demonstrate a pattern of interaction in which high balances preponderate. Only 2 children show a pattern in which low balances predominate. Six children show patterns that fluctuate widely from high to low. It would appear, therefore, that 8 of the 16 children had uncomfortable emancipation processes from their families.

Comparison of security scores at six, nine, twelve, and fifteen years of age with the yearly emancipation scores clearly demonstrates that, despite the wide fluctuation observed in many of the emancipation scores, the security scores remain relatively constant. Furthermore, while smooth emancipation usually coincides with high and consistent security, this is not necessarily the case. In some instances a constant state of security is maintained within a child while the parent-child interactions are either consistently uncomfortable or are fluctuating widely from balance to imbalance.

Recognition of the critical period in emancipation which normally appears in the pre-adolescent or adolescent years would lead to the expectation of a decided drop in emancipation balances as the study terminated. Such expectation has not been borne out as the balances show both a decline in some instances and an incline in the direction of smooth emancipation in others.

An examination of individual life histories in conjunction with emancipation patterns through time allows evaluation of outcomes of the parent-child interactions. Child 19, who was placed at age four with his adoptive family shows an initial interaction which fluctuated between balance and imbalance for the first few years. By nine years of age the parent-child relationship had stabilized and smooth emancipation took place thereafter. The outcome of this relationship at age 21 has been rewarding. Child 19 (see George, p. 124) has graduated from a university where he payed for his own residence and tuition. He has maintained his comfortable ties with the family (after a short period of feeling critical of his father) and has returned home with a plan to work for a year prior to returning to university for post-graduate training. There seems to be mutual respect between child and parents. This boy has become a well-socialized, self-directed young man with clear ideas of his future goals and a determination to pursue them.

Child 6 (see Mindy, p. 134) demonstrates a pattern of erratic relationships with her parents. The relationships fluctuate widely from severe imbalances in the first years of her placement to a temporary period of balances from six through eight years. After eight years there is again wide fluctuation with final decline in balances after eleven years of age. The pattern of this relationship is indicative of troubled waters through which parent and child seemed to seldom maintain a stable interaction. The outcome of this emancipation process has been unhealthy. The ongoing struggle between the child and her family to find compatible goals has terminated in the child's leaving home and drifting into a life-style which requires her to maintain only superficial relationships. This is not a well-socialized, self-directed young person with long-term goals for her life. She is a drifter with short-term goals and a seemingly frail system of values. As such she is open to manipulation by the persons with whom she makes casual encounters in the course of her life. One cannot resist raising the question that some basic lack of affect on the part of this child precluded the stabilization of the parent-child interaction during her growing years.

Examination of the emancipation pattern of child 15 reveals a consistently low number of balanced interactions from the time of his placement at four years of age until age fifteen. The history of this family is replete with conflict between father and mother over the rearing of their two adopted sons. This conflict is extended to their interaction with their boys. Family therapy was resorted to on two occasions to help gain insight into their actions and to allow freer communication among its members. Child 15 took some of his schooling in a treatment day school. As he moved towards his adolescence, his withdrawn, secretive behaviour was replaced by overt hostility and rebellion towards his parents. School achievement remained at a low level despite an increase in measured IQ, which indicated his potential to function at a superior level. He had no friends throughout his growing years. A long-term interest in taking organ lessons culminated in his acquiring an organ for his home and in providing money for his lessons from odd jobs. Relationships between parents and children seemed chronically irritated and worrisome. There was little joy in rearing these two boys. By age 18, number 15 had acquired a job in a Trust Company, was saving money towards entering the priesthood, and his behaviour began to reflect a more comfortable feeling about himself and his relationship to his parents. An unexpected visit to the Child Care worker after he had been working for some time revealed his pride in himself. He was able to spontaneously confess that he had been a 'stinker' to raise. A more stable relationship seemed to have come about and a report from his mother appeared to reflect a more objective view of this boy than had been achieved previously. He was now contributing money to the household, was driving a car, and was taking some responsibility for housekeeping. He continued to make extra money playing the church organ.

At present this 6'7" young man, now almost twenty-three years of age, has abandoned his idea of going into a seminary. His interest in children has prompted him to move into the Child Care field where he acted as an untrained Child Care worker with disturbed children in a group home. Disagreement about how to treat the children has led to his removal from this employment. He has now returned from the group home to live again with his family. His mother reports that he is goal directed about his future but does very little at present to help at home. He is determined to enter university as a mature student, where he hopes to study philosophy.

In overview, the erratic and troubled pattern of emancipation of the early years has had a relatively salutary outcome. This boy has remained on good terms with his family and is still using them as a base from which to step off in his own direction.

The emancipation graph of child number 25 reflects a highly unstable emancipation pattern from age four through age fifteen. The history of this child and his parents reflects a long-term struggle between dependence and independence which seems only to be resolved by age twenty-one. This boy was adopted into a family whose mother had been his volunteer. From his initial withdrawn and passive state he quickly moved to a demonstration of determined and demanding behaviour regarding his own desires. This proved irritating and frustrating to his high-powered and equally determined mother. This boy's need was for control and consistency in routines and for limits to freedom in play and social aspects of his life. His mother interpreted this in a rigid way, insisting on conformity to her wishes while at the same time denying his need to regress to a predictable state of dependency. As a result, this boy became highly resistant to parental expectations. Each crisis in his life produced new tensions which could be reduced somewhat by the intervention of the guidance worker who was quickly accepted as a friend. Hence the emancipation process swung erratically from one extreme to another as a reflection of new events or new crises. Placement in his home, entrance to school, the arrival of a newly adopted brother, new expectations around school achievement or around community involvement created disabling imbalances in the parent-child interaction. Parents and child seemed in a suspended state of hostility. Parenting provided few rewards. Mother expected emancipation by the child but according to her rules. The child, fearing to be overwhelmed, resisted and demanded dependence. Such incompatibility of goals led to delinquent behaviour. By age eighteen, minor infractions of the law by this boy proved an ultimate discouragement. Despite their feelings of failure, his parents supported him through this crisis, and the relationship settled into a more stable pattern. The final note at age twenty-one indicates acceptance of his limitations and a greater respect for him as a person than had previously been observed. He has continued to live at home, taking over the basement as his domain ('I think we will have him till he is one hundred!'). His family now welcomes and approves of his friends whom he entertains in his own quarters. He has shown little interest in girls yet. Since our contact at eighteen years he has experienced health problems which have required a pace-maker. Chronic infections behind this have necessitated almost constant dosage of antibiotics. He has a job in a machine shop which pays him a small wage. His health forces him to be quiet through the week although he keeps busy on week ends. Some kind of reconciliation has been achieved between this boy and his family. Whether or not the emancipation process is continuing, the interaction between the two has arrived at a balance.

8

Intellectual function

The intellectual functioning of this group of children was assessed on the Binet Intelligence test at six, nine, and twelve years of age. At age fifteen, their performance was measured on the WISC. The initial expectation, in view of the severity of their early and prolonged deprivation, was for possible depressed performance which would evidence some improvement through time.

Studies of the degree of damage to intellectual function by early severe deprivation and potential for future recovery provide conflicting evidence throughout the literature. There is considerable evidence that severe and prolonged sensory restriction can create long-term deficiencies in intellectual function or in particular aspects of it. Several authors believe that verbal intelligence is more vulnerable to early deprivation than is visual. Haywood (1967), Tizard (1969), and Ainsworth (1962) all point to the vulnerability of language and its resistance to later reversal of damage. Goldfarb's earlier study (1945) on adolescents who suffered early deprivation indicated consistent disability, not only in language performance but also in capacity for abstract thinking.

On the other hand, Dennis's final report (1973) of a group of foundling children first observed in Lebanon in the 1950s indicates that recovery (as measured on Binet scales) from experiental deprivation can take place if adoption occurs under the age of two years and is followed by normal, everyday cognitive experience.

Dennis's original study of creche foundlings demonstrated that this group of 61 children achieved a mean of 63 on the Cattell Developmental Test when measured between four and twelve months of age. A further drop in function was apparent between one and two years of age when the mean developmental quotient sank to 52, with no difference appearing between boys and girls. Later testing on these children up to six years of age indicated that this low level of function stabilized, the mean IQ of the group between ages one and six years remaining at 53 (Binet IQ).

A separate group of children reared in their own homes but brought into the creche for care between one and five years of age, was measured shortly after entry. These children achieved a mean IQ of 92 on measures comparable with those used on the foundlings. This difference of 40 points demonstrated the destructive effects of institutional deprivation on the foundling group.

The follow-up of the foundling children after removal from the creche and placement of the boys and girls in two different institutions provided evidence that modifications to this level of function could take place after such a disadvantageous beginning. The girls were placed in a highly institutionalized, unstimulating, rigid environment and later measurement of their level of achievement on Stanford Binet tests between ages twelve and fifteen years remained at a low 54 (range 30-60). They remained unskilled and largely illiterate, doomed to a lifetime of menial tasks. The boys on the contrary, were placed in a more favourable institutional environment after removal from the creche. Opportunities were present for indoor and outdoor play, contact with people in the local community, exploratory trips, and considerable interaction within the school among the pupils themselves. Family reared children came to the school from the community and mingled with the children in residence. The boys were expected to find occupations to support themselves in the community in contrast to the girls who were expected to remain as menial workers within the institution for a lifetime.

Measurement of the IQ of the boys on Stanford Binet tests between twelve and sixteen years of age indicated a mean IQ of 81, a significant 26 points higher than that of the girls at the same age. Furthermore, the range of scores was greater than that achieved by the girls, the lowest being 60, which was above the mean of 54 achieved by the girls. Two boys had scores above 100, quite unlike the achievement of the girls. Follow-up of the boys at a later date indicated that most of them were self-supporting and were in better mental health than were the girls.

Another facet of this same study resulted from some of the creche children being released for Lebanese or American adoption between one and six years of age. Subsequent testing demonstrated that the children adopted prior to two years of age overcame their earlier deficit and soon reached a mean IQ of approximately 100, which was maintained through time. On the other hand, those children who were adopted after two years of age never overcame their earlier deficit, maintaining an absolute level of deficit which had been established within the first years, i.e., those children who were retarded by two years when adopted at age four were still two years behind when measured at ages ten through fourteen (CA, 10 years, MA, 8 years).

Less intensive data collected on the creche children regarding school progress, social, psychiatric, marital and vocational adjustment indicate that the children experiencing the most severe and prolonged institutional deprivation unrelieved by adoption were the most seriously disabled in their life adjustment. Skodak and Skeel's (1949) long-term study further supports the recommendation that adoption from institution prior to two years of age can overcome earlier intellectual deficit.

Rutter's (1972) monumental survey of the literature on deprivation contradicts partly these conclusions as he states that 'the absolute restriction of sensory stimulation undoubtedly can impair development, including intellectual development.' He concluded that all forms of perceptual restriction may impede cognitive growth and different forms of restriction will affect different aspects of intellectual skill. He notes that language is of singular importance to the healthy development of human children and the quality of a child's language environment is crucial for his development. This quality is viewed not so much in terms of how much he is talked to but rather in terms of the richness of the communication between himself and his caretakers. An adult's capacity to make verbal stimulation meaningful to a child seems more important than the absolute level of stimulation supplied.

Our particular study focuses on the reversibility of early deprivation, but cannot point directly to the remedial effects of home placement after institutional deprivation. Although the original institutional milieu had severely discouraged cognitive development, the following remedial programme within the residence provided a cognitively stimulating environment designed to initiate cognitive development and further its future sponsorship after placement in homes. Out of the first milieu which had failed to provide a stable relationship between any child and his caretaker grew the therapeutic programme designed to assure the child of the reliability of his caretakers and the consistency of his experiential world. The first dependent relationship between adult and child was regarded as of primary importance in the provision of a stable and consistent environment which would encourage a child to learn. The consistency of his caretaker enabled him to achieve a meaningful network of communication and interchange. It provided further a secure base on which to make prediction and try out hypotheses. Both these factors assured a benign environment in which healthy emotional and cognitive development might take place.

Hence, in the rehabilitative programme, the aim was to provide sensitively aware staff and volunteers who would develop a stable relationship with the children through consistent and predictable attention to their needs. The success of this effort was demonstrated in the response of the children to reach out first to the warmth and affection of the adults and secondly to move into their world with expressions of self-initiated action. Intellectual stimulation through play materials gave opportunities for manipulation, experience of shape, colours, properties of movement, and function. The adults stimulated a deliberate interchange with their charges to provide words to label experiences and objects in their world. This programme eventually led to the children's exposure to directed, but ever widening experiences in his community.

As the children responded and were placed eventually in foster and adoptive homes, the aim of the guidance programme undertaken by the child care worker was to help the new parents maintain consistency in the children's lives. The consolidation of feelings of basic trust which had been initiated in the therapy programme was one of the goals of guidance. The inevitable impact of an enormous variety of new experiences and stimuli which resulted from placement in homes led to confusion in the children's conceptual organization of this experience. Entry into school put even more extensive demands on them to comprehend, label, and integrate new information. There was an obvious impairment in their capacity to learn.

This period of confusion which resulted in erratic behaviour led the research team to recommend that the children be allowed to regress for a time to a younger level of functioning. This might allow them time to comprehend their experiences and to arrange them into a more meaningful system of reference. One practical expression of this was to encourage teachers and parents to allow their child to mark time for a second year in either kindergarten or Grade I. It was believed, further, that their dependency needed reinforcement. Hence parents and teachers were encouraged to assume extensive control of the children's environment. On the assumption that the children could not discriminate in their response to a variety of stimuli, techniques were designed to emphasize structure in their environment and to impose direction on their thoughts and behaviour. It was hoped that such techniques would allow the children to focus their attention on the more critical cues in the environment and reduce their attention to the peripheral stimuli which distracted them.

These measures were sufficiently successful that by nine years of age an observable change was noted in their Rorschach responses. There was a move away from global, disorganized responses evident at six years of age to a more meaningful, although still immature conceptual framework. At the same time they maintained average levels of intellectual function. Such development pointed the way for increasingly healthy intellectual function as evidenced on later testing at twelve and fifteen years of age.

The course of the children's adjustment to school was carefully monitored by the research team. Whenever difficulties arose, the help of the teacher was enlisted to look at a child's strengths and weaknesses in an attempt to find the best way of overcoming the problems. The parents also were involved in the planning of appropriate strategies to help the child proceed through school maximizing his potential without overwhelming threat to his total personal adjustment.

An overview of the children's progression through school indicates that after the initial set-back on entry when most of them marked time a second year in kindergarten or Grade i, there was orderly progression through the expected grades. Most of the children went through the normal school stream, but a few had special classes and placements planned carefully to minimize their weaknesses. By age fifteen, when the final official testing and reports were complete, there were 23 children who had complete records. Of these, 15 were enrolled in academic schools, 2 were in trade schools, and 6 were in vocational schools. Our attempt to relate the marks on their records to some criteria for comparison indicated that 13 children were performing satisfactorily, 8 were performing poorly, and 2 were totally unsatisfactory.

As the result of our long-standing relationship with the parents, teachers, and children, the research team continued to gather information informally after the official data collection had been terminated. As a result we became aware that after fifteen years of age, approximately at the Grade ix level, all but 4 of the 15 children originally in the academic stream transferred to vocational schools where the demand for academic performance was less stringent and more value was placed on practical skills. By age eighteen, three children had left school and the remainder were completing their chosen courses. Presently, two children are in university, one is completing a course in a community college and another is a registered nursing assistant.

An examination of the data on the testing of our group yielded results in Table 4. Because of attrition and children's illness at testing points the numbers of children available for testing at each age level varied from 25 to 21.

Analysis of the WISC at fifteen indicates a continuance of the level of functioning within the Average Range demonstrated on the Binet at the earlier ages (Table 5).

The distribution of scores at age six approximates the normal curve while by twelve and fifteen years of age it is positively skewed. (See Appendix, Figures 5 and 6.)

The mean discrepancy between Verbal and Performance Scores was 11.69, with Performance Scale IQ higher than Verbal Scale IQ. This difference is significant at the .001 level. (Value 4.465)

DISCUSSION

In overview the intellectual functioning of the children in this study appears not to have been significantly depressed by their deprived early circumstances, where intellectual function is defined as performance consistent with age norm expectancy. The scatter of IQs for the group is found to fall generally within the aver-

TABLE 4
Level of IQ at ages 6, 9, 12 on the Stanford-Binet (L–M)

Age	N	Mean	S.D.	Median	Range
6	23	93.35	8.5	92	72-116
9	25	94.32	12.4	92	66-114
12	21	95.19	12.2	98	67-117

TABLE 5
Level of IQs on WISC at 15 years

	N	Mean	S.D.	Range
Full Scale	23	103.57	11.39	76-128
Verbal Scale	23	97.74	14.69	71-121
Performance Scale	23	109.44	15.56	76-138

Note; Mean discrepancy between Verbal Scale and Performance Scale: 11.69.

age range of intelligence, with an approximation to the normal curve of distribution (range 90-110 on Binets).

Dennis's study has shown somewhat comparable outcome as has the work of Skodak and Skeels (1949). If overall IQ is considered, the children reported by these authors performed up to average expectation providing they had been adopted prior to the age of two. Apparently the early depressed intellectual function was relieved by normal home environmental stimuli if experienced by age two. On the other hand, such response was not evidenced in the children adopted after age two. From this age on, earlier deficit was not recovered. It is within this context that our data differ, as most of our children were adopted between ages three and five. Some were adopted even later. The mean age for adoption was three years, eleven months. The range was one year, seven months, to six years, six months. Even the rehabilitative programme which relieved the earlier deprivation was started after most of the children were two years of age. The mean age at its inception was two years, three months. This present group had home placements of the following nature: two children below age two, five children between ages two and three, four children between ages three and four, eight children between ages four and five, three children between ages five and six, and two after six years of age. It is evident that deprivation can be relieved even after four years of age and in the case of some children quite spectacular improvement in function can take place. Although there was no significant change in the means of intellectual measure for the group from ages six through fifteen, individual children showed outstanding gains. Nine children gained more than 15 points and of these six gained 20 points or more. Two gained more than 35 points.

While the children's level of functioning appears unimpaired, specific aspects of intellect seem to reflect the damaging effects of early deprivation. Ainsworth (1962) has pointed out that language is particularly vulnerable to impairment which is not reversible by later experience. Rapaport (1956) also states that vocabulary as measured in tests (i.e., the defining of words) 'is primarily dependent upon a wealth of early experience and is refractory to improvement by later school and life experience.' Our study supports these experimental and clinical findings. On the Binet, half of the subjects show a depressed performance in the vocabulary test which is one measure of verbal strength, and this is apparent at all three test ages six, nine, twelve. There is a decline rather than any improvement in this capacity over the period recorded. Their achievement on the WISC Vocabulary confirms this fact. Here, the Verbal Scale IQs are significantly lower than Performance IQs, with 19 out of the 23 cases being superior in the Performance area, and 30% of the whole group having a discrepancy of 20 or more points. Vocabulary, a subtest calling for definition of words, has been regarded as especially susceptible to early expriences, and on this subtest the raw scores obtained by this group indicates a functioning at the 13.5MA level, with an average scaled score of 9.1. This suggests there is some relative weakness but not a striking one. These children do not appear to have suffered a severe impairment in this area.

Goldfarb (1943) showed in his study of adolescents who had suffered early deprivation that in all cases there was severe impairment to the ability for abstract thinking, as well as to language. While the present study does not use the same measures, the children are able to perform on the Binet in the area of verbal reasoning (Similarities, Verbal Absurdities, Finding Reasons, Induction) with some competence, even to levels above age expectance, while on the WISC they performed best on the Similarity and Block Design subtests, both of which are recognized measures of abstract logical thinking. Their mean score on Block Design is above average expectation (mean scaled score 11.6) (see Appendix, Figure 7). This would infer a difference from Goldfarb's group and suggests unimpaired function for abstract thought.

The competence demonstrated by these children in verbal reasoning over their ability to define words as tested on vocabulary is rather puzzling. Could it be that verbal reasoning items supply a framework for thought in that the answers are either right or wrong? This is not so in verbal definition items which are open-ended questions. These children's greater facility with reasoning and difficulty with defining suggests that they can function better when a context is provided than when they are required to furnish a structure themselves. Defining words calls upon a greater flexibility of thought and larger resource of descriptive items than does verbal reasoning, where the child is required only to draw on his own limited fund of words. The gain which was observed in verbal reasoning items through the years six to twelve leads to speculation that these children have, or are in the process of, developing capabilities of thinking and making adaptive adjustments to living which serve them adequately but which they are unable to verbalize with a richness and flexibility such as an extensive vocabulary would give them. Their capacity to make these adjustments extends to their school life where, barring emotional upset, they have been able to function sufficiently well to progress according to expectation, but where their impoverished vocabulary does not make for academic excellence. Even so, these children's competence in using words is striking in the light of their pre-school record when most had 'developed only a very limited vocabulary and made no attempt to organize words into any structure' (Taylor, 1968).

The question has been raised that there may be similarity in performance between brain damaged or emotionally disturbed children and those experiencing early institutional deprivation. A comparison of the patterns of functioning on the WISC of these three different groups show that our experimental group has a weakness in vocabulary not shared with the other two groups and has more strength on the coding subtest (Bortner and Birch). The pattern shown by our group does not appear to bear close resemblance to either of the other two groups. This suggests that they do not share a common aetiology.

One must speculate on the surprising superior performance of this group on the coding item. This is remarkable when it is recalled that these children had striking difficulty in concentrating during their early years. It was the recognition of this weakness that led to a programme designed to promote an ability to focus selectively on stimuli and to maintain attention. Apparently this earlier disability has been replaced by a capacity to concentrate on an immediate task. The further evidence of healthy intellectual adjustment was supplied by the children's high level of motivation noted for the most part by the psychologist throughout their test performance. This was confirmed by parent and teacher reports as a characteristic of personality.

What is the relevance of these results to the hypothesis that a dependent trust relationship between caretakers and child is essential for further healthy development? It was our conviction that such a relationship would provide a reliable and trustworthy environment in which a child could make predictions, act on his assumptions, and evaluate the consequences. Such an environment should support cognitive function. The present levels of the children's intellectual measures support the appropriateness of the hypothesis.

These children's developmental behaviour in the institution up to the inception of the rehabilitative programme when they were approximately two years of age showed distortions and a dearth of intellectual responsiveness. This disorganization yielded over time to the structured and purposeful plan designed to promote a secure trust relationship with adults. The present behaviour of the children supports the success of this approach. However, while their overall intellectual functioning is good, these children's language capacity bears the characteristic impairment noted by earlier researchers. Their capacity for achievement and their highly motivated performances are beyond the expectations we would have had when the children were in institutional care. Beyond demonstrating general improvement in the quality of intellectual function we have shown that certain areas of intellectual functioning such as reasoning do yield to deliberate intellectual stimulation and guidance. In addition to this, some capacity for concentrated attention can be engendered. These particular aspects of intellectual function are critical ones for successful adjustment to living. Nearly all of these children have developed the capacity to attend to critical aspects of their environment and to gain mastery over them.

9

What our measures tell us

INTERNAL MEASURES

Final analysis of the records collected on the behaviour of the children from six through fifteen years of age consisted of running Spearman rank order correlations to demonstrate relationships between the various measures.* The subcategories of the Security Ratings (Immature Dependence, Dependent Trust, Self-Worth, and Effort) examined the internal validity of the Security Theory. These in turn were related to the external measures of IQ, SQ, and (IQ-SQ). Such procedures allowed for external validation of our measures. All the above measures were then related to the length of time the children spent in the institution, both before and after the therapeutic programme was initiated. (Appendix, Tables 5, 6, 7, 8).

The assumptions of the theory of Security had anticipated a high positive relationship between Effort and Self-Worth items, Dependent Trust items, and final Security Ratings at all ages from six through fifteen years. Such expectation was confirmed. At age fifteen the relationship was more significant than at six, nine, and twelve years, which bears out the assumption that the children should be increasingly self-directed as they become older. The recognition that an immature dependent relationship in infancy is responsible for the initiation of the desire to be effortful on the child's part was further clarified by the data at six years of age, which demonstrated no significant relationship between these two variables at six and nine years of age, and an increasingly significant negative relationship from twelve to fifteen years of age. It would appear that a state of immature dependence which characterizes the early first relationship discourages effort by six years of age and continues to do so with increasing success through fifteen years of age.

* Siegal and Fagan's method of correction for ties was applied to these data.

The assumption that a child maturing beyond infancy and early childhood reflects security which is comprised of a combination of feelings of Immature Dependency and Dependent Trust, the latter being the more mature form, is confirmed by the data. First, there is a negative relationship between Immature Dependence and Dependent Trust from six through fifteen years of age. This is to be anticipated since they are considered counter-balancing functions, each of which compensates for the other. Secondly, the evidence indicates that Immature Dependence is predominant in this balance at six and nine years of age and shifts by age twelve to a predominance of Dependent Trust (Table 1, Chap. 5). The fact that Dependent Trust is increasingly correlated with Effort and Self-Worth after age twelve confirms the supposition that Dependent Trust feelings generate the confidence which leads to Effortful behaviour and a sense of self-worth. Hence, while in theory dependence of an immature nature is a necessary step towards Dependent Trust and has, in fact, been demonstrated through the infant and pre-school years to support effortful behaviour, it is evident that after six years of age, effort can only be predicted by the presence of a Dependent Trust relationship. As we believe effortful behaviour to be the manifestation of feelings of self-worth, we must therefore look to a Dependent Trust relationship as the key to a healthy adjustment between parent and child.

EXTERNAL MEASURES AT FIFTEEN YEARS

The use made of the Vineland Social Maturity Scale developed by Doll (1953) has provided an external source of validation for our use of the Security Theory as have the data collected on intellectual performance at six, nine, twelve, and fifteen years of age. Doll's own studies and others carried out later have supported the expectation that Social Quotient and IQ are highly related. Our particular group demonstrates this relationship. Furthermore, the positive relationship between Social Quotient and Security Ratings demonstrated by our children confirms our expectations that the mental health assets represented by the security rating should coincide with the level of Social Maturity. The positive relationships among the variables, Dependent Trust, Effort, IQ, and SQ further confirm the expectation of our model. The negative relationship between Immature Dependence and SQ is to be expected because Immature Dependence implies reliance on parents for support, help, and direction and would not be likely to coincide with advanced Social age.

The significant discrepancy between IQ and SQ in favour of IQ for the total group seems to indicate that there is a consistent deficit at age fifteen in social maturity. Such social assets have not yielded to intervention with the same resilience as the capabilities which are reflected on IQ measures. The result has been the emergence of the child's intellectual abilities to a far greater degree than his social abilities. The highly significant discrepancy between (IQ-SQ) and IQ is indicative of considerable social inadequacy in terms of intellectual capacity. Furthermore the greater a child's intellectual capacity the lower is his social maturity.

This measure of under-achievement of the children as a group reveals an expected negative relationship to both Security Rating and Effort, i.e., it is expected that the children showing the least effort would be the greater under-achievers socially.

TIME IN THE INSTITUTION

In view of the general hypotheses that the length of time spent in institutional care in early childhood could be directly related to later failure in adjustment, our data were examined in several ways. Because of the introduction of a period of therapeutic environmental manipulation prior to the discharge of these children from the institution, it was evident that the change in the quality of care would have a direct bearing on the effect of the length of time each child spent in the institution. Further, discharge from the institution had been predicated on the success of the therapeutic programme in modifying the children's behaviour in the direction of 'normalcy.' Those children remaining longest in the therapeutic programme would have been the most seriously disadvantaged and the least ready for placement in homes.

Hence, four variables were examined in our analysis, time in the institution; time before therapy; time in therapy; age at discharge. Expected highly significant ratings were evident between all three of these latter variables to time in the institution. It is evident that the longer the children had been in the institution before therapy was begun, the greater was their need for prolonged therapy and the older they would be when they were placed in foster or adoptive homes.

A seemingly paradoxical negative relationship between the length of time the children spent in therapy and effortful behaviour is indicative of the fact that the least effortful children needed longer periods of the therapeutic programme than did the more effortful children – hence the delay in discharge. Incorrect interpretation of this figure might lead to the mistaken assumption that the therapeutic programme was unsuccessful in its effect. In addition, the strength of this particular relationship is reduced further when the fact of time in the Institution is partialled out. At six years of age this relationship between effort and the therapy programme is barely significant and by fifteen years of age it disappears entirely. Hence we may assume that experiences which entered the lives of these children after the therapy programme were more powerful in the mediation of the outcome than was the therapeutic programme.

A similar interesting result appears at six years of age where the level of IQ displayed by the children is negatively related to the length of time they were in the institution before therapy began, i.e., the longer the time before therapy the lower the IQ. This would seem to point to the effect on the children's mental function of the prolonged unstimulating environment. This significant relationship dissipates by age fifteen, indicating that the measures taken to stimulate the children in therapy and later in placement were more powerful contributors to their present intellectual level than were their early depriving experiences.

10

Concept formation

The information collected on these children by means of the Rorschach test opened the opportunity to investigate some aspects of the children's cognitive processes. The nature of the Rorschach test called upon the children's capacity to impose their own conception of order and meaning on to unstructured material. Their approach to this task should reveal the nature of their attempts to interpret their experiences and read meaning into their unique perception.

Our intimate knowledge of these children's early deprivation allowed us some insight into their lack of conceptual organization in the early stages of their life. The disorganization evident in their behaviour seemed indicative of confusion in the processing of information once the early deprivation had been relieved and they were exposed to the impact of family life and later to the expectations of the school.

Because norms were available which claimed to reflect accepted stages of conceptual development (Ames, Learned, and Métroux, 1971), it was possible to contrast these norms with the level of concept formation demonstrated at various ages by our group. Presumably the limited past experiences of our youngsters and resultant problems in their understanding of their environment should be revealed.

The analysis of our Rorschach data was carried out on 10 children selected as representative of the group. Results were tabulated at six, nine, twelve, and fifteen years of age and compared to the accepted norms. In the Rorschach analysis, diversity of thought is reflected in the use of Rorschach determinants in producing a response. Specifically, one can rely on form alone (F) or one can

---

* The analysis and reporting of the data included in this chapter are largely the work of Mrs Ann Taylor, research associate. Portions of this chapter have been reprinted with permission of the American Journal of Orthopsychiatry.

combine form with a number of different percepts, i.e., human movement (M), animal movement (FM), inanimate movement (m), colour (C), etc. To the extent that these alternatives are employed, thought is said to be diversified. Flexibility is observed in the choice of location responses. (W) reflects use of the whole blot area and is the simplest of responses. Large details (D), small details (d), rare details (dr), etc., as they are used alone or in combination, reflect flexibility in approach. Most important, however, quality of thought and keenness in perception are implied in the form level rating accorded to each response. A rating of 1.0 implies a minimally adequately perceived concept. Scores below 1.0 (ranging from 0.0 to –3.0) reflect increasing confusion in thinking. Scores above 1.0 reflect increasingly mature, integrated thought.

The longitudinal nature of the data allowed us to examine the final outcome, at age fifteen, as well as to trace the maturing process of the children's conceptual organization from six through fifteen years. Our central concern was to identify for the group any remaining residual weaknesses or distortions at age fifteen which could be attributed to their common early deprivation. The developmental sequence demonstrated in the concept formation of these children, starting at six years of age, follows.

The trend in the response patterns of 9 of the 10 children moved from considerable diversity in location and determinant scores at six, to considerable constriction in the use of alternatives at nine. Case No. 10, however, followed the expected sequence. Moreover, the responses at six which were evidence of mature 'integrated' thought in many cases diminished somewhat at nine (notably FC), or failed to be more extensively incorporated as would be expected in the normal sequence. At six, these children appeared to be on the threshold of integrating their concepts within normal expectations. At nine, they appeared to be regressing to a functioning level more consistent with what is described as the 'intermediate' stage of conceptual organization. At the same time, form level rating universally improved. This picture is the reverse of what is observed in the family-reared child. At six, he is moving towards the conceptual integration of material which he has previously organized at lower levels. By nine, integration is well established and is reflected in the use of a wider variety of location and determinant scores (1.8).

The question arose – what happened between six and nine to these children who suffered early deprivation? Why did their mental processes become more constricted instead of more flexible and more diversified? Finally, was this trend necessarily indicative of failure to adjust to the new environment?

Since the longitudinal project was still in its early stages at this time, a tentative hypothesis was set forward. It seemed to suggest that since a common pattern emerged in 9 out of 10 cases, factors inherent in the institutional environment affected the development of conceptual functioning in a consistent fashion. The task, therefore, was to isolate these factors and examine their influence.

The most obvious factor thought to affect later conceptual development was the lack of experience in infancy with the objective, perceived world. There was nothing in their environment to stimulate the senses. These 10 children, with little chance when infants to explore the physical world, manifested minimal interest in their surroundings. As a result, the processes of perceptual differentiation and concept formation functioned poorly. For example, they failed within the first year to grasp the concept of object permanence. Further, they did not appear to discriminate between objects and people.

A second factor in the institutional experience which affected the conceptual development of these children was the lack of opportunity to develop language skills. They were almost never spoken to, and as a result were not stimulated to use their vocal apparatus. From the beginning, physical care was administered on a strict schedule and the babies learned that crying did not bring help. Consequently, the children did not experiment with their voices and the wide variety of sounds one hears in the family-reared child did not appear. Moreover, no one provided verbal labels for any of the objects in the environment, labels that would have helped organize their perceptions. As a result they had little interest in trying to form words, or to effect any communication at all. Many were three and a half years old before they began to vocalize meaningfully. Most developed only a very limited vocabulary and made no attempt to organize words into any structure.

After placement in homes, certain characteristics appeared in the children's conceptual functioning which we assumed later affected their ability to adjust to the expanded world of family and school.

In the first place these children were distractible. Their focus on the world was less organized than that of family-reared children. It included much more of the environment, as they had difficulty in separating the relevant from the irrelevant simuli. Consequently, their concentration was poor because they attended to sights and sounds that had nothing to do with the task on hand. Because they could not impose selective 'blinders,' their eyes were wide open and their attention was pulled first one way and then another. This distractibility impeded selection and direction of thought and behaviour.

Since these children had difficulty in selecting and directing thought, they could not integrate experiences as readily as the normal child. This hindered the quality of the concepts they were able to form. According to Piaget (1952), in organized thought one incorporates a new experience into a base of acquired meaningful information, and thus integrates the new thought by comprehending it in terms of what is already known. These children had an impoverished, poorly organized base of information to begin with. When they experienced something new they had great difficulty in relating it to past experience in a meaningful way. Thus they tended either to graft or to force a new concept into their poorly organized store of acquired information, or they failed to comprehend it at all.

This impediment in the assimilation of information was evident in the lack of consistency in thought. These children characteristically failed to comprehend the underlying functional relationships between ideas. Because they had difficulty in relating ideas to objects or one idea to another, they were slow to form the mental links between their thoughts which give direction to thought, and meaning to behaviour. Thus, their thought processes were characteristically haphazard and poorly connected. For example, one child could not grasp the concept of 'family.' He understood 'house' and knew who lived in it, but he failed to see the underlying relationship between his parents and siblings. Hence he used the word 'family' inconsistently and often inappropriately.

Rigidity in thinking was another persistent characteristic of the children's approach. They did not have a large fund of verbal concepts to draw upon and could not look at data from different viewpoints. They usually perceived only one central meaning for familiar words or objects; nor could they re-think events in other terms. Thus, definitions and meanings suffered from their inability to elaborate. For example, one child never heeded the command 'watch out,' as to him a 'watch' was something worn on the wrist. He could not understand the term used in another context.

At six these children's Rorschach responses demonstrated severe handicaps in processing the tremendous flow of information from their environment. Initially, they handled the environment in much the same manner as infants in the 'global' stage of approach. However, they quickly breached the confines of this level of functioning. With a rapidly expanding vocabulary they attempted even higher levels of mental organization in a short time. However, their introduction into new homes and the level of complexity inherent in the school and community programmes outstripped their abilities to incorporate many of these experiences well.

Hence at six, what appear to be signs of maturing thought must be re-examined on the basis of quality of concept. In all cases form level rating at this age was low, indicating a weakness in keenness and quality of thought. On numerous occasions, ideas were confused and disorganized and the children would weaken a concept by introducing inappropriate details, thus lowering form level rating. Often they changed their minds, having no clear idea of what they thought. They used form unrealistically. Again, they would try to integrate form and movement or colour but in a senseless combination. Thus, the observed evidence of flexibility and diversity in approach was undermined by considerable confusion and disorganization.

As a result of this analysis, guidance procedures were developed to facilitate the children's adjustment. Between six and nine years parents and teachers were urged to support them in doing things one at a time on their own. They were urged to simplify tasks and to direct the children's activities towards single and short-term goals. Thus, supervision of activities and interpretation of ideas were provided at a level which the children could utilize and comprehend. In school all of them had experienced severe difficulties with reading and writing. They found it impossible to concentrate on complex materials and to deal with the distraction of other children. Consequently, seven children repeated a year in order to grasp familiar material more fully. In this way they had an opportunity to develop a larger fund of information and skills to support them later on.

It was thought that this 'narrowing of the environment' was necessary if the children were to perform more effectively, and the evidence of the nine-year-old Rorschach demonstrated the success of this technique. By nine most of the former signs of conceptual confusion and disorganization had disappeared. The universal rise in form level rating indicated that what was perceived at nine was organized with greater clarity and meaning. However, while the constricted focus on the environment did result in a better quality of concept, much of the variety and dynamic nature of ideas disappeared at the same time. Thus, at nine the children were better able to organize their conceptual approach to the world but at a lower level of mental functioning.

It was believed that if these children learned to perform realistically and meaningfully at lower levels in the conceptual sequence, only then would they be able to proceed satisfactorily to the more complex levels. Therefore, this reversed trend in Rorschach performance was judged to be a not unhealthy regression but a very necessary step in their conceptual adjustment to their new world.

Another indication that the regression in conceptual organization was not unhealthy for these children was their performance on the intelligence tests. Although their mental processes grew simpler and less diversified between six and nine, the average IQ of the group did not suffer. At six the average IQ was 89; at nine it was 93. In eight cases their IQ rose slightly. Thus again it is seen that the forced de-stimulation of the environment did not reduce the children's ability to acquire and comprehend useful and meaningful information.

At twelve, the children were assessed again. The results demonstrate, as hypothesized, a partial return to the six-year-old pattern of greater flexibility and complexity of thought. At the same time, however, form level rating at twelve indicates a far higher level of thought than that which occurred at six. At six, the children were attempting to incorporate new ideas and to integrate their experiences, but much of their thinking was confused and unrealistic. By twelve, this same approach to the environment was characterized by a keener perception of reality and a firmer grasp of appropriate ideas. Further confirmation of improved adjustment during these six years is evident in the rise of IQ. By twelve, only two children tested below 90 (one at 82 and the other at 84). At the other extreme, one child obtained an IQ of 112. At six, the majority of children had tested below 90.

As stated earlier, the constriction of responses between six and nine was considered an essential process in the adjustment of these children to their rapidly expanding environment. At six, insufficient development in the language area, coupled with an immature and highly distractible approach to environmental stimuli, prevented an adequate conceptual grasp of the material presented, both at home and at school. Hence the confusion in the children's attempts to process information.

By nine, several important steps had been taken. Most children had been held back at least one year in school. The question of how they reacted to 'failure' was often raised. As far as could be determined by their responses, 'failure' was not a concept they had acquired in its full emotionally laden context. This indeed was characteristic of their response to many conventional concepts. Universally they preferred the company of younger children to age mates. Being held back placed them therefore in groups of younger children where they felt more comfortable. Moreover, the programme was familiar and what was expected of them easier to anticipate.

In addition, home life had been simplified as much as possible. Parents were highly aware that much of the behaviour of these children was inappropriate and impulsive. They had discovered that pressure only produced highly negative responses. Conversely, freedom of choice and/or lack of supervision resulted in aimlessness. At six, these children appeared capable of no higher level of behavioural organization than the toddler.

In the conceptual area, parents had been advised to structure the living pattern of these children along firm and consistent lines. Routines (according to the parents' lights) were to be established and followed. Emphasis on routines was judged the most meaningful and obvious method of promoting consistency in the children's thinking. An awareness of what was expected, plus interpretation geared to the ability of the child to understand, induced an awareness of the mechanics of daily life and their meaning.

Free time was largely abolished. Instead 'spare' periods of the day were structured by the parents. The parents were encouraged to select tasks or pastimes of interest to the children and to supervise their efforts. Tasks were to be one-dimensional, suitable to their talents, and goal-oriented. The rationale was to provide a framework for thought which would condition the children to think serially and logically. Much help and encouragement was needed in this programme – far more than would be necessary for the normal six-, seven-, or eight-year-old.

Socially, the children were unable to control their behaviour or respond well to group situations. Parents were urged, therefore, to maintain simplicity in the social area. Since the children were more comfortable with younger playmates, they were encouraged to play with such children, one at a time. Friends were brought singly to the home or taken on family outings. Parents were advised to be aware of where their children were when outside in case trouble should arise, as indeed it often did, e.g., bullying and impulsive aggressiveness. Again, in this area, supervision and control were the crucial factors.

By age nine there was progressive decline of confusion, arising from environmental stimuli. The children responded to the programme by demonstrating an increasing ability to comprehend relevant data and adjust their behaviour with greater appropriateness. It was evident that keenness of perception and meaning were being acquired.

The de-escalation of environmental stimuli had been judged a necessary, but temporary step. Clearly, if maturity were to be promoted, external supervision and control could not be maintained forever. Once a sound, though immature, foundation to conceptual functioning had been established, it was necessary to expand the complexity of environmental events. By age twelve it was judged that, if conceptual development continued to progress satisfactorily, symptoms of more complex and diverse thought patterns should have begun to emerge.

Such symptoms, evident in the Rorschach method of assessment, had, in fact, appeared by age twelve. Not only was there an increase in response categories (diversity of thought), but those most indicative of maturing concept formation were selected with greater frequency (complexity of thought). Form level rating remained constant, indicating that, while thought was growing more complex as expected, keenness of perception remained at only the 'adequate' level. Superior perception of the varying components of reality eluded the children.

But what of the adolescent years? While at least six years had to pass before improved concepts began to reflect the normal sequence, the pressures and consequences of adolescence remained unknown factors. An immature state of dependence (fostered by the parents) coupled with delayed school entrance or slowed progression through the school system had resulted in maturer thinking. However, by age twelve, these children, although more competent to form concepts, were immature conceptually, socially, and emotionally compared to their peers. Most were one grade behind chronological age placement in school. What would happen to conceptual function when they were placed under increasing peer influence and increasing freedom in the school and community system? Would thinking continue to mature, and if so, to what level in the normal sequence?

At fifteen, as at twelve, nine, and six, an analysis of data was carried out. According to Ames, Métraux, and Walker, normal fifteen-year-old responses to the Rorschach yield a 'typical' profile. This, in fact, is true of all the ages between ten and sixteen covered in their book. Comparison of the group-average Rorschach scores of the 10 children who suffered early prolonged deprivation with the group averages reported in Ames, Métraux, and Walker, revealed the differences outlined below.

Several changes between ages twelve and fifteen were observed (Appendix, Table 9). The most noticeable change was the substantial increase in the use of unrelated form. Use of colour, however, had decreased. While these two changes are in the direction of the nine-year-old response pattern, they did not reflect the same degree of constriction as seen formerly. At the same time form level rating had decreased between twelve and fifteen to a value reflecting minimal adequacy of response. Paradoxically intellectual functioning (IQ) rose.

Moreover, comparison of typical patterns of twelve- and fifteen-year-old children with those of the present subjects (Appendix, Table 10) demonstrated a pattern among the present subjects more closely resembling the twelve-year-old profile than that typically elicited at fifteen. While unrelated form is slightly lower, M responses are equivalent and FM responses are closer to the typical twelve-year-old values than the typical fifteen. Use of m for normal twelve-year-olds and the children in this study is also equivalent. In the location category, W% in both normal twelve-year-olds and these subjects is approximately equal. There is, in fact, little difference between normal twelve-year-olds, normal fifteen-year-olds, and the present subjects in W%.

It would appear from these results that, while steady progress in the organization of conceptual function has been acquired by our subjects between the ages of six and twelve, maturation has failed to occur beyond the level expected by the typical twelve-year-old. When these subjects were twelve they had negotiated a very constricted period in their conceptual development, but had not yet closed the gap between their level of function and average expectation. At present, they appear to have achieved a level closely resembling that found in the normal sequence. While this acquired level is three years below chronological age expectation, it actually represents a considerable achievement for children with a history of severe prolonged early deprivation.

According to Ames, the typical fifteen-year-old is going through a period of temporary restriction of activity and withdrawal from authority figures. He has the necessary maturity to be aware of his own problems and to know that he must be, to some extent, responsible for their solutions. He has, however, not reached the stage of resolution. He is often self-critical and introspective as well as extremely sensitive to his own emotional reactions. He often appears moody and apathetic. It is an age of withdrawal and reflection.

How do the present subjects fit this picture? The main indicators of intellectual and behavioural control (F% and FM% respectively) clearly do not reflect the trend towards withdrawal and reflection so evident in the normal fifteen-year-old. Rather they strongly suggest the more active mood of twelve inferred by the higher proportion of M and FM responses. This is particularly true of the FM category. The subjects in this study are typically outgoing in terms of effort, and impulsive in their reactions to stimuli. There is nothing in the records to suggest a temporary retreat into the mechanisms of reflection and examination of emotional reactions characteristic of the typical fifteen-year-old's search for an identity or new relationship to society.

At the same time, however, the decrease in colour responses between twelve and fifteen could signal a withdrawal of another kind. While inner dynamics at fifteen are impulsive and unreflective, a weakening in the tendency to respond affectively is strongly suggested. These subjects appear alert to external stimuli but prone to participate impulsively at a superficial level without a corresponding engagement of emotional depth.

The qualitative aspects of the current fifteen-year-old records suggest, too, a strong dependence on the structure of reality without much ability to interject subjective material by which to elaborate or expand on what is provided through the senses. The failure to increase form level rating suggests a limiting mechanism in the development of keenness and quality of thought. Current form level scores are consistent with only the minimally adequate level of response rather than with an increasing ability to combine and integrate various components of Rorschach alternatives with meaning. Complexity of thought associated with increasing awareness of deeper levels of meaning to experience appears to have eluded these children. In fact, form level rating at age fifteen is lower than at age twelve or nine. Perhaps the pressures of adolescence have forced these children to depend upon simple structures offered rather than to re-interpret structures for themselves. The recognition of the world of interpersonal events and the impulsive approach to it which characterizes their efforts is a product of structures imposed on and provided for them rather than on structures generated from the resolutions of their own reflections.

In an independent portion of this study social maturity at fifteen was measured on the Vineland Scale. Results reveal an average SQ (Social Quotient) of twelve years. This finding is consistent with the Rorschach results reported here and suggests an equivalent level of development in both the social and the con-

ceptual areas. The relationship is understandable in Rorschach terms. Characteristics such as dependence on external structure and immature behavioural controls account for the lower than chronological age social ratings.

The larger question of recovery from the ill effects of early, severe, and prolonged maternal deprivation must now be raised. In this sample of 10 fifteen-
year-old subjects there is no evidence of gross pathology in personality development. No child has required psychiatric intervention. No child has been expelled
from school or been truant. Certainly numerous conferences between members
of the research team, the parents, and the schools have been held, but suitable
placements within the school system have always been found. No child has been
in any difficulty with law enforcement agencies.

In terms of overall development, the children reported here have all acquired
an intellectual functioning level within or above the average range. Full-scale
wisc's at fifteen range from 96 to 124. Again, social quotients show an average
developmental level of twelve years. Concept formation also appears to have
developed to a level closely resembling the normal twelve-year-old. Scholastic
achievement has been variable. In terms of family life at fifteen, all of the children were at home living as full members of the family. However, by eighteen
two had left home and were leading independent lives. The remaining eight function as integral members of their families.

In his exhaustive review of 'Deprivation in mammals and man,' Bronfenbrenner (1968) states, 'there is no evidence that the debilitating effects produced by
early deprivation of the type encountered in institutions are irreversible.' The
evidence for this statement is based on three studies, two of them, unlike the
present study, retrospective in nature. First, Beres and Obers studied 30 adults
who had been institutionalized between early infancy and four years of age.
They divided the group into diagnostic categories according to present adjustment. They discovered that seven subjects did not exhibit classical symptoms of
any recognized pathology. These were diagnosed as 'satisfactory adjustment.'
The remaining subjects ranged over many diagnostic categories of pathological
disorders.

Secondly, Maas (1963) studied 20 young adults who had been evacuated
from London during wartime between the ages of one and four and placed in
residential nurseries. Later adjustment was determined through interviews. The
investigation concluded that most of the subjects in young adulthood gave no
evidence of any extreme, adverse reactions. However, they also state that the
data support the prediction that children placed in residential group care during
the first year of life will show evidence of some damage in their young adult
years in terms of relationships with people, performance in key social roles,
inner controls, self-esteem, and intellectual functioning.

Finally, Pringle, and Bossio (1958) investigated a group of children who had been institutionalized at varying ages, the youngest placements being described simply as under five. They followed the children up to fourteen years of age. These children fared better on all personality and intellectual functions than did Goldfarb's (1945) subjects who, although placed in a comparable institutional atmosphere, were six months of age or younger at the time. By fourteen, Pringle and Bossio conclude that 'intellectual and language defects attributable to early deprivation were no longer discernible.' These conclusions were based on WISC results where mean verbal and full scale IQ's fell only in the high eighties.

The hypothesis underlying the guidance procedures of this project is that 'enriched' programmes are of little value until a meaningful framework around which to organize thought has been established. Moreover, until sufficient experience with the objective world has been acquired, the child cannot conceptualize the functions of objects or categorize their properties. Increases in stimulation prior to the acquisition of this basic orientation to thought lead to confused conceptualization. Furthermore, inadequate language robs deprived children of the opportunity to grasp normal age graded experiences at home and at school. Regression to simpler modes of expression and training in word skills was also an integral part of our programme.

The improved degree of conceptual adjustment in the present group by age fifteen demonstrates that even the most severely deprived school age children (six, seven, and eight years old) benefit significantly from an infant pre-school programme of conceptual training. Their ability to focus their thought processes within the accepted framework of conceptual development supports the view that what has been witnessed is not only the absence of obvious symptoms of pathology but rather the acquisition of a positive conceptual basis for behaviour. Our aim was to promote this in as many of the severely deprived children as possible; not merely to identify the 'few' who might eventually recover from the ill effects.

Summarizing analysis of our findings, it was demonstrated that the reverse of the normal sequence occurred between ages six and nine. While at six normal children reflect only the beginnings of integrated thought, by nine they have moved to considerable diversity and complexity in thought processes in association with improved keenness and quality of concept.

In conclusion it may be said that these children have survived and developed many signs of health within their adoptive families. The only negative finding is the above-mentioned immaturity of development in both the conceptual and social areas. These adolescents may always be dependent upon external systems for orientation and direction. Lack of imagination and reflection may always be an intellectual weakness. Sophistication in behaviour and subtlety of thought are probably lost. However, if, indeed, these are the only residual effects of deprivation, potential for recovery in a stable home environment may be said to be high.

The crucial factor in these three studies reported above appears to be age. Pringle and Bossio's (1958) subjects were fourteen when assessed. Maas's (1963) subjects were young adults. Beres and Obers emphasize that satisfactory adjustment in five of the seven 'satisfactory' cases did not become evident until latency or early adolescence. The implication is that recovery from the ill effects of deprivation is a process that requires considerable time, and, while possible, may not become evident until childhood has been negotiated.

How does this hypothesis compare with the evidence here? At nine the children were undergoing a regressive stage of conceptual development. By twelve they showed signs of increasing conceptual maturity. Furthermore, in all cases, the onset of maternal deprivation occurred in the earliest months of life, i.e., before the six-month level. The children suffered from what Bronfenbrenner terms (1968) 'stimulus restriction' of an extreme degree. This is judged to be the most damaging of all degrees of maternal deprivation. Yet by twelve all are showing signs of maturing conceptual thought and all obtained IQ's close to or within the normal range. Time, it appears, is indeed a crucial factor. This, however, is a very meagre statement. Our focus, while recognizing that personality changes do not occur quickly, has been on the process of change rather than the period in which change occurs. How, not when, is the theme.

De-stimulation of the environment and the opportunity to regress to infantile and pre-school levels of conceptualization were perhaps the two most important steps in the re-training of over-extended cognitive processes. The initial hypothesis that living experience must follow a consistent pattern so that future events can be anticipated was the first order of business. Hence the establishment of daily routines to ensure regularity in specified events provided an opportunity to order thought in those behaviours where most of life appeared chaotic and meaningless. Once the children could think consistently about routines and predict future events, mental links between past and future were within their grasp. Instructions and interpretations of these behaviours were kept simple and logical. Beyond this, simple goal-oriented tasks were provided as play material – again to provide order and direction to thought and behaviour. In play concepts such as 'beginning,' 'middle,' and 'end' were emphasized to promote an idea of limits and why and where they are set. Constant adult supervision in the social area attempted to promote and reinforce a grasp of the rules of social interaction, i.e., sharing, co-operation, emotional control, etc. Every technique geared to pinpoint a structure and indicate a direction to thought or behaviour was employed. Should this appear too regimented a programme it can be pointed out that the process does not differ (except in degree perhaps) from techniques used in the normal home during infancy and pre-school years. The former programme was deliberate, the latter is often carried out unconsciously. Human beings cannot avoid superimposing a framework on their lives; our intention was to impose a framework that would best benefit children who had been given little opportunity to understand family and community living.

In contrast to many thinkers pondering the problem of how best to raise the conceptual level of deprived children (whether the deprivation be cultural or emotional) the present researchers opted in favour of toning down the degree of environmental pressure impinging on the children. As typical products of early institutional life, they could not select relevant from irrelevant stimuli in many situations. The attempt to de-stimulate therefore took the form of ensuring that only cues relevant to the situation were present. This involved 'stripping' events of extraneous people and objects. Again, typically, the frustration level of the children was low. Presenting too many ideas, too many materials, too complicated a pattern only ensured loss of attention and emotional control. Therefore, simple tasks, simple explanations, simple materials to explore were presented, one at a time, to promote focus of attention and reduce confusion.

Perhaps the clearest implication emerging from this particular study is the amount of time required for unhealthy maladjustment to shift to potentially healthy growth. Those children who demonstrated chaotic conceptual function at six years did not begin to show evidence of healthy cognitive function until the age of twelve. This required the opportunity to regress to quite immature forms of behaviour, lower expectations, and often delays in school during the first six years of their school careers. Significant change requires considerable time in which to occur and judgments on similar children should not be made hastily.

A second equally important implication lies in the different levels of functioning reflected in Rorschach and WISC productions. In the latter category, IQ can be seen to rise slowly but steadily from six to fifteen. The present group norm is within the high average range (compared to the normal population). In intellectual terms the subjects of this study compare favourably with the normal fifteen-year-old.

This favourable comparison might consequently lead teachers and others to expect average scholastic achievement and average behaviour based on normal intelligence. However, one must examine the nature of the intelligence test in order to understand the difference that exists between intellectual and cognitive productions. The WISC (like most intelligence tests) is composed of a series of questions to which there is one correct answer. In other words, the nature of the content is highly organized and all the subject must do is fill in the correct word or phrase. It is precisely in these well-organized, right-or-wrong situations, where all the structure is provided, that these children show to best advantage. They do not have to employ imagination or their unique understanding of experience to score well.

Conversely, the Rorschach taps those very facilities. It is a projective technique implying that the subject must respond in terms of his unique understanding of reality and his own inner resources. The nature of the given stimulus is almost totally unstructured - one can only respond in terms of how one is disposed to interpret experience. To score well one requires judgment and insight - two characteristics weakly represented in the personality structures of these subjects.

The discrepancy between intelligence and achievement (whether it be academic, social, or emotional) is thus clarified. These children are able to function appropriately in structured situations, but react considerably less maturely in situations which depend on independent decision-making, insight, and judgment. Nor should they be expected to do so. Average or above intelligence, as a single indicator of development, places them in a position of unfair advantage relative to society's expectations. The equally important components of social and cognitive level of maturity must be considered by teachers and others for these children in particular, and for all children in general.

11

The child care worker

Although officially designated as a child care worker associated with this long-term study, the very human person whose life intertwined like a facilitating thread with those of the children in the study, was a many-faceted person. Mary Kilgour, the woman who carried out the original security study which initiated this intervention programme, was above all a warm human being. With her background in obstetrical nursing, short-term courses in social work practice, a diploma in Child Study from the Institute of Child Study, University of Toronto, she was essentially a person convinced of the individual worth of each human being. Her conviction that every child had potential to grow in a healthy direction sustained her throughout the many years of this study despite setbacks and disappointments in the on-going development of each of the children whose lives she touched.

From the inception of this study in 1956, when she acted as a research data collector to evaluate the security status of the infants in the institution, through the time of her appointment as director of the therapeutic programme within the institution and through the final stages of the study after the children were placed with families, her purpose in her work was to ensure the greatest possible potential for each child under her care. At the time of her appointment as supervisor of the rehabilitation programme, Miss Kilgour had just received her diploma in Child Study, a degree conferring on her recognition as a specialist in child development and a person with some capacity to arrange programmes to guide the well-being of young children. Initiation of the rehabilitation programme was an enormously taxing job and most of the long-term planning, as well as the daily organization, fell on her shoulders. Administrative capacity and leadership was one of the essential qualities needed and this she was able to provide. Working out the details of staff training and new placements for staff, implementing the suggestions and directions of the specialists of the Institute of Child Study, who were interested in the programme, and making the difficult decisions about which staff members would have to go and which might remain were part of her job. While coping with staff difficulties, her determination to keep the welfare of the children a prime objective of the institution enabled her to plan both for long-term goals and for daily changes, despite difficulties emanating from dissident colleagues along the way. Not only did she deal with the administrative problems of the staff, but her knowledge of child development and programming proved invaluable in mustering the assistance of other experts to help train staff. In addition to this practical aspect, her conviction that record taking was a worthwhile endeavour allowed her to set aside time at the end of a long day to record the progress of several children. As a result each child had monthly records of his progress which were used not only for staff training but for evaluation of the changes in that child's adaptation to his changing environment. Her capacity to respond to the personal concerns of all her staff members enabled her in turn to promote the well-being of the children under her care. Daily meetings with individual staff members, or on a group basis, enabled her to interpret the progress of the programme when understanding seemed to be elusive. To set up and arrange a volunteer programme and see that it was carried out were also her responsibility.

As the therapeutic programme within the institution began to show signs of success and as each child in turn became ready for placement, she participated actively in the selection of what would seem to be an appropriate home for each child. The records that had been kept on each child gave insight into the capacity and characteristics of each individual which enabled, insofar as possible, a matching to take place. She was able to assist the social worker in charge of the placements to evaluate the capacity of each individual family to cope with the weaknesses of the child with which it was to be matched. When the therapeutic programme drew to a close a shift in roles took place.

Once more Miss Kilgour was designated as the worker to keep track of the ongoing development of the children after their placement in homes. The advantage of knowing the children well was an asset in the interpretation of their behaviour to their new parents. In addition to carrying the practical guidance role, she was affiliated with the research unit of the Institute of Child Study and as such was the data collector. Each of her interviews with the family and with the children was recorded for entry in the research files. She became part of the planning team which set up a long-term study and decided the kinds of recording and testing which should take place in the progress of the study. It then became her responsibility to appoint appropriate people who would routinely keep the records as designated. However, her own sensitivity in her dealings with the children and families led her to many measures of intervention beyond the routine aspects of the study. Setting up of appointments for testing, for hospital visits, eye clinics, for special teacher and school interviews, arrangement of appointments for family therapy whenever needed, encouraging parents and children to proceed in certain directions, and conferring with the psychologists at the Institute of Child Study, all took place as the result of her initiative. Relating both to the families of the children and to the children themselves was another facet of the skills she had to draw upon. The way in which she did this and the basis of the thinking which enabled her to successfully 'pull it off' are worth recording. Working from a sound base in security theory as a result of her association with the Institute of Child Study as well as with her use of the security records within the institution, she was able to apply a theory of personality which allowed her to give guidance within a consistent frame of reference, identifying both short-term and long-term goals for development.

After launching into the role of social worker to the families with whom the children were placed she maintained a highly flexible point of view regarding her relation with them. Her familiarity with security theory allowed her to continue its application in her work with families, but now rather than having to think only of moving a child along in the development of his security feelings she had also to think of the capacity of the families in which the children were placed to allow the child to develop to his fullest extent. The security theory gave direction to the total case work relationship both in its application to each individual child's mental health and also in the case worker's ability to assume a supportive role within a family.

In addition to the attempt to individualize the application of the security theory, three other principles were largely followed. One was that of meeting each family at the point where they could accept or seek whatever guidance was available. Some families were aware of their need for help and were willing to seek it from the worker. However, when a family was unable to perceive a child's need, then suggestions were unwelcome and rejected. This led to the second principle by which the worker functioned and that entailed a variety of methods by which to make families aware of problems that could be anticipated in the course of the child's growing up. Because the worker had a unique role, moving in and out of homes and collecting information, there were many times she could see potential problems of which the families were still unaware. It was not her practice to leave a situation until the problem became sufficiently evident that the family would ask for help but rather to take steps to forewarn and sensitize families to the kinds of difficulties in the offing. By such methods she was able to intervene in such a way that in the long term the problems were deferred and the welfare of both the child and his family was promoted. A third principle on which she operated and which was directly related to the security theory was that each child, when faced with the stress of a new placement, would need to regress to a less mature stage of development. His behaviours would be likely to reflect levels below that of his chronological age and such behaviours might not be accepted or thought normal by the parents. For this reason, when each child emerged from the institution and went to his home and whenever he faced exceedingly stressful situations such as entry to school, she would forewarn both parents and teachers, if necessary, that the child would likely regress to more infantile ways of dealing with his problems. These would be spelled out in behavioural terms. Hopefully, this would help the parents and teachers to cope with such behaviours and accept them as temporary measures until the child felt the assurance that he was supported by his human environment. Such theoretically based practice proved in application to be very sound and, wherever parents and teachers could allow the children to regress, the period of time required for adaptation to stressful situations proved to be limited and the emergence through such stages usually came to a happy conclusion. On the other hand, an unwillingness on the part of the parent to allow regression frequently delayed the child's happy adjustment to a new environment and sometimes distorted his continuing development.

That the total venture in human relations would never have happened without a Mary Kilgour is self-evident. Had she carried out only the operation of the institutional rehabilitation the children would have moved to homes. The fact that she was able to carry her convictions and will to succeed into the last phase of the programme has undoubtedly had much to do with the relatively successful final outcome. The dual role as research data collector and child guidance worker has put its unique stamp on this project. As data collector, she maintained an official role on the staff of the Institute of Child Study. As a child care cum social worker she continued to carry duties on the staff of the Catholic Children's Aid.

Her close relationship with the families over thirteen years reached an unusually rewarding level. Four years after the termination of the study the worker still received Christmas cards, invitations to family events, and telephone calls about the children. In overview, an evaluation of the worker's achievements would lead to the conclusion that there has been no failure in relationships over time with any of these families, despite the fact that some of the worker's aspirations for the children had not been achieved.

There are many aspects to the worker's success during this final phase and we constantly seek explanations for her dedication to the welfare of the children and her capacity to sustain her serenity and strength as she helped some of the families through very difficult adjustments. We suspect that the research aspect had something to do with this as it not only supplied her with relatively objective data about the children but also guaranteed the presence of a supportive team of psychologists and researchers. The existence of this team provided her with a sympathetic ear to which she could talk out her discouragement as well as reinforcement and guidance about appropriate decisions which might shape the course of the children's lives. Another factor in the success of this programme must have been the long contact maintained over the years. Many questions need to be answered if we are to discover what alchemy was responsible for the high level of success.

Looking first to the nature of the families who opened their hearts and homes to these children, we see a few factors common to them all. One of the most important seems to be the fact that they all had a Christian value system that was important to them. Although there was great variation in the degree of adherence to Roman Catholicism, none of these families had totally rejected their adherence to their church. The second common factor was a willingness to share their experiences and give information to the staff engaged in the research project. Many of the mothers had been volunteers in the rehabilitation programme and were acquainted with the research aspect of that phase of the study. All these families demonstrated a willingness to accept 'high risk' children into their homes. An attempt was made to forewarn them of potential difficulties although their exact nature could not be determined. None of the parents were extremely young and nearly half of the families were childless.

At the time of placements all the fathers had stable jobs and owned their own homes. Over the following years all these homes remained relatively stable with little mobility or change. From time to time more than half the mothers supplemented the family income with part-time jobs. All but three were lower middle income groups. Two families lost a parent by death and one family separated. Of the six children in foster homes three had sufficient trouble to be transferred to treatment institutions and later entered group homes.

The second question is how the worker applied her knowledge of the children to their placement in homes. How did she adapt her understanding to create in each family a unique bond of goodwill which held them together for the following thirteen years? The first prerequisite was a knowledge of the attitudes and expectations of each household to the arrival of a new child. In the initial stages this required her accurate evaluation of their need for an adoptive or foster child. Secondly, she had to estimate their capacity to cater to the needs and demands of these particular children. Even more important was an estimate of the parents' ability to be flexible in the face of the child's changing needs as he moved from an uncertain newcomer to a more confident and permanent member of his household. Failure to recognize change required interpretation, for example the mother, who having given an opportunity for trusting dependency to develop, then thwarted further healthy development by failing to allow her child to move away from his reliance on her.

Since the mother was probably the central person in the family constellation, the worker was sensitive to the interactions between her and the other members of her family and particularly with her husband. Although the worker's interaction was largely with the mother, it was affected by reservations, jealousies, or the degree of support the father felt towards the new child and his intrusion on the family. The worker needed also to be sensitive to the subtleties of the shifting role between the mother and the other children in the family and to be aware that at times the other children were suffering from a feeling of alienation when emergencies arose with their foster or adopted child.

Beyond this, after a relationship had been established with a family and some of the initial problems worked through, the worker had to define and accept her role with each particular family. She was ready to be used when needed and rejected when things went well. At the same time it was important for her to try to carry no resentment and remain always available. Should she anticipate problems which seemed insoluble she needed to maintain her faith that the ultimate outcome would be acceptable to the child and his family. An abiding faith in the worth of each human being dominated her point of view. She needed the ability to see beyond the immediate situation whether in a state of quiescence or stress and to keep her goals oriented to the future. This implied a recognition not only of her own goals of what constituted a healthy adjustment for the child, but also a recognition of the family's unique goals which may have provided unconscious motivation for some of the frustrations imposed on the child. The worker needed sufficient confidence in her own judgment to indicate her convictions to a family. Such a situation might have arisen when parents were unable to accept the emotional and intellectual limitations of their children and as a result pressured them for unrealistic school achievement. In such cases she was ready to attempt modification of the attitudes and expectations of a family in the direction she believed to be healthy. This always required great patience, ability to withstand years of frustration, and consummate skill in maintaining rapport; an ideal aim, but one rarely fully achieved.

An important aspect of the worker's role with the families in this study was the mustering of outside resources to facilitate the child's adjustment to his home and his community. Specific solutions to problems were recommended after extensive consultation with a psychologist working on the project. After discussion with the parents, the worker might then act as a mediator between home and school or make an effort to elicit the help of some community resource in the child's life. She would prepare psychological reports and make appointments in mental health clinics, hospitals, and residential schools. She extended her support to the parents by sometimes accompanying them to hospitals or clinics.

The methods used by the worker in giving support to families, adapting to their needs, and at the same time pursuing her own goals were focused on her use of security theory. This theory gave directions to the total casework relationship, both in its application to each child's mental health and in the worker's ability to assume a supportive role with the family.

The task of the worker was to put into practice a conceptual framework based on a concept of 'security' or 'trust,' and this was to be her guiding principle. Trust in others and trust in oneself and one's world is the core of mental health. The attitude of trust begins its development in early infancy as the result of predictable and dependable care. As a child grows in trust he begins to impose an order and meaning on his experiences and eventually recognizes his relationship to the trustworthy people in his world. Through his relationship with people he develops feelings of self-worth and as he becomes progressively more confident he can extend his good feelings to encounter new experiences. The two requirements for mental health in early childhood are (1) a dependable, consistent adult who can be relied on for care and encouragement, and (2) opportunity for independent action which leads to the development of self-confidence.

In practical application this means that parents entrusted with the development of a mentally healthy youngster must give sufficient care and guidance to permit a child to develop first a sense of dependence and trust in them and then, second, trust in the world about him. This means that a child must learn to rely on the consistency of his parents' care and at the same time be ready to accept any opportunity to show independent action and take up the challenge of his environment wherever he is capable.

The difficult role of the worker was to individualize the application of this concept for each of the children in the study. This implied two dimensions. One was a recognition of the level of function of each child as reflected in his behaviour and the second an assessment of the depth of dependent trust already established in his personality prior to placement. Having once made this assessment through familiarity with a child and his past experiences, the next challenge was to interpret the information to either adopting or foster parents. Such interpretation was hampered by the parents' expectations for their child and their capacity to identify the ways and means of building dependent trust in a child of vulnerable mental health. Such a task for the worker required many interviews and a constant reassessment of her relationship with the families.

Generally her task was to help the parents provide an opportunity for an appropriate balance between the acceptance of controls and allowing the child to show independent effort in those aspects of his life over which he had control. While this balance (which is a constantly shifting one) was being resolved, the worker was also sensitive to the emotional depth of the relationship between parent and child. To do this, she had to be aware of the behavioural manifestations of both parent and child and to interpret them within the developmental context of the security theory.

Hence she was always alert to the first sign of mental health which was an *immature dependency*,* displayed by the child's comfortable acceptance of parental care. The second sign she watched for was *dependent trust and effort*, displayed by a child's grasping the opportunity for independent action. The third sign was *mature dependent security*, observable in the child's successful interaction with his contemporaries. The fourth sign was an indication that the child was dealing with insecurity by *defence mechanisms* such as excuses, lying, rationalization, sour grapes, stealing, compulsiveness, denial, cruelty, etc.

Because the security theory provided a comprehensive frame of reference for all human behaviour, it was also applied at a different level by the worker in her relationship with her families, particularly with the mother. In her role as a consultant, supervisor, researcher, and broker she was able to see how she could support the well-being of her families. Some highly dependent families were viewed as in *immature dependent relationship*. Such families were the recipients of constant guidance, specific directions regarding child management, use of community resources, and written information. Over a period of time a highly dependent trust relationship was established by the worker, and in the case of very unsophisticated families this relationship did not change in quality. On the other hand, there were families who permitted the worker to assume this role when the child was first placed but as they gained confidence they moved into a *mature dependent relationship* with the worker whereby they shared information and the worker in turn offered assistance when it was needed. There were other families who very quickly moved into a relationship with the worker which was largely independent of her guidance and based on their own successful past experience with children and their own good sense in dealing with the child placed with them. There were the *independently secure* people who acted like collaborators on the research project in giving information as requested. There was yet another kind of relationship between some families and the worker which had an openly *deputy agent* flavour. Such families, although unwilling to make use of the worker's guidance, clung to her visits and maintained a strong relationship over the thirteen years. Such a family might have viewed the worker as a status symbol in the context of a university research project. One of the characteristics of such a relationship was a frantic and immediate

* Terms taken from W.E. Blatz, *Human Security*. Toronto: University of Toronto Press, 1966.

demand on the worker's time when an emergency arose and, at the same time, an inability to accept her recommendations.

The role of the worker was, therefore, characterized by two levels of parallel functioning within the frame of reference of the security theory; one, the quality of her relationship to the family, and secondly, the methods by which she persisted in the pursuit of her goals for each child.

Mark, Age Four

To illustrate how the worker functioned within the framework of the security theory we might take a look at Mark, age four at the time of his adoption placement. This boy of low average intelligence gave the superficial impression of a normally developed youngster. His response to the therapeutic programme within the institution had been heartening, but his personality structure remained fragile and his intellectual functioning uneven. After placement his greatest need was to be allowed the privilege of being consistently cared for and supported through new and difficult experiences until immature dependent trust in his new parents was consolidated.

His superficial outgoing sociability accompanied by his physical size gave the impression of an eager, alert four-year-old. His excitability in new situations, expressed in distractible hyperactivity led his parents to believe that this was merely the expression of an eager, interested child. They failed to grasp the implication that distractible behaviour indicated a lack of inner and outer control.

Mark's institutional behaviour pattern was exaggerated on placement in his home. He continued to procrastinate and ask for help when dressing. He ate well, but dawdled. He was restless and had difficulty falling to sleep on going to bed. He played in an immature way with playmates. His constant need for support from his mother was expressed by his following her everywhere, and constantly demanding care and attention when she believed it was unwarranted. Her persistent attempts to push him too soon in the direction of independence resulted in his exaggerated clinging. She then attempted to reduce his demands by nagging.

The worker struggled with the problem of convincing his parents of his need for dependency. She pressed them to allow such practical manifestations of this as giving him help in washing and dressing activities and closely supervising eating and play. Co-operative family activities were encouraged on the basis that Mark was their little boy and need not demonstrate four-year-old competence to achieve his parents' approval. Their desire to have a boy who might satisfy their need for high achievement and exemplary behaviour in their family and community blocked their acceptance of an immature child. Hence they were unable to allow their child to regress and could not respond to his demand for immature dependence. This resulted in a deterioration in Mark's mental health and a high-strung, irritable youngster began to emerge.

Throughout the course of his growing up, many crises arose. Mother and child would collide in stubborn rebuttal of the other's desire. The ensuing panic would prompt Mark's mother to call for immediate help. However, having once talked the situation over and relieving some of the pressures the family would once more resort to the former nagging and pressuring in the pursuit of more mature behaviour. To provide support for her recommendations the worker would draw on extensive community resources. Mental health clinics, reading disabilities clinics, resources of the staff of the Institute of Child Study, were all made available for further diagnosis and arrangements for these were made by the worker.

The worker, sensitive to the significance of the child's behaviour, persisted in her attempts to interpret his needs to his over-striving parents, but without success. They continued to press him towards independence and in time he developed a pseudo-independence characterized by bravado and 'smart alecky' behaviour. By age fifteen this conflict was still unresolved. At fifteen years of age, despite some personality strengths, there is still evidence that this child is seeking an immature relationship, while his parents continue to complain about his inadequacies. There is excessive friction between the teenager and his parents and his behaviour is lippy, arrogant, and defiant. At the same time he is strongly identified with his family and has told them, 'you cannot make me leave this house.'

The refusal to allow Mark to regress in order to give him time to develop an immature dependent relationship distorted the course of his development and precluded the comfortable emancipation from his parents which characterizes the truly secure child. His present conflict is an expression of his past experience whereby he is attempting to cling to his family, still seeking the reassurance of their guidance, while his parents persist in their desire for him to prove his competence and independence.

The second level at which the worker functioned in her relationship with the family is demonstrated by the way she allowed Mark's mother to use her. Ideally she would have based her work with this family on a relationship whereby Mark's mother could use her in a maturely dependent context. This would have meant that Mark's mother could view her as a wise and thoughtful resource person whose recommendations for guidance could be taken seriously and an attempt made to implement them. Such a relationship was impossible because of his mother's insecurities about her status as a homemaker and a worker in the community. Her striving for superiority had an unrealistic quality which was expressed in many deputy agent manifestations. She had a compulsive need to control her environment and the people in it. Her need to feel completely competent as a mother precluded her acceptance of advice, even when she requested it in moments of severe stress in which she panicked. She insisted on her relationship to the worker being that of one of a team in which she held the reins and which she could abandon on her own impulse.*

We active participants in this on-going rehabilitation programme had our own convictions about the worth of the guidance worker in this project but were uncertain if the parents would also regard this role as highly. We therefore developed a short questionnaire as the study drew to its completion to which we asked each parent to respond. Every parent did so. The questionnaire was accompanied by a letter from the chief investigator requesting the parents' assistance in describing the role the worker had played in their lives so that we might have useful guidelines to pass on to other workers.

The questionnaire was a brief one-page document as follows:

(1) *How would you describe the role M.K. has played in your life?*
– at the time your child was placed in your home
– after your child's initial adjustment to your family
– over the elementary school years
– at present
(2) *What are the most helpful things she has done for your family?*
(3) *What are the least helpful things she has done?*

Additional information and suggestions may be written on the back of this sheet.

Because the children had been living with their families 10 or 11 years we were aware that accurate recall of events would be difficult, if not impossible. However, we believed that the flavour of their relationship with the worker could be described.

The responses of the parents were analysed first by taking statements off the records verbatim and then by classifying them according to three criteria which seemed relevant.

Under each of the four sections designated by the questionnaire it was possible to classify three main categories: (a) attitude of the worker; (b) type of involvement – supportive/intervention; (c) intensity and duration (for listing, see end of chapter).

In summarizing the results it was possible to look at the answers in several ways. It appears first of all that the involvement of the child care worker with the family can be thought of as (a) supportive, and (b) steps in intervention. Throughout the questionnaire there is a consistent indication of the parent being aware of the worker's concern, not only for the particular child in the study but

* From *The Social Worker*, vol. 41, no 1, Spring 1973 (by permission).

for the total family. Guidance and intervention were supplied for any child in the family in need of it and at times this kind of support was extended to psychological testing and personality assessments by our own research psychologist on the study.

In reference to the supportive role carried by the worker we find the parents describing the worker as 'a reliable friend who provided them with a ready ear to listen to problems.' Afterwards she could offer suggestions which were knowledgeable and reflected good judgment about the practicability of the problems. In addition, she was viewed as a resource person who could provide books and information at the appropriate levels of development for the children. She gave the parents a new view of their children through her discussions about the children and through the use of books which she thought were important.

At the level of intervention her knowledge of children's development and her insights into children's feelings and problems made her diagnoses and recommendations reliable. The parents learned to trust her judgment. This quality of insight was extended beyond providing help in times of crises to an anticipation of potential developmental, school, or family problems. The child care worker had an ability to forewarn parents and to prepare them to take steps to prevent problems arising.

The worker's contact with these families spread over many years. In some cases her visits and recording would take place only twice yearly. In other cases there would be prolonged and frequent visits. Despite this discrepancy, there is never a suggestion that some families were neglected or on the other hand that there was too much intervention. Regardless of the frequency of contact there is a consistent reflection that the worker was considered a friend of the family (one exception). Her visits were welcomed. Even where no problems existed it was a pleasant opportunity to talk about the family. Those families which required frequent visits relied on her to help them over crises. In many instances her capacity to interpret meaning behind a child's behaviour avoided what might have seemed in its initial stages a potential rejection of the child. The parents gratefully accepted her interpretation and tried to act on it.

There is some indication on the parents' part that their active involvement in record keeping and supplying information over time in a consistent way was valuable. It gave them an opportunity to consider all aspects of a child's behaviour and put into perspective those aspects which seemed to be out of focus in the day-by-day course of living with their children. It also afforded the opportunity to look at the progressive steps in the child's development and prevented too much concentration on transient problems. On the other hand, when real problems were emerging it helped the parent identify the symptoms and opened up channels for discussion with the worker.

PARENT QUESTIONNAIRE

(1) How would you describe the role M.K. has played in your life?
- At the time your child was placed in your home.
- After your child's initial adjustment to your family
- Over the elementary school years.
- At present.
(2) What are the most helpful things she has done for your family?
(3) What are the least helpful things she has done?
Additional information may be written on the back of this sheet.

ANSWERS TO PARENTS' QUESTIONNAIRE

(1) *How would you describe the role M.K. has played in your life at the time your child was placed in your home?*
- Always ready to help and advise. Parent felt 'very much alone' coping with new member of family – comfort someone there to turn to.
- Great friend. Helped parents with child not understood by parents of CCAS. Helpful in advising parents how to handle a child who had spent three years in an institution, 'in a vacuum.'
- Parent felt M.K. knew everything there was to know about children, not only what she said but by kindly attitude to everyone.
- Played large role in family's lives. Gave advice so parents felt they were doing no wrong. (tactful)
- Parents were told of little problems beforehand and child's ways so better able to cope as things arose.
- Without M.K's help one parent would not have kept difficult foster child.
- Selecting type of child that would be a challenge to parents.
- Kept in close contact, guidance.
- Genuine interest in our children – advice re each member of family.
- Helped *our* adjustment to children.
- Made us realise we *are* a *family* – with ups and downs like most families.
- Suggestions, guidance, genuine interest – no insistence.
- Made transition from institution to home easier for child and parents by helpful practical suggestions.
- Initiated phone calls and made encouraging visits.

How would you describe the role M.K. has played in your life after your child's initial adjustment to your family?
- Frequent telephone calls and visits if needed.
- Resource person and adviser once satisfactory relationship established.

- No real problems, but glad to know M.K. there if needed. A very good friend.
- Adjustment not easy. Many trials. Parents needed M.K. – a friend who understood child's ups and downs, a knowledgeable consultant.
- Advised how to handle discipline problems, constructive suggestions.
- Always there if needed. Listened graciously.
- Advice on family as a whole and what to expect of our children.
- More than a Social Worker – a friend of the family.
- Explanations of disturbed behaviour.
- Reports of adjustment of the other children from the institution proved supportive.
- Visit to male psychologist to talk over adjustment (child, mother, father) was very helpful. M.K. sensed husband would rather talk to a man.

How would you describe the role M.K. has played in your life over the elementary school years?
- Warned age 14 would be difficult.
- Advised what parents could expect of child's development. Suggested ways of solving school problems to school as well as to parents.
- Parents given inside view of what child will be able to do in school.
- Helped with specific discipline and school work problems.
- Three way meeting with parent, teacher, and M.K.
- Go between – between home and school, explaining to school difficulties re child.
- 'Went to bat' for child at school – persuading principal to let child go to school of her choice.
- Insight into problems of youth from her overall experience.
- Coping with specific problems, e.g. emotionally disturbed child – got him into Boys' Village for treatment, sent to YMCA camp. Guidance and leadership to foster parents. Got child a sort of Big Brother.
- Her interest in children never waned. Saw their needs always met, medical and psychological.
- Terrific source of ideas for problem solving.
- Kept up to date on movies, lectures, TV programmes which would be helpful to needs of families.
- Periodic assessments for research provided genuine insight and appreciation of our children which we wouldn't have had without it.
- Mediator between school and home.
- *M.K.* provided a support and confidant for child outside of her family.
- Interpreted special 'Indian' qualities to family.

- Foster parents *need* someone to question.
- Practical suggestion, to repeat year, was correct.

How would you describe the role M.K. played in your life at present?
- Dear friend of family – over abundance of love, understanding, patience, ability, education. Best type of social worker.
- Dedicated life.
- Still interested in the children – all children of family, and *does* things for them.
- Encourages all.
- Builds and maintains parents' self-confidence by constant reference to their achievements and faith in their judgment.
- Still a good friend with good ideas and solutions.
- Continues to be a warm human being that parents can call on without feeling guilty. Has helped with 'ALL our children.'
- Parent saves up problems to discuss with M.K. on visits, knowing they will have them solved before she leaves, and parents again able to cope for a time to come.
- Friendly interest – discussion without prodding.
- Has been comforting and non-critical.

(2) *What are the most helpful things she has done for your family?*
- Always available.
- Nice to know she was there if needed.
- Made better parents, more aware of children as individual human beings.
- Helped parents understand the needs of child.
- Made parents aware how complex human beings are, and encouraged them to have a positive approach.
- Parents grateful for her help in crises.
- Easy person to talk to, full of experience and knowledge to help raise a growing family.
- Never singled child out in front of other children.
- Showing foster parents what satisfaction they could get out of letting a little boy know he was loved by *someone* and wanted. Pointing out he had no one in the world but them made quite an impression.
- Advised parents to seek help for older child in family – for the good of all. It worked.
- Gave foster mother incentive to start a career.
- Showed *sustained* interest for 11 years – always willing to visit home repeatedly.
- Reminded me to be firm – mean what I say.

Suggestions from parents
- More people like M.K. needed – mature, uncritical women as trouble-shooters. But would the people who need them most make use of their services?
- Has knowledge plus experience gained through visiting homes. Comes right into your environment and lives the good and the bad with you. Interested in the family as a whole, not just foster child and family like most social workers.

SUMMARY

Attitude of the Worker
- Interest in children – friend to children, does things for them.
- Interest in parents
- Interest in other members of family
- Friendly and enjoys talking:

  Frank   Considerate
  Kind   Reassuring
  Understanding   Tactful
  Encouraging   Good Judgment
- Listens graciously:

  Parents have confidence in M.K.
  Sincere; warm; dedicated.

Types of Involvement
- Counsellor: resource person – re background of child
- Offers suggestion – specific, trouble shooting
- Teaches, suggests methods of parenting
- Parent education – general
- Diagnosis – insights into children's problems
- Prodding
- Supports – discusses
- Knowledgeable: Good judgment: Advisor
- Acts as mediator with school – helps school as well as parents
- Provides opportunity for professional help: Psychologist Mental Health Clinic; Hospital; Boys' Village
- Anticipating problems – preparing parents
- Watchdog for the children
- Offers material re child rearing, literature, movies, lectures
- Builds parents self-confidence
- Friend

Supportive	*Intervention*
Friend	Trouble shooting
Support	Mediator
Builds self-confidence	Parent Educator

Intensity: Duration

- Back-up if needed – rare
- Large role in family
- One parent would not have kept child
- Selects children challenging to parents
- Always there if needed – frequently
- Dear friend of the family
- Sustained contact (11 yrs): readily available (telephone) initiates contact: frequent – regular visits
- Record keeping gives parents an idea of progress (may be threatening)

SUZANNE

The importance of the child care worker to many of these children is apparent through an examination of her relationship with Suzanne, a child with Indian heritage, who was placed from the institution into a middle class suburban family when she was two years of age. This rather rigid family, expecting high achievement from their five children, had firm religious values and aspirations for a high standard of living (big house, several cars). Suzanne made a satisfactory adjustment to this family as they did to her. Her immaturities and relatively slow rate of development were accepted well, despite their high goals for their other children. Suzanne's three main developmental problems which recurred throughout her life centred around her somewhat fearful relationship with her strict foster mother, her struggle to be fully adopted into her foster family, and the reconciliation of her Indian heritage. In the initial stages of her placement her passive nature led to rather poorly developed relationships with her family. She related much more comfortably to her foster father and siblings than she did to her foster mother. It was not until she was eleven years of age that she seemed to be a fully integrated member of the family. By this time she was expressing a strong desire to be adopted by them, rather than fostered. Despite this, foster care was continued out of the perceived necessity of her family to recover expenses for her care from the agency. Adoption was not to be completed until she was nearly eighteen years of age.

At the same time that Suzanne was pressing her family to adopt her she was reconciling her conflict over her Indian origins. Her child care worker was able to help her with this in various ways. A visit to an Indian reservation and discussion with some of its admirable residents, the provision of literature and a study of the history of the Ojibway tribes provided an opportunity to understand some of the strengths of her background. This interest led to Suzanne's collecting a book of Indian poems, many with contemporary themes. These she presented to her worker.

One of the facets of this child's personality was her rather limited ability in verbal communication but an increasing admirable capacity to communicate in writing. Her feelings poured out of the letters she wrote to her worker from time to time. She was increasingly able to make use of the written word. In these, one finds a progressive zest for life as she passed through rebellious feelings against her mother, unhappy feelings about North American prejudice towards Indians, and resentment about parental supervision. Her constant stream of letters to her case worker seemed to provide a safety valve for the resolution of resurgent, uncomfortable feelings. They are replete with accounts of personal interaction of which she herself is the focus. The following letters reveal some aspects of her development from age fourteen through seventeen:

(Age 14 years 11 months)

Dear Miss Kilgour,

Hi, I love my bike! I rode it one Saturday and I couldn't stop riding! I nearly got myself lost! I rode all over the place. I usually ride with my girlfriend, Nancy. Remember her? Were going skating on Thurs I think. Then swimming on Friday for sure and my two girlfriends, they're both Indians, one's straight from India. They might come. My girlfriend, Joti, she's Indian and she's so dark, and I was wondering why I wasn't that dark. My other girlfriend, Manisha, she is so fun to hang around with. She's a Hindu Indian.

Nancy had to stay one night for english, and her teacher said I could wait for her and so I did, and her teacher asked me what nationality I was and I said Canadian Indian, Ojibway, and she asked me what tribe I was from, Six Nations or around Lake Huron? and I said I don't know and I wanted to tell her so much to and I didn't know! Unless I forgot. I felt so stupid when I said I didn't know. I want to know.

You know that dog I never stop talking about, Kelly. Well one night she was hit by a car, and they had to put her away. The day I heard about it, I cried so much because I loved her very much and now she's gone and I'll never see her again. I was so close to her and she could hardly wait till I got out of the door before she jumped all over me and that little tail of her's nearly wagged right off. I always had a bone for her or a piece of meat. During the winter when she came to see me she would shiver and I would pick her up and wrap her up in my coat.

During the summer I would take her swimming every night. She would run back and forth and bark at me and sometimes fall right in. Then we would be on our way back and my dad would be sitting there ready to go for a walk with her. She loved my dad and my dad really was fond of her. She would protect me from the paper boy every day. She would make us laugh when she would get excited and run all over the place barking. Now she gone.

Thank you for the letter and the picture. I really like it and I will keep it forever. My mom is really proud of me and same with my dad. The neighbours are pretty surprised about it.

Thank you Miss Kilgour

LOVE

Suzanne

March 1972, Age 15 years

Dear Miss Kilgour,

hi, we finally got are report cards. I did pretty good. I'm happy about it anyway. So are my parents! Well anyway, here's my 1st term marks:

Subject	Mark	Class Average	Personal Average
Consumer Education	56	59	
English	62	56	
Geography	58	59	59.1
Home Economics	67	68	
Math	51	67	
Phys. Ed.	62	66	
Science	52	55	
Typing	64	62	

I'm above average in typing and English. The others are close to average except Math. I was lucky, I thought for sure I would fail that one. I'm really happy I did fairly good!

You know something, I've been hearing things from books, magazines, people that Indians are stupid, and lazy! I've heard that liquor wasn't allowed to be sold to Canadian Indians because they can't handle it. Who can? I hear about men killing themselves in cars, killing other people, really causing things. I don't see the right in that!

And that silly thing about Indians losing their right as an Indian if they marry a white man. I don't see the point in that because no matter who you marry, you were born Indian, lived Indian and nothing can change that!

I'm reading this book Indians are for Reservations, *and I am so surprised at the awful things some people actually say! Its those people who write awful things about Indians and then it spreads and as a result, we end up with a bad name! That's just not right!!*

This is one paragraph:
"Indian kids don't seem to be taught why you don't do things. They don't know the difference between right and wrong. They're not psychopaths, they come from broken homes, often their parents are in jail. The reserve is a kind of no-man's land."

Why can't Indians live where they want? Eskimos live at the North Pole, why doesn't everyone bother them about living there!

You know I think its all got to do with the race. Because I'm reading this book, Black Like me *and its a true biography of a white man who changed his colour with medical treatments and he went down in the deep South and he wrote on how Negroes were rejected by the whites. And it all has to do with colour. I sometimes think its the whites. They don't seem to except other races. Boy thats so sad. Oh well, I hope someday, this world will change!*

I'm so sorry for writing such a rotten letter, but you've been telling me so much good things about Indians I was wondering about the bad things.

Oh well, I still proud to be an Indian.

I guess I better go now,

Love
Suzanne

Dec. 1973, Age 16 yrs 8 ms

Dear Aunt Mary
hi. How's everything with you? I mean it, I just don't know *what the hell's wrong with me. I feel like dying. So what else is new?*

I don't know why, *but I told my parents Peter's 10-speed bike was stolen from the garage and it wasn't!! I lost it up at the plaza. I lied to them, I did tell them the truth and they're mad at me, which I don't blame them. I have to pay Peter $60.00 and for my punishment is that I can't buy my own 10-speed that I've wanted so bad. You don't know how much I wanted that bike. I sold my old bike for $30.00 and I was going to help pay for my new 10-speed, now I can't even buy one. It was probably Mother's idea of a punishment and my dad announced it, because he never knew I wanted that bike. I hate her so much, she makes me so miserable. She's not my mother, my mother's DEAD. She's constantly checking up on me, last weekend, a friend of mine, John called me, and I asked to go to Michele's, like an idiot, she says 'what, are you going to meet John there?' God, she's gets me mad.*

I think I'd be happier an orphan, I don't care if I would be poor or what, as long as I was happy. I don't know, but I think she's got something against me. What's the age adopted people can leave there homes legally? Please tell me.

Don't mention anything to Mrs. Chalmer. I like her, but I don't need another social worker.

NO ONE *in this world can take your place Aunt Mary. I'm* happy *your my social worker. I thank God I've got you.*

Believe me, I honestly believe she likes yelling at me, making me so miserable. I'm not going to talk to her, I've just given up. Just one more year of school and off I go to Vancouver for a permanent job. I hope I'm happy out there, cause I'm not coming back. I'll come back to see you for sure no matter what.

Some Christmas. I just can't wait to see my neice, Katey. She's 1 1/2 now.

I'm going X-mas shopping this Saturday downtown Eaton's (EATON'S COLLEGE STREET) I'd like it if you could come with me. Please give me a call. I'm dying to hear from you. Please don't tell them about this letter, to me it'll only mean more yelling, tears, and believe me, I've HAD ENOUGH. Don't talk to my mother, she'll probably tell you a pile of crap! Anything to get you on her side. Please give me a call and let me know, I'd love you to come shopping with me. I don't work this Saturday.

One of the patients at the Bayview Villa called me a dirty Indian Bitch. Friendly aren't they? For no reason. She had asked one of the tea girls for cereal for dinner, and Louise the cook said no cereal for anyone cause there suppose to eat their dinner, so I told the tea girl and she said to the old lady that it wasn't allowed. She she told her friends I was a Dirty Indian Bitch.

Oh well, I don't care. I think I'll go for a long walk, try to settle down. So please think about it ok. I do hope *you can come, if you can't there will be other times.*

Love
Suzanne

May 1, 1974.
(Age: 17 years 2 months)

Dear Aunt Mary,

Hi, I miss my favorite aunt you know! When you don't phone, or write, I write to you and tell you how I'm doing! Well, I'm just doing GREAT!!! I'm just bubbling over with happiness!! Believe me, I couldn't be happier!!

The fighting with my mom is ALL FINISHED!! I could actually feel myself grow out of that 'age period'! I'm not fooling! All of a sudden, I wanted to talk to my mom, I wanted to go places with her, I wanted her around, I wanted to be around with her! It was so amazing! Every day after school, I come home, I have coffee with her, we talk.

Sure, she gets mad at me for something, but I don't take it the way I used to! I'm going to a shower with her this Sunday. My cousin is getting married pretty soon, so I'm going to the shower with my mom.

My dad was showing me how to act at a shower, I have to balance a cup of tea on my knee, and he was telling me how everything is, he starts off by giggling like a girl, saying 'Oh, thats what I just wanted,' in his high voice, giggling away, I was laughing! He's a joke!

School is going great! I got my report, and I failed my typing, 41! So this term, wow, I gotta get at least a 59! I pray to the Lord I get 59!

Last semester, I failed Graphic Arts, the final report, a fail. So I went to the guidance councellor, and he straightened me all out, and now, Next year, I only take four courses, and I get my grade 12 diploma, then I can go on to where ever I want to, so I think I'll go onto Seneca College.

Our school is in a semester system. Four the first half, that is equal to a full year. So I failed one of the four subjects, so I lost a credit, and this semester, I have four other subjects, so if I get all those subjects, I'll have altogether 23 credits. I would of had 24, but I failed Graphic Arts, so I have 23, and the guidance counseller, said, I needed 27 credits to get a grade 12 diploma, so I need four more credits to make 27, and I picked them out for next year, and since were on a semester system, I only go for half a year, which is equivalent to a year! So I graduate in January '75. Do you understand?

So I'm thinking of taking swimming courses to lead up to Therapy courses, so I can work in hospitals, you know theraputic pools. So my mom and I are looking into it. That'll be great! Because I'll be into something I like. Besides that, weekends, or some nights, I could teach swimming lessons. So I registered for my Bronze Medallion, and I start on May 27, three nights a week.

So I gotta work like a fool idiot this term! I can't fail my typing, I just can't!

Guess where I'm going this summer? I'm going to fly to New Jersey on my own, to stay at my Brother's place, with Doreen and my neice, Katey. I can't wait! Probably at the end of June sometime. I can't wait to see my little neice! She'll be two this June! Little Katey Krackers will be two years old! I love her so much! I'll buy her the best present she could want! Last time she was here, she followed me all around, we'd play peek-a-boo, every morning she would run to the bottom of the stairs and yell out Dabin! This would be about 7:30 in the morning to! So I get up, and she'd come running to see me all excited with a sweet little smile on her sweet little face! I just adore that little one! Everytime we phone long distance, you can hear Katey in the background saying, I want to talk to Dabin! You gotta see her this summer! I just LOVE her to pieces!

I've still got my job. I'll be stayin' there all summer. I'm trying to save my money to go on that trip to New Jersey, and I want new good clothes for when

I go, because I want to look nice rather than look like a tramp in jeans! I'm so excited about everything! School, this summer, after grade 12, Seneca, and to top it all off!

I hope to get my driving license this summer some time! I'm studying for my 365, and my sister is teaching me. So I'm hoping!

My brother Peter just bought his own little MG Midget, and so that might mean that I can have my dad's car a few nights! I'm just hoping right now!

I still have my two little fish! One of them was born in the big tank, and we kept it, and now he's almost full grown, and he's a year and 2 months old. We've had him since he was born! Watching him grow. He's a swordtail. I'll have to get a female and watch their babies grow. They're so cute when there small, little fins, little eyes!

I can't part with him though. He's only a fish, but I had him since the day he was born, I watched him grow, took care of him when he was sick, we almost lost him on Christmas day, and I was almost in tears, thats how much I love the little guy! When he was little, he played this game with me, I'd be watching T.V. and he'd swim to the glass and just stare, and I'd look at him and put my finger to the bowl and he'd swim away, and I'd take my finger away and he'd come to the glass again, and I'd put my finger to the glass again and he'd swim away! He was a cute little thing when he was a baby. Now, his coloring has changed, he used to be bright, bright, orange when he was 7 months old, now he's dull orange, with a white stomach! The same markings as his mother. His mother died of a disease. But he's still with us, and I'm really attached to him, I'll talk to him and he still comes to the glass. I just hope I don't lose him for a long time. His name is Little Orange Juice!

I'm doing embroidery right now, on material. I read this beautiful poem, and I wanted it on material, so away I went, and I'm almost finished. The poem goes like this:

> *If you Love Something;*
> *Set it Free,*
> *If it Returns,*
> *It is yours;*
> *If it doesn't,*
> *It never was.*

Isn't that beautiful? So I've got a white bird flying in the sky, and then the poem underneath it, and below the poem, I've got a black horse walking through tall grass, and along the sides I'm going to put in some flowers. I hope it turns out, cause if it does, I'll do more!

Oh Aunt Mary, You don't know how HAPPY I am! I just feel like running across a field screaming at the top of my lungs;
I'M SO HAPPY!!!!!!!
Life is sunshine with Occasional rain. I read that somewhere, I've never forgotten it, and I often say it in my mind. Its so true, isn't it?
Come and visit sometime! I can't wait to see you!

Love
Suzanne

Feb. 8/76
(age 21 years, 8 months)

Dear Aunt Mary:
hi, thanks so much for the beautiful Indian note paper. It's really beautiful. They're all so cute. I'd like to frame a few.

Its been so long since I've written to you and I have so much to tell you. I haven't seen you since September.

How was your Christmas and New Year's? Mine was really great. We had the whole family together, 2 new members. Geoff & Doreen had a baby boy, his name is John, after my dad. Is he ever, ever cute! He is just the happiest little guy. The sweetest little smile in the world. I just love him so much I was constantly picking him up and playing with him. He loves Katey. Katey is 3 1/2 now, almost 4, her birthday is in June. John will be 2 in July. I can't wait, because when Katey turned 1, I made her a rug with her name on it, so I'm going to do the same with John.

The other new member of the family is Bob's wife, May. They were married in October. It was a really beautiful wedding. I invited my boy friend Bart to come with me. I just got out of my cast a week before the wedding. I was still on crutches, which was so frustrating in a long gown! I really wanted to dance but I couldn't. Little Katey was the flower girl and at the reception she was running around in her little long gown that my mom made, giving every one a piece of wrapped wedding cake. It was so cute.

At the end of September, I lost my job at Montreal Trust. My manager said she didn't think I was suitable for the job. I think it was my leg, all the time I had off, and they needed someone full time.

On December 1st, I got a job at a publishing Co., its called Houghton Mifflin Canada Ltd. It's a small Company, not even 2 years old yet (in Canada). It has 5 offices across Canada, and the head office and the only office in Ontario is at Steeles & Woodbine. Our office is only 7 people and 2 are part time. Its really tiny. But I love small offices, they are so close and friendly. At times it doesn't even seem like your working, because we're all joking around. The age group is all young. There's a girl there 18, and we get along just great. The president of the company is about 34 and we call him Peter. Right now I am being trained on key punch.

We moved home about 2 weeks ago. We fixed the basement up, put a rug down, our furniture, table, lamps; set up the stereo and its really cozy.

Right now I'm saving for a $600.00 stereo. Then after that I'll save for an Apt. The rent around here is ridiculous.

Bart and I are still going out together! Its been a year and a month now! You never met him, we'll have to get together. Right now he is going to University in Hamilton. He comes to Toronto every weekend. I just love him so much. He's made me so happy.

Last week I met my brother Benjy. Is he ever nice. He's just like Al, so friendly and always laughing. Benjy is 31. He lives in North Bay with his Indian wife 'Jo' from Six Nations Reserve. They have 2 boys, and a new born baby girl. Benjy just applied for a job in Toronto and he has a good chance of getting it, and if he does he'll be moving to Pickering which is great because they'll be closer. My sister Bonny just had a new baby girl. She called it Michelle Nicole. My sister Sandy is supposed to be having her baby anytime now. Bonnie and Marlene and Sandy live in Collingwood.

I also met my sister Nada. She lives in Toronto. She's 21. She lives at The Indian Girls' residence on Spadina. She is really mixed up – confused. I really don't know the whole story but the whole family is rejecting her. I think that is stupid! She tried to kill herself once and to me that is a cry for help and there's no one to help her. I don't care what the others say I like her and I want her to know I'm there if she needs someone. Bonny also likes her. Bonny likes everyone and everything. She's so sweet and sincere. I really love Bonny. She's such a lovable person and she's my sister!! Wait till you meet her, you'll just love her. I have so many pictures of all my nieces and nephews! They're all so cute, big brown Indian eyes.

Well, I guess I better go now. I'll write more often I promise.

Bye Aunt Mary, and thanks again for the beautiful gift.

Love,
Suzanne

12

George

'I am right in there. I wouldn't miss this experience for anything,' was the enthusiastic greeting of George, age eighteen, to his mother on his first home visit from an out of town university.

This appealing young man's development, although not all comfortable, has moved along in a heartening way since the intervention in his young life. It also illustrates in a rather clear way how the worker in this study has been able to help release this child's greatest potential, first through her influence within the institution, secondly in helping to find a congenial home for his adoption, and thirdly through her constant support of his family in the course of his growing up. Her life became intertwined with theirs in such a friendly and salutory way that even now she is regarded as a good friend of the family. (George is nineteen years old at the time of writing.)

We search George's history in an attempt to clarify some of the assets that contributed to the highly successful outcome of his maturing. As he was not placed for adoption until four years, seven months of age, it would appear that he must have had inherent strengths which enabled him to withstand such prolonged deprivation within the institution. In retrospect we can see that he had sufficient intellectual capacity to overcome the institutional deficit, once given an opportunity to respond to a stimulating environment. His second asset seems to be some kind of emotional resilience which allowed him to overcome his initial tendency to withdraw from any new situation and to experience the elation of having achieved and enjoyed an event despite his initial fears. His third asset seems to be a capacity to respond at an emotional level to offers of support from the people in his environment. The good luck to have found trustworthy adults on whom he could depend permitted him to use this asset to form healthy attachments to the central persons of his life.

What environmental supports nourished these assets? A normal delivery, one month of breast feeding, and a second month as a resident in a maternity home with his mother would point to a relatively benign beginning, although no records are available about the emotional state of his mother either prior to his birth or after as she prepared to release him for adoption. The sudden transition from this situation to becoming a resident of the institution with eighty-five other children seems barely to have created a ripple in his well-being. The first brief notations about him at three months indicated that he was a contented baby who was taking his feedings well and responding to whatever attention might come his way. Even by nine months of age he was described as alert and interested in his surroundings, confined as they were. Some aspects of his development seemed close to normal as he was described as 'standing on his feet and creeping whenever he got the opportunity.'

By eighteen months of age the next earliest record of his progress indicates that deprivation was taking its toll. His developmental status was described by the comment, 'slow progress.' His emotional state was 'fearful and lacking confidence.' And further, 'as long as he was in his crib he was friendly, but placed on the floor he became timid and nervous,' and 'although interested in things around him he was afraid to attempt anything and would venture nowhere with an unfamiliar adult.' A social worker's plea at this time was, 'This child requires individual attention and lots of affection but both these needs are not being satisfied.'

From this time, at eighteen months, until the inception of the rehabilitation programme at twenty-six months, we see a declining mental health picture with few remaining strengths. During this period George suffered from many infections, cellulitis, colds, measles, chicken pox and was hospitalized seven days with tracheitis. He was still considered an attractive baby despite his frequently unhappy and expressionless face. His play was aimless. He was demanding a great deal of attention from familiar adults, but withdrew fearfully from anything unfamiliar. He ate and slept well and still ran about his confined nursery quarters with an 'active spirit.'

At three years of age there was no behavioural record but he was observed casually with several other children of his age group. He was now in a senior infant nursery consisting of one large room with seven cribs. The only other furniture was a long eating bench where, in addition to sleeping, George was served a bowl of nourishing mush, with his six companions, three times daily. His play consisted of scrambling for two or three cartons thrown into the room and left lying about. He was still in diapers and as there were no bathtub or toilet facilities, a 'potty' was chained to the crib for toileting. The only time George had an opportunity for outdoor activity was in the summer when he was corralled with thirty-three other children for two hours daily in the yard. Supervision of activity in this situation was minimal and frequently there was none at all.

When George was three years, two months old, the rehabilitation programme was instituted. When first observed by new staff, he was a compulsive, ritualistic child, lacking trust in adults, unable to tolerate interference, frequently screaming and having temper tantrums. He was apprehensive of anything unfamiliar, indifferent to play materials and appeared passive and withdrawn a great deal of the time. He had physical characteristics which the rehabilitation team labelled 'the institutional droop, flabby muscles, mouth hanging open and lips protruding.' These characteristics were common to all of the children.

Four months later the influence of the worker whose presence was to wield such benefit on his life had begun to exert itself. As a result of her planning George had been placed in a room with five other children of similar age. Here he was sufficiently lucky to have acquired a warm, loving woman as a house mother – a fortunate circumstance at the beginning of this programme. His response was heartwarming and encouraged further investment in his well-being. As time went on his physical bearing reflected his improved feeling about himself. His posture straightened, he walked with his shoulders back, and his total body musculature became firm. His face began to awaken from its blankness and he was able to relate to a few familiar adults. As his world opened up and as more varied experiences became part of his environment he began to display temperamental qualities which were to remain part of his personality structure in the future.

The first quality was his capacity to relate to consistent adult caretakers. The second quality, not so easy to live with, was his undue fear of any unfamiliar situation or persons. Fortunately, his capacity to form a trusting attachment to familiar people allowed him the possibility of being introduced to and carried through new and unfamiliar events. For example, a picnic planned by the staff was eagerly anticipated by most of the children, despite their uncertainty as to the meaning of this first event in their lives. When the day arrived most of the children moved eagerly with the adults to the waiting taxis. George, contrarily, collapsed kicking and screaming on the doorstep and was finally carried sobbing to the taxi by his concerned house-mother. Once at the 'picnic' he began slowly to participate in the activities until, caught up in the pleasure of it, his exuberance spilled over to include everyone. This characteristic, to respond with resilience once supported through stress, was also to be a consistent quality of his person throughout his young life. This quality, which reflected his enjoyment of effort, was the second asset we always looked for in a mentally healthy child.

As the focus of treatment in the rehabilitation programme was to sponsor each child's assets until they took precedence over the disabilities, George's personality qualities could be strengthened in a very clear way. Evaluation of his progress was also relatively clear cut. The monthly recording of his progress showed heartening step-by-step gains and almost no incidents of prolonged regression.

During his fourth year, after fifteen months of treatment, his assets were far more impressive than his disabilities and pointed the way to sufficient health that adoption placement could be contemplated. He had demonstrated a consistent capacity to rely on and to respond to the trustworthy adults in his world. Furthermore, he was able to make use of them to carry him through his ever-present fear of whatever was new. He began to show solicitous feelings towards the younger children and would comfort sick companions (a rare occurrence with these children and even for some normal children). He was curious about people and how they lived, asking many questions, 'Where's your home? Where's your bed? Have you got a sister?' He had successfully negotiated a week-end trip by train to the home of one staff member and was able to relate to her family, particularly to her father. He appeared to have developed the two main facets of mental health – dependent trust in familiar people and a desire to be effortful in his world.

Once more the worker made crucial decisions in George's life. She helped find adopting parents and worked out a programme of preplacement which she believed would sponsor his best interests and that of his family. These visits covered a period of many weeks and started with the parents casually meeting George in a park and later visiting in the institution to play with him. This gave him sufficient courage to allow them to take him for walks outside the institution, to church, to shops, and finally for many visits to his future home. A community nursery school was used at the same time to help broaden his relationships beyond the institution. When George finally stayed with his adoptive parents he had relinquished his dependency on his well-loved house-mother and was eagerly anticipating living in his 'own home' with his own possessions and his new parents.

Despite all this pre-planned visiting, the worker anticipated his need to regress in his new home once the impact of all his experiences were felt. Hence, she elaborated on paper recommended steps which could allow this to happen. Consistency in discipline, clear cut and simple rules of behaviour, clearly defined steps in the procedures of eating, sleeping, dressing, and toileting were established. Such ideas were stated in practical detailed procedures which the parents could clearly understand and were willing to follow. Rules about the amount of time to be spent in social and play activities were recommended in order to keep his world simple. Discipline was to be enforced in an affectionate and kindly way. Follow-up of these procedures was carried out by telephone calls within a few days, 'dropping in' after a week, going over with the mother the established procedures and being assured of George's reaction to them. Within a few weeks the changes in George's behaviour would lead the worker to assist his mother to revise or modify some of the procedures in order to respond to the changed behaviours. This close relationship was maintained throughout the first months of George's placement.

These first few months of George's arrival were particularly well managed in this way. Both parents were able to permit George to regress and to act out behaviours appropriate for a much younger child, while at the same time encouraging whatever independent and effortful behaviour he was capable of. Both parents were friendly, open people with few defenses to block a satisfactory relationship with the worker. After his initial demonstration of his need for a dependent attachment when he carried about his possessions in paper bags, participated eagerly with his mother in household chores and was generally cautious, anxious, and conforming, he began to move ahead more independently into new situations, asking questions, exploring, and expecting answers. The consistent dependability of his life was giving him reassurance. He took pride in achievement and throve on approval.

By age six, the routine data collection which included psychological testing revealed something of his function and allowed evaluation of his progress and consideration of how close he might be to 'normal' six-year-old behaviour.

PSYCHOLOGICAL ASSESSMENT

His emancipation scores at age six showed a healthy balance in most areas. Those aspects which were not in balance showed him relying on parental care. His psychological test revealed an IQ level of 102. The record stated that 'he functioned consistently at age level.' His vocabulary was adequate, but he used immature phraseology. However, the Rorschach test revealed considerable emotional immaturity as he seemed to be relating closer to the two-year level than his six-year level. He was concerned with safety and protection of the home. He looked to adults to provide protection and guidance. Other children and the world outside the home were still largely interesting and exciting, but potentially unpredictable and unsafe. He was learning social skills, the right things to do at the right times. However, he did not trust himself to respond spontaneously to others. His identification with adults was largely on immature dependence. His self-definition would be largely in terms of his attempts to be a 'good boy.' There was, however, some strength in his acceptance of himself as a child whose dependence extended over a wide range of behaviours. His controls were largely of a heavy reliance on conformity in the obvious social situations.

He was wary of such situations and his lack of confidence in his own social controls was a source of continuous anxiety to him since they threatened the equilibrium he had reached by the use of conformity to adults. Since his sense of self-value was still largely dependent on his extreme dependence on adults, there was anxiety lest his lack of control socially somewhat threaten this dependence. Accordingly, he would be expected to feel pushed or pressured if adults urged him into social activity with which he felt incapable of coping. For similar reasons, he would be very upset by the possibility of failure to please adults by his performance at school (grade 1) and would tend to withdraw or revert to silly behaviour when put on the spot.

Although George has made considerable progress in his personality development, he is still largely organized around an immature dependence on adults. He would need considerable reassurance that he has scope to regress at home, considerable attention and reassurance as to his own value regardless of his performance.

These results were always reported back to his parents by the worker.

SECURITY ANALYSIS

The analysis of behaviour symptoms according to our security theory at age six shows 23% Immature Dependence, 61% Dependent Trust, and 16% Lack of Dependent Trust. The Rorschach and Security analysis show minor divergence insofar as George appears more heavily dependent on his family according to the Rorschach, which implies a frailer dependent trust than that seen in the Security analysis. This conflict in interpretation could be due to his heavily conformist behaviour, which seems based on anxiety as reflected through the Rorschach, but appears as comfortable dependent trust according to security theory. The Security analysis reveals a healthy degree of effort – 67% Effort and 33% Lack of Effort and Self-worth.

So comfortable a relationship had been developed between George and his parents that by the time he was six years, nine months of age, a four-year-old sister was added to the family by adoption. George took on a superior, but protective role towards his little sister which did not preclude some expected rivalry, bossiness, and feelings of jealousy towards her. Once more the worker was called upon to assist the family through the strain of this new adjustment. The new sister was quite unlike George and did not respond to the kind of management strategies that the mother had developed in her first adjustment to George. She needed further support in that she was continuing to sponsor George's best welfare while at the same time making a place for a young daughter in the house-hold. The worker was able once more, not only to discuss the shift in family roles, but to outline specific directions of child management on which the mother was able to act.

Through his seventh and eighth year George continued to mature in a satisfactory way. His anxieties were covered by defences of a perfectionist nature. He was able to overcome his initial anxiety about swimming lessons and then participate with keen enjoyment. If he allowed himself to be drawn into games and sports activities, he would bow out if he felt he might not win. Although he was developing some facility in peer relationships, his uncertainty led him to be overly aggressive with them. He was expending enormous effort at school as he was progressing through Grade III, at age eight and keeping well up to the top of the class. He was attentive but hesitant to express himself for fear of making mistakes. Through nine years of age these characteristics were largely the same, with evidence of his worrying about disapproval both at home and at school.

NINE YEAR OLD PSYCHOLOGICAL ASSESSMENT

At age nine his second progress report was completed on the basis of the test battery. It was felt his relative level of intellectual functioning IQ, 92, did not reflect his potential. His general level of conversation was adequate for his age. According to the Rorschach there seemed to be some potential for meaningful relationships but he had problems in this area because his perception of both others and himself were still somewhat infantile. Although he suppressed impulses, he remained basically dependent on others for the satisfaction of his comfort needs. The mother figure was regarded as authority. George was still in the process of developing a differentiated concept of self and a clear sexual identification. There was evidence which caused concern about his constricted personality as the formal and intellectual aspects of experience were emphasized at the expense of emotional elements of both his inner life and outer environment. Thus inner control was achieved through repression of impulses and the external environment was dealt with intellectually. George's method of achieving control was potentially hazardous. It was recommended that to overcome his inhibitions he would continue to need a great deal of assistance and encouragement in expressing himself. He needed to 'take more chances.'

At nine years of age the Security analysis indicated a continuation and intensification of his immature dependence (55%) on his family. The healthy nature of this dependency was balanced by a continuation and intensification of his effortful behaviour (75%) and expressions of self-worth. It would appear that his value of himself at this age was closely tied to comfortable support and help offered by his family. His emancipation analysis indicated a comfortable relationship between mother and child.

Between nine and twelve years of age, the worker's contact was not so much a matter of active guidance but rather that of dropping in for friendly visits, discussing the children and family, and making sure that the regular research data were collected each year. Reporting back to the family on any analysis of data collected always provided a ready opportunity to confirm our continuing interest as a research team in their events. At ages nine through eleven, maturities and immaturities appropriate to George's age level were in evidence. An understanding teacher encouraged him at school where he took his work seriously. He was meticulous about homework and projects and his average marks were around the mid-seventies, a surprising achievement in view of his prolonged deprivation. He was taking responsibility for helping his mother with her office work, doing considerable amounts of household shopping and chores and looking after his younger sister. He spent time with his father at the summer cottage, in the workshop, and in discussion. At the same time he was 'lippy' and assertive and occasionally would go off and sulk in frustration. He still had to be encouraged to involve himself in a new situation and still hesitated at the thought of possible failure. There was the normal amount of bickering with his sister.

TWELFTH YEAR PSYCHOLOGICAL ASSESSMENT

The emancipation analysis at twelve years of age indicated continuing easy interaction between mother and child. His Stanford-Binet IQ rating continued to reflect a performance level of 92 – a suspected underestimate. George's Rorschach indicated a capacity for warm relationships and some difficulty in controlling agressive impulses. His attempt to control took the form of intellectualizing his approach to people. He had enough insight into the dynamics of the interpersonal world to do this successfully at times. His aggressive impulses were organized and related meaningfully to events. Although aggression formed a central part of his ego, he could use it to advantage in the intellectual sphere. Underlying this was a conscious striving towards others. George now had a clearly differentiated concept of self. His personality was much less restrained and his impulse life more fully expressed. His developing ego had acquired a very healthy degree of organization and enrichment: George's former over-intellectual control had decreased markedly. There was more evidence of emotional content to his thought, which was organized into an aggressive drive pattern. There was a totally marked change in the protocol. The only concern was the amount of aggression rushing out of a formerly dammed up personality.

The security analysis confirmed this present healthy picture with a dependent trust score of 75% and an immature dependence of 0%. It appeared that George had taken a huge step towards emancipating himself from his immense dependency on his family, firmly rooted in a dependent trust relationship which was highly flavoured with faith that he would pursue goals which were compatible with those of his parents. Hence he continued to be a highly effortful (82%) young person.

George's effort was also being put into his relationship with others, a fact confirmed by his social competence quotient of 108, a good average expectation for his age.

By age fifteen, George was a rather admirable teenager, creating friction with his father because of his assertive opinions and accepting the role of his mother as mediator between them. He also was sharing healthy interests with his father and with his aunts, uncles, and cousins in his extended family. He protected and helped his sister on one hand and competed with her on the other. His peer relationships were highly satisfactory as he had one or two 'good friends,' and a variety of boys and girls with whom he associated and went to activities, such as school dances. His 'nice personality' with everyone had allowed him the confidence of selling advertising for the school magazine, an art at which he was highly successful. His warmth towards others was expressed in his 'doing things for people and not for favours.' He continued to be highly motivated and effortful in his self-appointed goals. He earned money at a variety of jobs and spent it on week-ends in pursuit of his own recreation – a show, games, or a dance.

FIFTEEN YEAR PSYCHOLOGICAL ASSESSMENT

The psychological report from testing at age fifteen showed a heartening increase in function on the WISC, and was thought to reflect a truer level of ability than was achieved in the past. His verbal IQ was 116, his performance 118. His Rorschach reflected the continuation of his characteristic intellectual control over his emotional life. The security analysis continued to show a healthy pattern of a high degree of dependent trust combined with extensive effort and feelings of self worth. This effort and worth were confirmed by the Vineland Social Maturity score which was once again of average expectation.

SUMMARY

By age fifteen, George's personality was a healthy one. He was functioning well within both his family and the community. Furthermore, he was enjoying life. His anxieties about his competence were reflected in his perfectionist tendencies but could not be construed as a weakness in his personality. Rather they were supported by well-directed effort which led him into healthy achievement.

George is now nineteen and seems well launched on a healthy young adult life. He has been fortunate in his family life and has been able to develop his potential to an admirable degree. He demonstrates the best of what can happen to the children of this group. Thinking back to the little boy in the institution, one can identify certain behavioural assets which seemed present then. His capacity for relationships with grown-ups seems to have been one of his greatest strengths through his lifetime. It was this capacity in early childhood that supported him through terrifying new situations when he was first encountered in the institution. Furthermore, it was this asset that was used to support him through his persisting tendency to withdraw from anything new as he grew up. The fact that the guidance worker, supported by the research team, was able to recognize his assets and was successful in counselling his parents in the continuing sponsorship of them after his placement has been a facilitating catalyst in his development.

Our predictions are for George's future healthy development. These are based on the many assets which are now built into his personality. After the conclusion of this work we learned that George has now graduated in psychology. He plans to work for one year before returning for post-graduate work.

13

Mindy

Mindy is an attractive young woman whose history has many puzzling aspects. She was more fortunate than the other two children discussed by being placed at an earlier age than they in a warm, highly organized, and accepting home. Insofar as one can judge the environment was a healthy one, high powered and lively, and apparently responsive to her welfare.

Searching her history leads to the conclusion that undetermined constitutional factors were more powerful contributors to her development than all the extensive environmental intervention that took place throughout the therapeutic programme within the institution, and later in her home, which was closely supervised by the child care worker throughout her growing years.

It was noted on her records at four months of age that she had been placed in the institution because of unsatisfactory living conditions which were attributed to the instability of her mother. It was observed that 'She was a long, slender, dark-eyed responsive baby who seemed well settled.' Physical progress was good, she had gained 3 1/2 lbs since her birth weight of 6 lbs 2 ozs. A month later it was recorded she was gaining weight and was a strong, lively little girl, satisfied with her formula and sleeping well. At one year, development still seemed satisfactory but slow: she was generally content, a weight gain was showing, and she was sitting without support. She was responsive to attention, but was doing a good deal of rocking. By two years, development seemed less healthy as Mindy was retiring, apprehensive, and sucking her thumb continually. She was vague and aimless in play and 'when in a mood would not respond to attention.'

At three years of age, just after the commencement of the rehabilitation programme in this institution a psychological assessment was attempted. She was found to be quiet and rather shy. 'She is not yet asserting herself as an individual and needs help to gain confidence in herself and others. Her rating is just in the dull normal range. A retest should be made within this year to gain a more reliable rating.' At that time a staff member remarked that Mindy was very conforming and co-operative in all routines. However, she seemed to lack trust in adults as she was superficially pleasant and sociable but never asked for help from any adult. She was very distractible and easily frightened. Six months later another psychological assessment reported she was still functioning in the dull normal range. 'Today's test indicates Mindy's progress has been of similar quality over the past six months and she seems to be at a point where she needs the learning experiences of a private home for fuller development.'

Thus when Mindy was placed into her one and only home at three years, eight months of age, she seemed to be a child whose abilities may not have been tapped. She was a conforming rather fearful youngster who had not related strongly to staff and it was suspected she needed a warm dependable family to give her the opportunity to relate and to encourage the use of her intellectual potential.

Fortunately a very strong family was found which it was felt would be able to provide for this little girl's needs. Mr and Mrs Brown had a well-organized child centred home where their four children ranged from one to eight years of age. Both Mr and Mrs Brown had come from very large families and in this home there were flexible, dependable, and consistent rules and requirements that all the children seemed to accept naturally. Mrs Brown was receptive to this research programme and was anxious to contribute in any way possible. Very quickly the worker and mother became a team consulting together to support Mindy. It was soon found that Mrs Brown needed a great deal of help through many periods of frustration with Mindy, who sometimes seemed to be a child 'without feelings.' As reported by the foster mother at the time, 'John and I feel Mindy has a definite mental block. Of course she missed being a two year old so we have let her have a run at abnormal activity for her age. Mary age eight can get through to Mindy better than I can at times.' Four months after placement Mindy was still indiscriminate with all grown-ups. She could respond to her foster father but would not seek affection from her mother. She never displayed intense feeling by having a temper tantrum; never disobeyed a play restriction; and would often 'draw a blank' when her parents attempted close physical contact.

After Mindy had been in the home eight months another baby girl was born to this family. A few months later the foster mother complained that Mindy's inadequate demanding behaviour was causing an added burden on such a busy household. They felt pressured and spoke of giving the child to a family where she would be an only child. 'If Mindy is in the garden, I am out there 100 times. If the other children are out there, I am out there 10 times.' She appeared insensitive to the attitudes of others. She responded indiscriminately to unfamiliar adults but withdrew from unfamiliar children. She displayed nervous tension by scratching on her hands, thumb sucking, rocking, and picking her fingers. She was a compulsive eater, hoarding food and showing jealousy of sharing it. Her activities were perseverative and aimless. 'She talked at people not with them.' Discipline and simple direction were a threat to her, especially from her foster mother. By five years of age she was still called a 'very superficial child.' She tattled a great deal, clammed up or day dreamed and 'tuned off' her parents. However, she showed more trust than earlier by coming to her mother with hurts instead of going off alone. Occasionally she would accept the consequences of her behaviour. Her mother stated, 'She needs help in relationships.'

A year later when Mindy was six, many family problems had been resolved and the Browns with help had changed their attitudes towards her. Now she was regarded as one of a family of six, and was not talked of as a foster child. She now seemed to feel 'safe' with her mother. Her foster mother was able to lower her expectations for this child as it was apparent she could not function as well as her own children. A series of problems such as stealing and losing possession were overcome by the mother's acceptance of suggestions by the guidance worker – for example on the basis Mindy had never owned her own things, a box was provided in which she could collect the kind of oddments she was taking from others.

At that time the picture of Mindy in her home environment looked good. There was a good deal of consideration for each individual's differences in this household. It was recorded, 'This household has given Mindy both acceptance and a sense of security by its orderliness. It may seem controlled – this dictated by the number of children; it sounds somewhat like a pleasant small boarding school.' She was now in Grade I and holding her own. She tried very hard to achieve and was always overly tired when she came home from school. The teacher remarked that when outside pressure bothered her, school work seemed to disintegrate and the older pattern of not reaching Mindy would reappear. She needed a great deal of support and approval and consistency in rules. All play activities with children were very imitative.

On her six-year-old assessment Mindy was a responsive co-operative youngster. Intellectually she functioned within the low average range, but showed a deficiency in her ability to express herself. Her personality assessment on the Rorschach showed surprising strengths in affect. It was stated she had real warmth in her response to children and adults and was developing both a sense of self-worth and a dependence on the adults who were providing her with both physical care and external guides to behaviour. On the other hand the tenuousness of her adjustment was evident in the fact that her controls were based on her conformity and she saw herself in terms of the skills she was learning to master.

Between the ages of six and nine, Mrs Brown's pictures of Mindy were usually positive. She stated she really loved this little girl, but the quality of her love seemed different from her feelings towards her own five children. She thought perhaps she wanted to prove that she could resolve the challenge of Mindy, whereas she did not have to prove anything with her own five children. She felt strongly that Mindy would always need more outer controls than her own children as there were times when she seemed more confused than they when under stress. Another concern was Mindy's inability to initiate and put forth much effort in activities. The nine-year-old psychological assessment confirmed the foster parents' feelings that Mindy was doing quite nicely at that period in her life. Her IQ was 88, with successes from six years to eleven years suggesting that her potential was not completely tapped but that there was still some interference in performance. Her vocabulary was a little beyond the eight-year-old criterion on the Binet. The Rorschach indicated she could relate to others. However, she had considerable concern for interpersonal relationships, indicating that they were not yet satisfactory. She needed people but probably found it difficult to cope with situations which were threatening to any extent.

By the time Mindy was ten, Mrs Brown, feeling quite confident about her ability to rear children, commenced taking a child development course in preparation to becoming a Nursery School teacher. She was out of the home (which she now had well organized in absentia) every morning. Mr Brown had a serious illness and was off work for two months. The children were given more responsibility and more freedom. All the Brown children handled this new change of life style quite well Mindy, however, commenced using Bob, age nine, instead of her parents, as her confidant. She would not go to them for help and gave up very easily if things were at all difficult. She was repeating Grade IV and was enjoying the superficial social contacts she was making because of her reduced academic pressure.

By the time Mindy was eleven years of age, the mother was still involved in her course and in Nursery School work. Mindy seemed much more on the defensive. The subtle jokes which were part of this family's rapport were beyond her. She could not tolerate criticism or ridicule. Regardless of consequences, she seemed more devious in her behaviour. As her mother stated, 'when she was caught, she would completely "tune us out" using the old familiar blank stares.' However, in spite of Mindy's apparent hostility against her mother, Mrs Brown's attitudes towards her were positive. She cared about her and accepted her limitations.

Mindy, by twelve years of age, was having real difficulties in the family environment. She again commenced taking money from the other children's piggy banks – and then became very aggressive with them when the bickering over her misdemeanours occurred. Her older siblings commenced calling her 'Weirdo.' She needed constant reminding of all family rules. She was lashing out in all directions to hurt people's feelings and showed no sensitivity to their reactions. At school she had to cope with a rotation system in which there was no one teacher with whom to identify. No longer was a structured classroom system available to give her a consistent predictable environment. Her academic work was only fair. She became very forgetful and was lashing out at her classmates just as she was at her siblings at home.

Although her mother was now more involved in Nursery School work, she became quite concerned and asked for extra help in guiding her child. The psychologist reported that 'Mindy was striking off into a pseudo independent approach to family. She was becoming aggressively alienated in the sibling area and noncommunicative about school. Her lack of dependence was reminiscent of her early lack of dependence when first placed – the difference being that the present lack of dependence seemed willful whereas in the past she withdrew passively.'

When tested in the twelve-year-old personality assessment, her intellectual functioning showed an IQ of 84. The spread indicated her potential was close to her functioning level. It was noted her visual memory was poor and vocabulary weak. Verbal communication was difficult for her and it was hard for her to explain ideas or express feelings. The Rorschach revealed Mindy's processes of relating were breaking down. Her perception of the world of interpersonal relationships was fearful. Her attitude to others was one of fear and uncertainty. Her panic in the interpersonal world was interfering with the establishment of good identification. Her ability to acquire structure and meaning from events in her life had slipped badly. Thus she had few values and a vanishing frame of reference to guide her behaviour. Control was slipping in both thought and behaviour.

During Mindy's fourteenth and fifteenth years, the guidance worker resumed more intensive guidance with the Brown family. Mrs Brown, although a busy Nursery School supervisor, kept a close eye on Mindy's activities and tried to encourage and steer her as she felt Mindy was 'incapable of being selective.'

Our research psychologist was consulted frequently and reported 'Mindy continues to live on the surface which is complicated by the teenage models she sees around her. She is growing increasingly egocentric and moody – a pattern very difficult to break through. Mrs Brown still tries to reach her and talk to her which is successful at times. Mindy bribes others to like her and copes with situations by being a follower. There are very few areas of satisfaction perhaps only the chores and basic routines. It seems likely Mindy is doomed to superficiality and the Browns to watch dogs.'

Concern for this child involved many people. About this time a conference was held at the School Board including school principal, inspector, school psychologist, school board clinical psychologist, and research workers from the Institute of Child Study. The considered opinion arrived at was that Mindy should continue in an academically limited setting with academic pressures removed. Thus a very small girls' high school was planned for her.

The environment at home was changing again. It was growing into a teenage household, each member vigorously pursuing his own interests. The children were less communicative with each other but reported back to mother, the 'hub' of the household. Mr Brown seemed to be taking a more passive but still involved role. The fifteen-year-old psychological assessment recorded that the picture was somewhat improved from the previous tests at twelve. However, Mindy's vocabulary and memory for factual data were extremely weak and further testing to investigate the possibility of organic impairment was advised. On the wisc her intellectual functioning was within the dull normal range. Her Rorschach responses lacked maturity but were directed towards involvement and self-expression. Emotional needs continued to be dominant and she still lacked means of relating at a deep personal level. She was growing more aware of others but tended to project a feeling of remoteness and unreality.

At that time, according to mother, Mindy appeared to be a tense, emotionally flat youngster who could not be reached by her father or brothers or sisters. She was unable to tolerate any criticism and used many 'avoidance techniques' – 'I can't help it, I don't want to, I have to go now.' She was unable to remember the simplest explanations of what was expected of her. Her foster mother stated she had become very aware of the opposite sex and was doing everything in her power to attract her brother's friends and any male she met. As Mrs Brown stated, 'I am basically worried about her, as she is breaking all the rules of home, community and school.' She was lying, stealing, and manifesting behaviour that made no sense to the family. At school she skipped classes, was extremely distractible, and was unable to organize herself. She could not follow through in assignments. The guidance counsellor mentioned, 'She could not get along with others due to her devious activities. She was uncharitable, ridiculed, and had no sympathy for those in need. She played on other's differences, bragged and used tall-tales.' Her interests (always few) deteriorated. She no longer sewed or finished anything. She gave up early or would not try. In fact, she was not coping socially, emotionally, or academically in her environment. She gave the impression she was determined to do whatever she wanted, without regard to the consequences.

The following two years were ones of heartbreak for the family. In spite of more neurological and psychiatric consultations, the worker's weekly contacts with the girl herself, and family interviews, Mindy's behaviour continued to deteriorate. Mindy, with her limited intelligence, was no doubt receiving double messages in this household. Although still a member of this household she seemed to have waning status. Over the years the Browns had not committed themselves to adoption. Mindy began to doubt that she could ever meet this family's expectations. 'I am dumb, I won't fit into society. I stop talking immediately even if I think I am right because I can't win any argument.'

Just after Mindy's seventeenth birthday, she left school and left home. An alternative was presented by the Children's Aid Society in a supervised 'halfway house.' This home could be a base for Mindy to go to school or work and yet have a place of her own where she carried some responsibilities. After two months this arrangement also broke down. Mindy, however, proved sufficiently effortful to find three jobs. On the other hand, she was becoming indiscriminate in her selection of companions and seemed more openly superficial in her relationships. She was caught lying and stealing without any apparent guilt and when last heard from at eighteen years of age, she was having liaisons with numerous men and showing no interest in contacting the only family she ever knew.

Looking back on the more objective measures taken at six, nine, twelve, and fifteen years of age, we see a child whose social quotient was always lower than that of the group. By age fifteen she was functioning four years below her chronological age according to this measure. Similarly her intellectual function was consistently lower than that of most of the group. Her final assessment indicated a dull normal level. Her ratings, according to security schema, indicated a lack of development in the essential qualities of mental health. At six and nine years of age she showed a relatively healthy amount of immature dependence and this was supported by an average amount of effort on her part. By twelve years of age she deviated from the group pattern insofar as she was unable to make the transition from immature dependence to dependent trust and the continuing decline in this quality by fifteen years of age was accompanied by increased passivity expressed in an overwhelming lack of effort score (88%).

When one speculates about the outcome of this course of development, one can hypothesize that Mindy's limited range of competence precluded her growing up according to the pattern established by the other children in the family. As the other youngsters became capable of taking responsibility and carrying out the tasks and expectations required of them, there was a diminishing need for specific direction and supervision. Hence they became more self-reliant and less dependent on their mother. This quality implied a base in dependent trust and was observed in increasingly effortful behaviour in Mindy's siblings. Under these circumstances the foster mother would naturally have expected the same quality of performance from Mindy and could conceivably have resented the continued burden of Mindy's immature dependency as she grew through twelve and fifteen years of age.

Whether or not continuing immature dependency support would have sustained Mindy beyond the twelfth and fifteenth year level and allowed her to remain effortful is an open question.

14

Tom

The child who shows inexplicable resilience to overcome life's misfortunes has always posed a human enigma. Scientists are prone to establish antecedents to account for outcomes and are called upon to explain away as best they can the exceptions which bedevil the laws. So it is with Tom, an eighteen-year-old youth who has emerged from a severely deprived infancy and early childhood, who has survived three traumatic attempts to become part of a family, and who still yearns intensely for a family to call his own. Possessing warmth, charm, and an ability to muster people to his aid, he has agonized his way through his young life, defying all orderly predictions and revealing no plausible explanation for his capacity to rebound from soul-destroying experiences. He still holds his heart in his hand and seeks someone who will take possession of it.

Why is Tom not the traditional affectionless character? We watch the unfolding of his development with a sense of wonder.

Tom's mother came of an apparently stable middle class family but, surprisingly, would give no information about his father. After the normal delivery of her baby she spent the following six weeks with him in a maternity home prior to relinquishing her claim to him.

At seven weeks of age Tom was separated from his mother by transfer to the institution in which he was to remain until he was six years of age. Brief notations by the social worker in charge of his case noted his adjustment to this situation at eight weeks by stating, 'Tom is an attractive, good natured baby who responds well to people and takes his feedings well.' Not so happy, the notation at nine months of age – 'This infant is sickly, unresponsive, subdued, not playful, and seldom smiles.'

Continued decline in Tom's well-being was reflected in the brief recording at eleven months of age. He was sitting alone and was trying unsuccessfully to pull himself to his feet (an indication that his motor development was delayed). He showed little interest in either his surroundings or the people in it. He was very susceptible to colds. Little physical gain was taking place, as his weight at twelve months of age was eighteen pounds, an increment of less than twelve pounds since birth.

From eleven months to fifteen months of age, Tom was one of the sixteen children studied in our initial investigation of mental health. His monthly scores declined from +.39, +.11, +18, +.10, to +.03. His environment was constricted and lacking human warmth. The babies in the room, including Tom, were isolated from one another by dividers and he was seldom out of booties or placed on the floor. Feeding was frustrating and unpleasant for both the staff and the child, as his refusals to eat were met by harsh forced feeding methods. His behaviour expressed misery as he rocked in the corner of his crib with his back to the world, his head lowered, sucking his fingers. His chronically disgruntled expression made him unattractive and he showed little interest in any aspect of his world. He never vocalized, but would crawl slowly and pull himself to stand by the sides of his crib. He fed himself his bottle in a listless fashion.

Tom was not observed until after more than another year of institutional life, at which time he was living in a nursery with six other children of similar age. The only furniture in the nursery consisted of cribs, from which the children were set free for one hour in the morning and one hour in the afternoon. The formidable, harsh caretaker seemed to be concerned totally with the cleanliness of her charges. Outdoor activity was non-existent. The only attempt being made to push the children in the direction of maturity was the totally unsuccessful toilet training routine consisting of a pot tied to each bed on which the children were left for long periods of time.

Tom's behaviour was frightening. He had sustained a fractured clavicle from a fall and needed a brace for three weeks. His constant colds had created a need for confinement beyond even the usual twenty-two hours spent monotonously in bed. Tom now appeared to be a tense, apprehensive child who would startle if an adult put a hand out to pat him. Whereas formerly he had been a 'whiner,' now he was uttering intermittent piercing screams which alternated with hysterical laughter. No obvious cause was evident to precipitate these outbursts. Tom's usual posture was to sit silently facing a wall or a corner, immobilized, unless approached by another child. At such times he would scream. He still did not communicate. A notation at two years, seven months of age, indicated that he was now walking.

When the rehabilitation programme was initiated Tom was three years, four months of age and observation of its impact on him for the next four months yielded discouraging results. His behaviour was bizarre. He showed no overt response to his new kindly caretakers beyond responding to their new directives with screams and temper tantrums. His new exposure to the children created un-certainty in him so that he vacillated from complete withdrawal at one time to aggression and attack at another. When he was upset he screamed for long peri-ods of time. Under other normal circumstances he frequently burst into hysteri-cal laughter. His play with materials was perseverative and frequently was termi-nated by a piercing scream as of frustration. He clung to small objects which he might carry around in his hand for a full day. Bed time was very unhappy. Tom would remain awake for a long time, ever so often screaming piercingly so that removal from the room in which the other children were sleeping was necessary. (Looking back at age seventeen, Tom remembered being put in a small room away from children and adults, and shouting to get out.)

A slight ray of hope came from Tom's obvious enjoyment of the revised eat-ing routine and his reluctant permission to allow someone to dress him. Further-more, he was babbling sounds and even repeating an occasional word. Through-out his third year Tom's health continued to be poor. This was reflected in 33 notations on his medical files indicating chest colds and allergic conditions.

The extent of Tom's bizarre behaviour led to a psychiatric examination for the possibility of schizophrenia. The report indicating that he was 'an immature child whose behaviour disorders were secondary to disturbance of his environ-ment' gave direction to better planning for his treatment. The psychiatrist be-lieved that Tom had some ability to relate to people and some potential for development if placed in a favourable environment.

By the time he was three years, eleven months old, it was possible to place Tom in a small unit consisting of a self-contained room with beds, chests of draw-ers, tables, chairs, and room for a few possessions. Here, along with two other children, he was cared for by a warm, motherly person. Gradually he allowed a relationship to be established, first through accepting her care and direction within the unit (he refused this from unfamiliar adults) and later through trips into the community on buses, street cars, walks in parks, strolls through stores, and visits to church.

Attendance in the Coach House Nursery School gave him further opportuni-ties for a one-to-one relationship with another adult. He responded healthily to this and was co-operative about the play activity. Showing a capacity to respond to such stimulation for approximately one hour daily, he could play purposefully with a limited range of materials. His poor motor co-ordination was expressed in apathy towards outdoor play, but he was showing co-operation in such routines as dressing, feeding himself, and toileting. Signs of speech acquisition were appearing as he gesticulated and attempted the use of words to impart his mean-ing. His laughter still was loud and hysterical (age 3:11).

Five months later, by four years, four months of age, he seemed to be reaching out tentatively for a wider world. His participation in nursery school had increased to a half day, an indication of greater interest and self-control. A volunteer was taking him for weekly forays into the community. He was able to respond to requests of unfamiliar people in a formal way and was careful not to exceed any of the rules or adult expectations of his world. He was now interested in his peers and sought opportunities to interact with them. Although there was a general improvement in his behaviour, he still had unpredictable mood swings. Other children rebuffed him because he would take their toys, tease, and run about hysterically. He was happier when dealing with the purely material things of his world than when functioning in a social setting. He would explore ideas, often on the verge of fantasy, and he carried a small possession in his hand or pocket all day long. It was heart-warming to hear him talking to himself and humming as he played.

By age five, Tom was demonstrating healthy qualities which seemed to indicate potential for higher function than was evident at the time. He was able to elicit the affection of his immediate caretakers, of whom he was asking thought-provoking questions, quite unlike the other children around him. 'Why is the moon up there,' 'Where is it gone?.' With a glint in his eye, he would sometimes tease familiar adults. There was a decrease in his thumb sucking and hysterical laughter. He felt a strong sense of ownership over his possessions. There seemed more potential for relating to children as he could sustain play with one or another in his unit for a short while.

The assets which were emerging in Tom's personality led to the optimistic hope that he might gain by moving from the protection of his small unit to the more challenging environment of a larger unit. Such conjecture on the part of the staff revealed the fragility of Tom's gains. He reverted to his old pattern of excitable, disorganized behaviour accompanied by outbursts of hysterical laughter. He showed extreme mood swings, seemed fearful of the larger group of children, and sought adults for protection. He demonstrated obsessive behaviour in many forms, being concerned with fire, loudspeakers, and radios. He carried small possessions about and wanted to hide them. His use of toys was again bizarre. His inner world was revealed by 'continuous talking,' repetition of difficult words, experimentation with sounds, and making up of "jingles."'

The peculiarities of Tom's behaviour aroused the interest and concern of one of the Research Staff, Mrs Day, from the Institute of Child Study. Her observations of him led her to believe he had potential for normalcy and she arranged play therapy sessions within the institution. Mrs Day was to play a supportive role in Tom's life for many more years. In many ways she was to be the fairy godmother who, working with the child care workers, facilitated many of the good things which were to happen in the future. After five months of extensive therapy Tom was feeling very comfortable with his volunteer therapist and was having monthly week-ends at her country home.

Once more healthy assets began to make an appearance in Tom's behaviour. He sought the support of adults in a very immature way, enjoying being carried about (age 6 years) and seeking affectionate comfort and protection in a baby way. In his attempt to possess an adult he showed jealousy of other children, while at the same time demonstrating anxiety about his desire to be accepted by peers. His puckish humour would appear in flashes and was one of his most endearing assets. Intelligent questions about the world around him once more gave indication of hidden potential.

Our analysis of his security score at this time confirmed much of what we were observing in his everyday behaviour. His very high immature dependence score reflected his reliance on adults as his source of comfort and stability. His minimal dependent trust score was a reflection of his lack of readiness to move on to the next stage in psychological development, that of feeling a sense of trust and reliance on adults which could be counted on even when they were absent. He was still in the baby stage of clinging to the physical presence of grown-ups to maintain his sense of security.

The vulnerability of Tom's gains made it necessary for him to remain in the institution almost to the end of the programme. With only seven children left, it was possible for one staff member to give him daily periods of individual attention. The focus of these efforts was to bring him closer to reality in his self-expression and to pave the way for foster placement. Despite his age, he was obviously unready for school experience. Gradually his behaviour reflected change. Intellectual curiosity continued in such expressions as 'How do leaves turn colour?' 'How do seeds travel?.' Intense feelings were evident in his play when he continually knocked down bridges, smashed trucks, and 'locked people up in bad places with no windows.' Much of such play resembled that of a two-year-old.

When placement in a family was finally arranged, Tom went to a country home which was fortunately close to his volunteer therapist, Mrs Day. Ten preliminary visits covering a five-week span preceded his placement in the hope that his adjustment to his foster family might be facilitated.

No one anticipated the degree of confusion which could arise in this child whose first six years had been spent in institutional life. Family life was completely bewildering. The idea of two parents was incomprehensible. He could not accept his foster father. The five foster children seemed to ride on the fringe of Tom's awareness. His preoccupation with his adjustment to the whole event of placement seemed to sap his energies. He was most anxious to be reassured of his foster mother's affection and constantly nagged her in this vein. His fear of returning to the institution was evident in his extreme conformity and his verbalized, 'Will you send me away if I don't like Daddy?' His mind turned with interest to the real world to be found outdoors. Catching flies and examining bugs proved fascinating.

Tom's capacity to relate was taxed beyond its early stage of development. Despite his apparent acceptance by the five siblings in this family, he seemed unable to reciprocate. His fundamental need was the comfort and support of his foster mother in a very dependent way. The foster father was never able to accept Tom's immaturities. After three months of dependent conformity, Tom began to express some of himself and test the foster mother and she too began to resent him. She felt defeated by this bewildering child, so Tom was turned out of the house and left to play alone for long periods of time each day. When Tom's need for dependency was denied he felt rejected.

Once more, he retreated to his familiar fantasy world, playing for hours with a padlock and keys with which he locked up the 'bad people.' In order to support Tom through this failure, his volunteer, Mrs Day, once more intervened by taking him to her house for week-end therapy sessions. The friendship of her own adult family was a further source of strength to Tom.

Ten months after placement, the foster mother remarked, 'Our home to Tom is *mother* - nothing else about it has any meaning.' Tom's affirmation of this was, 'Mom is as pretty as a tulip - I will never let her move away from me.' It was evident that he was unable to relate satisfactorily to the other members of his family until he was assured of the affection of his foster mother. As he struggled to meet overwhelming expectations, his silly, self-conscious, unpredictable behaviour and irrelevant chatter antagonized the whole family. After fifteen months in this home the sad little fellow had to be moved. He had failed to find a place which he could call his own. The family had failed to recognize his limited stage of development.

At the age of seven years, nine months of age, still not ready for school, Tom was transferred to his second placement. Because it appeared that he could tolerate another home situation with all the demands it placed upon him, he was sent to a small residence of eleven children with various handicaps of mild emotional disturbance and mental retardation. This was a successful group home despite the discontinuity of care resulting from many staff changes and admissions and discharges of children. Each child was considered an individual. There were chickens, cats, a monkey, nature walks, a pony and outdoor equipment to enhance country living. The routines were sound and limits were structured. Because Tom was one of the more competent children he did not receive much physical affection. He expressed the conviction that he was at this place for the summer holidays and wanted to go back to see his former foster parents. When finally told by his child care worker that he was definitely not to return to his former foster home because the foster mother was not well enough to have him back, he said, 'Is mom still so sick that she can't walk or cook? Will she die? Can I go back when she is better? I don't know any prayers to get her better. Does that mean that Elizabeth is my home and I have no mother? Will I stay at Elizabeth's until you and Day find me another mom?' Then, demonstrating insight which was one of his greatest strengths, 'Will you find me a mom that will like little boys even when they are naughty?'

Despite this, Tom made a successful adaptation to life here. The supervisor saw him as a fascinating child, 'too conforming but coming out of it.' He still appealed to adults to protect his rights and was very conforming. He needed a great deal of approval. He did not withdraw from others into his fantasy world as might have been predicted, and was eager to do his special chores. He was very enthusiastic about all activities, especially was he 'eating up' all academic stimulation. He was aware of and sympathetic towards some of the retarded children. He seldom played alone. He had ideas and seemed less worried about mistakes than formerly. He was still extremely apprehensive about new situations, angry voices, rough play, and screaming children. In this group home he was getting acceptance and respect and finding a stimulating world.

At age eight, a psychological assessment conducted by one of the research team placed Tom's intellectual functioning within the Dull Normal range on the Binet and this was considered an underestimate of his potential. 'Inner controls had not yet emerged. He has a capacity to relate but is having difficulty in relating to adults as authority figures because he perceives them as frightening and threatening.' Continued psychotherapy with Mrs Day was advised.

In his ninth year Tom was introduced to public school. He was at school all day, going by bus and taking his lunch. The social interaction of being with children all day was stressful for this boy. His teacher for Grade I was warm and supportive. She stated he frequently came to school looking unkempt because he was expected to get himself ready for school. He began to show signs of academic gain. His teacher sensed his desire for affection and approval and took a personal interest in him. Mrs Day continued to see him and take him to her house occasionally. Unfortunately, regular therapy could not take place because of the distance he lived from her home. The research worker continued to act as his social worker, as she had through his placements, and saw him frequently.

Because Tom seemed to be in a healthier state than before and continued to ask for 'parents of his own,' it appeared that it would be better for his development if he were living with other than handicapped children. Hence, just before his ninth birthday (after one year in the small institution), Tom was placed into a recognized foster home where the foster parents had seven children of their own. Mrs Brown was a tense, highly organized foster mother who had gained some superficial academic knowledge of psychology and child rearing and was anxious to 'try this' on her children. This quality unfortunately did not reveal itself until the social worker began to work closely with her. Mr Brown was a warm hearted man who handled his children on the emotional level. When Mrs Brown's own intellectual goals could not be reached, especially for Tom, she became frustrated and unrealistic. Thus, three months after placement, when Tom's unusual behaviour did not yield to her guidance she stated that the only way to get any sensible response was through *firmness* and fear. 'It repulses me to do up buttons and comb hair for a nine year old boy. I didn't do it for my own children. I won't do it for him.'

At nine years, six months of age, Tom, once more in Grade I, now in an urban school, again found a sympathetic teacher who recognized that he was being extremely pressured at home. She stated, 'I have the impression that Tom is very fearful of his foster mother – more than anyone else at home. He has sad, moody days. He is a sad child who desperately wants to relate to human warmth. He is not vague with me. He is trusting of me. He wants to talk to me a lot. He is *starved*. He is a likeable kid, not mean; is kind and considerate. Everyone in our school likes Tom. He is distractible. He likes physical contact. I have many chats with him to let him know he is a person. He is eager to learn, curious; no academic problems, and probably could do more than Grade I work. He is the type of child who, if you ask what an object is, he will tell you *what it is for* and then what it is. With peers he is not ready for group activity. He will pick an intelligent six year old to work with. He is keenly interested in rocks and mountains at present.' His intellectual assessment on the Binet showed a minimal rating of 86. His potential was unknown. The Vineland Scale of Social Competence at this time showed him functioning around the level of a seven-year-old, his social quotient being 76. His security status was lower than his earlier rating in his first foster home. Both immature dependence and dependent trust were minimal and his potential for effortful behaviour was impaired.

By now, Mrs Brown felt Tom – nearly ten – would never fit into her family life. She felt her husband, who was more sympathetic than she, did not see Tom's behaviour from her frame of reference. He thought Tom 'was approaching normal but was struggling with a world which was fearful to him.' Mrs Brown became pregnant and quite emotionally upset. She insisted on a diagnosis of Tom's 'bizarre behaviour.' At the Neurological Clinic, Hospital for Sick Children, there was no evidence found of any pathological damage. His Bender Gestalt Test was up to chronological age without any obvious signs of disturbance. Moreover, it was found that in the past four years he had shown general and marked improvement. However, his perception, reasoning, and concept formation still showed odd gaps.

Having been rejected again by a foster mother and not accepted by siblings, who now believed that Tom had a 'distorted mind,' he was once more set adrift. Asked by his foster father one day, 'Tom, what would you like best of all?' he replied, 'I would like to live in a volcano.' 'You can't live in a volcano.' 'Well, when it stops bubbling!'

Once more, the support of his constant child care worker, now an old friend to Tom, helped him survive the misery of this rejection. His other friend, Mrs Day, was also in the background and together they pulled a rabbit from the hat which led to Tom's next experience – one of the most salutary of his life. Close neighbours of Mrs Day were unearthed to fill, for the fourth time, the unlikely role of foster figures for this boy. An active, warm-hearted woman, age sixty-three, living in retirement with her seventy-year-old farmer husband, was asked to accept the challenge of Tom and give the child a pleasant summer in the country. She was told he needed to be an only child and to receive a great deal of support and an opportunity to explore the country environment. Because Tom had already had two poor experiences with mothers, Mrs White and her husband were to be called Aunt Jennie and Uncle Bill.

The boy received a great deal of mothering from Aunt Jenny. Few demands were made on him during this summer. He was busy outdoors with contented, undemanding Uncle Bill. He was trusted by the old man in his workshop. He helped with chickens and chores. He made squirrel traps and a garden swing for himself. He enjoyed weekly swimming lessons at the community pool. He frequently saw his volunteer friend, Mrs Day, who now lived close by. His omnipresent child care worker continued to see the little boy almost weekly.

After placement Tom became very conforming and conciliatory. He told Mrs White, that, 'Mother Brown thought I was stupid. She was always watching me.' He could frequently verbalize what was bothering him. Later his noisy, loud whining and confused behaviour was hard to cope with. He was extremely restless and silly at bedtime. He whined a great deal when uncertain of what was expected of him. He was a compulsive, anxious eater. When inactive he constantly picked his lips and eyelashes.

At ten years one month (five months after his placement) Tom was speaking of Aunt Jennie as 'my mother.' 'My mother is proud of me today.' The child care worker was giving constant support to this foster mother, not only to interpret Tom's behaviour, but also to listen to the outpouring of her own personal needs.

Tom entered a country school 500 yards up the road. He commenced in Grade II but three months later was transferred to Grade III, which he handled well. Here, he had another warm supportive teacher whose own parents had died in a concentration camp and who put her *all* into this very deprived child. She worked very carefully to gain his trust. 'He responds to quiet, fair discipline if I don't raise my voice.' He was enthusiastic about school. It was noted in his school report, 'He was an impatient, compulsive child desperately in need of approval.' He was accepted only by younger children. He wanted friends, but was very much a loner. He became silly in unfamiliar situations. He would trust no one with his possessions, coat, pencil, or school books. The teacher also stated, 'I am very pleased with him. His vocabulary is remarkable. He uses it in the right context and knows what he is talking about.'

His behaviour at home was now more assertive. He was demonstrating more affection and wanted to give sloppy kisses. He showed increasing dependence on his foster mother. He still loved to be outdoors with Uncle Bill. He manifested less fear when criticized and was not so threatened by anger. He could be disobedient and over-talkative but accepted consequences and took blame if he deserved it. His characteristic over-excitable behaviour was in evidence in social situations he couldn't handle. He enjoyed and participated in family ideas and activities. He thrived on consistent and structured routine life. For the first time in his life he had possessions he could call his own. Every little gift was a big thing in his life. He would feel it, fondle it, and not want it touched by others. On receiving a steam engine for passing exams he expressed his joy by saying, 'Thank you, thank you. I am so happy. I can only say thank you. There is lots more I could say but it is inside of me and I can't make it come out!' He would play with toys in his room, build with Lego, and play with cars. He did a lot of talking to himself, 'making bombs in his laboratory.' His reading was at the stage of 'Jerry Muskrat.'

Tom's twelfth year was one of very healthy development in the White home. He had had an enriching and happy experience at a day camp all summer. His foster mother visited him on all overnights as he was so very dependent on her to move into any new situation. His relationship with her was healthy and productive. He was able to verbalize his two great anxieties, 'to live with Aunt Jennie forever and ever and to do well in exams.' Up to this time, Mrs White, an anxious perfectionist in her home and with her only daughter married and living away from home, was still enjoying the challenge of participating in this boy's improving development. However, if she was not given continual support and encouragement, little irritations became unsolved problems.

During the following year, Tom had the same understanding supportive teacher in the small country school. She felt Tom's progress was miraculous. 'He is a joy to teach and I feel he has a great potential. He is eager for approval and will work hard to do things properly. However, he is so excitable his concentration level is low but he is still motivated to succeed in school and to conform to his parents' requirements of behaviour.' He had an average of about 70% in Grade IV and was devouring 'How and Why Science' books. He was still a loner in the school yard.

Tom's twelve-year-old psychological assessment at the Institute of Child Study showed his intellectual functioning to be 92 on the Binet. It was still an underestimate of his potential. 'There were still signs of gaps in his knowledge of familiar events.' He was capable of relating in a meaningful way. 'He was still an impulsive child, but was beginning to develop some emotional and intellectual control despite the fact that his needs tended to dominate. There was growth in ego strength which, though immature, was being guided along appropriate channels.' The social quotient on the Vineland, when measured at 12 years, 6 months, was 72, showing his functioning in social competence at the nine-year level. His security rating showed a remarkable improvement. There was a marked move to a more mature pattern; immature dependence 8% – dependent trust 67%. This heartening increase in dependent trust was reflected in his putting forth more effort than formerly.

Until his thirteenth year his foster mother was still giving a very positive picture of her warm feelings for the boy. She herself was deriving satisfaction from the worker's constant visits and support, in addition to watching Tom's personality unfold. However, his habit of running about and screaming to let off steam and his increasing assertiveness was 'bothersome.' She stated 'no matter how often I bawl him out he always sticks up for me in every situation.' He continued to grow in dependence on Aunt Jennie. He verbalized his feelings and wanted very badly to belong to the Whites. He talked about his future, 'I never want to go behind an iron curtain like that baby institution again.' He was now going further afield, walking two miles into town to get library books on animals and science. He loved to experiment with chemistry set, steam engine, anything pertaining to science and seemed extremely inquisitive and knowledgeable. All was not easy. Tom was no longer accepting the very strict structure of the family routines without much pre-teen grumbling. He was monopolizing the family conversation at the table and eating habits were extremely poor. He saved his money for 'important things,' one of which was an apron for Aunt Jennie's birthday. He was a loner with peers at school but there was occasional interaction with boys in the community. His school report indicated that he was gaining more self-control in class but poor work habits were impeding academic progress as he sacrificed accuracy for speed.

In his fourteenth year everything was going well. His foster mother was still attuned to him. There seemed to be a growing bond between Aunt Jennie and her foster son. Tom hugged her, argued with her, and worried when she was not at home. Uncle Bill thought the boy was 'great.' He made no demands on the youngster. As Tom said, 'I really like Uncle Bill because he likes to teach me things and believes I can do things.' The boy and the old man still went trapping together.

Tom was changing. The changes in some ways made him more difficult, as he was distractible, impatient, impulsive, and very forgetful of simple routine procedures. He was no longer content to play or read alone. He wanted, more than before, companionship to share his projects and science experiments. His peers, like himself, were not always socially adequate; he was easily led in his eagerness to be accepted. He was doing a lot of clowning and his over-excitability got him into trouble. The boy was putting a lot of energy into social development to the detriment of the academic. He was extremely weak in mathematics so his friend, Mrs Day, gave him weekly sessions in that subject. Through time, Tom became a friend of her family with regular daily visits.

Another psychological test (WISC) indicated his verbal IQ to be 106 – performance 97 and full scale IQ 102. 'His strength lay in the field of abstract reasoning, general information and social comprehension. He demonstrated highly developed skill for verbal analysis and logical reasoning. His weakness lay in conventional arithmetic. Summarized, Tom's intellectual potential was far in advance of his fund of knowledge. He was a very bright lad who had incorporated information at an astonishing rate in view of his impoverished early background.'

By the time Tom reached fifteen years, Aunt Jennie was also showing a change of attitude. She had an interest in a new baby grandson. She was now 67 and was becoming more dependent on her married daughter. She also became extremely anxious about her own health. Uncle Bill's deafness and non-involvement in the handling of Tom's negative behaviour enhanced her anxieties. She was becoming the less healthy person in the mother-child partnership with Tom. Tom was now an argumentative adolescent whose social and emotional needs were reaching beyond the capacity of these parents to meet. Sensitive to the distress he was causing, but confused by his foster mother's inability to meet his needs, he attempted to repress their expression, recognizing that he should adapt to his older foster parents rather than they change for him.

That autumn he had an uneventful recovery from an appendectomy which left many somatic problems which were related to the deteriorating relationships in his home. He was distressed about his beloved Aunt Jennie's change of attitude. He felt strongly that the Whites were his roots. He had become more mature and more aware of his own impulsive, erratic behaviour. He was very excitable, but because he was now more comfortable with more adults he was able to talk out his problems when anxiety overtook him. He was extremely vulnerable and very sensitive to any indication of rejection or mistrust. He was trying very hard to be a good boy to get the approval of his foster parents. Once more he was dealing with confusion which needed to be worked through emotionally.

Now his activities and interests centred around chess playing and scientific experiments. He put forth effort in things he liked to do. He enjoyed taking responsibility at school in contrast to home where he felt pressed into too many chores. He was now in Senior Public School, Grade VIII. His male teacher and principal were sympathetic and supportive. His teacher made the comment: 'He is a good kid. I like him. He has all kinds of good qualities I hope we can develop. His mind is alive with things that interest him.' In academic progress, spelling and maths were difficult for him. His performance fluctuated from failing to hand in assignments to A- in a project on programming a computer.

It was also evident the boy was not having enough contact with peers in this country home. He worried that the kids thought him queer. It was interesting to note that his social competence at fifteen on the Vineland was eleven years seven months, a social quotient of 78. His security rating reflected his uncertainty of his home. There was a decline in dependent trust and a marked increase in clinging, demanding behaviour reflected in an immature dependence score. His effortful behaviour had declined.

Because of Tom's increasing anxieties and sense of rejection he began to show many somatic symptoms. A pediatric specialist was consulted. His report stated, 'I found no physical basis for his symptoms which were typical of an anxiety state. He impressed me as a capable boy with a good potential and I would regret to see any unnecessary damage to him emotionally by leaving these foster parents.'

Two clinical psychological examinations were also made of which the following was a summary:

Tom wants to stay with foster parents and work out any difficulties with them. He sees his foster mother as a controlling person who makes strong demands and at present he sees her as perpetuating early experiences. He seems to be controlled by rejecting factors. Rejection seemed to have played an important part in his life and was doing so again.

Tom's feeling of repression and withdrawal was in a process of expressing his hostility in somatic form.

Hostility is taking two forms, (a) cover up feelings of repression and (b) explosive physical reaction. He can be very responsive and attempt to give what he thinks others expect of him. Much of the boy's difficulties are from never being given adequate dependency satisfaction. He is a bright capable young adolescent but unless he receives a greater degree of warmth and consistency of the sort that he needs, then I am afraid he will have problems as he gets older. Presently it would seem that he would be able to go to University or be directed into vocational fields involving scientific, mechanical, biological or engineering.

Close to Tom's sixteenth birthday his world seemed very vulnerable. His foster mother was full of bitter complaints about his behaviour. Once more he was facing a crisis of overwhelming proportions. He desperately wanted to belong to Aunt Jennie and Uncle Bill, but at the same time his whole being sought expression in his maturing status as an adolescent. He needed someone to accept his questions and feelings. Aunt Jennie no longer could. Uncle Bill was deaf and withdrawn. In order to maintain some thread of stability in the relationship, his faithful case worker was busy on her frequent visits interpreting Aunt Jennie to Tom and Tom to Aunt Jennie. Tom struggled to be acceptable to his foster mother by clinging and being very dependent. He constantly sought her attention in unacceptable ways such as burping loudly. His nervous tension reactivated many of his earlier irritating habits. His foster mother responded by constant nagging which Tom interpreted as rejection. As a result of his conflict he was moody, depressed, impulsive, over-talkative and argumentative. Weekly case work by the child care worker with Aunt Jennie was not improving the feelings at home.

In order to provide a male figure to whom Tom could relate, a warm young man became his official social worker, while his constant mentor and child care worker who had been part of his life since his institutional days remained in the background, helping Aunt Jennie where possible and reassuring Tom that she would always be around. To take the pressure off the situation at home and to provide more social and intellectual stimulation Tom was once more sent to the summer camp from which he had profited the year before. He won a special award for 'the boy who made the most effort.'

A psychiatric report at that time recommended that, since his foster mother was ambivalent in her commitment to Tom, a boarding school should be explored. It was felt there was no need for intensive psychotherapy. Another psychological assessment on the WISC showed a verbal IQ of 113 – performance 114 and full scale 115 within the bright normal range of intelligence. 'His strength lay in the field of verbal symbolic thinking and in explanations of the world of interpersonal events. He was weak in arithmetic. He had a fair grasp of information and an above average vocabulary. He was thinking precisely and meaningfully. On the Rorschach he was shown to be highly drawn to the world of personal events. He was experiencing considerable anxiety, viewing other people as hostile and threatening. He saw himself as a victim of forces stronger than himself. He was trying hard to control situations by elaborate verbalization and an air of pseudo confidence. He needed constant structuring and feedback to maintain an appropriate level of communication.' In summary, the boy had made great strides intellectually but this was accompanied by considerable anxiety. A highly structured boarding school was again recommended to provide control and supervision and to relieve pressure at home.

Thus Tom entered Grade IX in a boarding school of 150 boys at the age of 16, going home to his foster parents on weekends and holidays. During that year relationships with his foster mother deteriorated. Mrs White became emotionally upset and thoroughly unaccepting of Tom's assertive behaviour. Her health also deteriorated and any added responsibility was too much for her. Tom's feelings about his lonely weekends in the White home were extremely heart rending. He was living in a vacuum. It was very difficult to convince this boy that the problem was Aunt Jennie's illness and age, and *not* his behaviour. When the time came to leave this home that he had struggled to make his own, it was mentioned that 'life was not a bowl of cherries and he would have to be strong.' Tom replied, 'I feel sick all over when I think of Aunt Jennie. Life is a bowl of pits and one has to dig very deep to find the luscious cherry.'

When Tom entered boarding school, he was given tremendous support by his teachers, and by the principal of the school. He was a tense appealing boy. While in Grade IX he was subject to rather frequent emotional breakdowns where he seemed to collapse and become unable to cope with life. This was accepted with passing concern by his teacher. His academic work was satisfactory, although he was disorganized and confused at times.

During the break with his foster mother, Tom's enormous need for belonging was filled in part by his continuing relations with the two people who had remained supportive from the time he lived in the institution. These two women now became his 'aunts' and it was to their homes (Mrs Day and the child care worker) that he went on long weekends from school. At this time a young married couple, who had taken an interest in him while he was at camp, actively entered his life and began to take him to their home also for some weekends. When he was not with his other two friends, he would be with them. This relationship blossomed into affection and in time Tom became their foster child.

The following two years saw more emotional stability and improvement in academic achievement. It was stated in a school report from the Dean of Students, 'I sincerely believe Tom has the makings of a fine person but that he needs at least two or three more years in an environment where people will take time to help him overcome his emotional fluctuations and still guide him in learning to get along more smoothly with others.'

Tom, now nearly 19 years old, is enthusiastic about his new life with his young foster parents. He is thoroughly enjoying Grade XII, working extremely hard to get into university in two years. He is now in a local village high school where he commented in a letter to this worker, 'At school the big question is computers. I hope that my interests will continue to expand. A teacher at present is working his butt off at trying to get me into a place in London so that once more I can sit in front of the big machine. New friends? Well, I am not pushing it but its coming, and soon I will be like the rest of the people at school. This is a great house we are fixing up. Our big problem is hot water and central heating. We have two of the happiest dogs in the world. Soon we will be ready for you to visit us.'

As one looks back over the life of this boy one cannot help speculating about the strengths within himself which were mustered to combat the destructive influences in his life. In doing this it is impossible also to ignore the extent to which supportive experiences helped to shape the outcome of his adjustment.

As we examine his record, we find reflected from infancy some inherent quality which enlisted a supportive response from grown-ups. With the exception of the period between 11 months of age and 3 years, we find indication that the adults in his world were moved to be helpful. After the rehabilitation programme was initiated, the flashes of intellectual curiosity encouraged his caretakers to think that he had untapped potential. The quality of his thinking was very different from that of the other children with whom he was living. There was a philosophical trend of mind and an unusually lively quality in his choice of words. Another of his redeeming qualities was his puckish sense of humour, again a rarity among the children within this institution. The degree to which he sought acceptance with adults and children was seldom dampened. His methods of attracting people to him were not always successful. This was particularly evident in his relationship with Aunt Jennie. As he sensed impending rejection his clinging attention-seeking nagging behaviour indicated his need for warmth and acceptance but arbitrated against it.

The most puzzling aspect of Tom's personality was his fantastic resilience despite the overwhelming difficulties which became evident at various times in his life. Hope never dies! One cannot help but think that this will be a constant characteristic for the rest of his life.

In tracing the supportive aspects of Tom's environment and putting them in balance against the destructive aspects one attempts to evaluate their divergent influences. Tom's early experiences, which could have crippled his development probably started at the time of his separation from his mother at seven weeks of age. By nine months of age his sparse record reflects that he was becoming disabled. As his care was prolonged in the institution his behaviour became increasingly bizarre and withdrawn. However, once a rehabilitation programme began he sought the help of grown-ups and was supported by them. He was unsuccessful in developing peer relationships within the institution. The three tramatic experiences of rejection from potential foster or adopted homes were shattering enough to destroy almost any child. That he was considered 'queer' should have created added disabilities. The heart-rending distress accompanying his departure from his beloved Aunt Jenny's and Uncle Bill's home would have been impossible for most children to bear. The histories of children subjected to many changes of foster home invariably show progressive failure in human affiliation.

How did it come about that Tom was able to move through these experiences and emerge with enormous insight into his own personality and the realities of his position? We have to then examine the supportive experiences in his life. At least two people have maintained this child through his development. The first person was the child care worker who came in contact with him at ten months of age while doing the initial study on security states. About a year after the termination of this study fleeting contact was again made by the worker during a brief experimental play programme. By the time Tom was three years, four months of age, the child care worker was in charge of the rehabilitation programme and was determined to rehabilitate the children in her care. Tom's needs were evaluated and he was placed in a small unit with a warm supportive house mother. Healthy maturation was proceeding slowly.

At this time the worker was able to interest Mrs Day on Tom's behalf. The ensuing therapy which was undertaken undoubtedly enabled Tom to be placed in a home. Once in his foster home, Mrs Day was always available to take him for weekends to her home and as the situation in his first foster home worsened the twenty play therapy sessions she had with him in her home undoubtedly helped him to work through some of his fears and hostilities and prepared him for his placement in another home. Meanwhile the child care worker was arranging for evaluation of his progress, and was seeking out the best possible placement for him through successive failures. It was she who decided the moves to be made and in a sense manipulated his life. If Tom felt a sense of helplessness over his own fate it was not openly reflected in his relationship to her. The reason for rejection and the explanation for the need to move on from one experience to another was done through her.

Other supportive experiences in Tom's life came from his good fortune in finding understanding, sympathetic teachers. When he first attended school at age nine, in a country school house, the social worker put his case before the school teacher who immediately devoted her talents to moving him ahead emotionally as well as intellectually. His second school teacher in the city was similarly understanding. While living with Aunt Jenny, he went to a rural school in a small town where both principal and teacher helped him. When final separation from Aunt Jenny came, Tom was accepted and supported through his emotional upheaval by his boarding school staff while at the same time his academic progress was encouraged. Always, the teachers felt that he had a unique quality to his thinking which was indicative of high potential.

Tom's difficulties in growing up were unusual. His early extreme immaturity made him almost impossible to live with in an environment which demanded age appropriate behaviour. When people were able to understand his immaturities (allow regression) he moved ahead. When they failed to understand, he slowed down and was overwhelmed. Something within himself, coupled with the intervention from his environment helped him over his serious hurdles. His final good luck in finding a young couple who liked him and wanted to offer him a home seemed a further extension of his capacity to enlist people to his cause.

One can seldom review a life history to pinpoint the critical moments in time which are responsible for the course and direction of development. We are able to do this in part with the children in this study.

Reading through the histories leads to the conclusion that few of these children were blessed with intensely caring people to make any early crucial decisions affecting their lives. Tom exemplifies this. In the sweep of his developmental history from seven weeks to eighteen years of age, one can roughly identify 21 crises at which time decisions have been made which have controlled the course of his life. Of these, nine would seem to have been made by the worker and research team whose greatest concern was to provide Tom with a grown-up who cared about him and on whom he could rely. Decisions around other events in Tom's life were largely dictated by expediency. Compromise between what appears to be an ideal plan and what was possible was necessary.

12 OCTOBER 1976

Tom, now age 22, is in his second year of a computer science course at university. He completed taking one subject at summer school which he failed at the end of his first year.

He still visits with his two life-long friends, Mrs Day and Miss Kilgour, spending an occasional week-end with one or the other. He is now the older brother in his young foster family who have had a baby which Tom adores. He spent part of his summer holiday on a trip with them to Western Canada. The remainder of the summer was used working on a nearby farm. Christmas and most holidays are spent with his foster family.

While in residence at university he had the good fortune to be welcomed by a local family who are relatives of Miss Kilgour. In this home he frequently joins the week-end activities of the boys in the family (ages 13 and 15). He is a willing helper with chores and repairs.

Tom is still learning by consequences as he continues to evaluate outcomes of activities and events. He is still sensitive to criticism but less vulnerable to moods as he seeks out someone with whom to talk out his troubles. He has made friends with some of his university instructors and assumes that they will welcome discussion with him about his courses.

He is still more comfortable with adults than he is with peers and states he will not get involved with girls until he obtains his goals at school. He is still young for his age and somewhat uneven in his progress towards maturity. His inquisitive mind and his delightful sense of humour make him a welcome visitor. Tom exemplifies the success of the philosophy that effort will grow out of dependency and some immature dependency is to be expected for many years to sustain a youngster who has had unusually difficult experiences.

15

Postlude

The lapse of fifteen years from the beginning to the termination of this study has allowed an accumulation of literature by other researchers having the same concerns as were identified by us in 1958. By the late 1960s it was evident that maternal deprivation had many facets and was far too generic a term to describe the mechanisms responsible for the variety of symptoms observed in severely deprived institutionalized infants. The first insight into clarification of the meaning of maternal deprivation came with a recognition that children living in understaffed institutions, providing minimal but adequate care, suffered not only a lack of consistent caretaking and attention from one or two persons, but also lived in an environment devoid of the significant stimulation provided in a home to initiate and sponsor healthy cognitive development (Bronfenbrenner, 1968). The consistent deficiencies in language abilities observed in such children led to the hypothesis that verbal abilities were more likely to suffer permanent impairment than other cognitive abilities. Further clarification of the different effects of separation and deprivation took place largely as a result of work of the Robertsons, with the identification of particular syndromes of disturbance resulting from separation of children from parents when attachment had already taken place.

ATTACHMENT

The assumption that attachment of a child to people in the world about him is essential for healthy development has been made by many authors. In common with this, the security theory used as the theoretical base for our study, used the concept of 'immature dependence' in much the same sense as 'attachment' is used in the literature. Both the therapeutic programme within the institution and later placement in foster and adoptive homes were deliberately designed to

foster dependency in the child on the caretakers most essential to his development. Although we regarded a caretaker-child bond as essential to the child's
future healthy development, we did not consider a biological mother to be the
exclusive mothering agent needed. However, the matter of continuity of care
was considered necessary in order to allow a child to construct a meaningful network of interactions between himself and his caretaker which would give structure, order, and meaning to the daily events of his life.

Satisfactory mothering was viewed as promoting a loving relationship in
which the child could feel a sense of warmth and belonging. In addition, the
mothering would be sufficiently stimulating to encourage a child to be effortful
in the exploration of his world and in looking after himself at an appropriate developmental level. The parent role implied the provision of an environment full
of experiences and play things designed to arouse the child's curiosity. Stimulation through physical contact and verbalization were also components of this
role.

These assumptions are still largely unchallenged. However, under discussion
is the question, 'Need the parenting role be exclusively assigned to a mother?' It
appears this need not be an exclusive relationship. Evidence to support the idea
that father-child attachment can replace a mother-child attachment is available
(Rutter, 1972). Furthermore, it would appear that support from siblings and
peers is also a potential source of healthy attachment. Harlow's work (1969)
with rhesus monkeys offers some of the strongest evidence for this assumption.
In contrast our group of children within the institution seemed to gain very little
from early peer relationships. In addition to the source of attachment figures,
evidence is accumulating to indicate that intensity rather than duration and constancy of interaction may be a crucial feature of parent-child interaction. Ainsworth and Bell's study in 1969 demonstrated that the degree of responsiveness
a mother could exhibit to her infant's signals was significant in the development
of attachment. Furthermore, children who were strongly attached to their mothers demonstrated a greater degree of curiosity than those less intensely attached.
Some studies point to the fact that the amount of social interaction from a
child's total environment might have some bearing on his degree of attachment
(Schaffer, 1969).

The second question on which there is less direct evidence is, at what time in
life might it be too late to form attachments? Is there a sensitive period? If so,
how long does it extend? Animal studies such as Harlow's (1969, 1970) link this
phenomena to sensitive periods in early childhood for forming attachment, and
it has been suggested that between the ages of five or six months and two or
three years in human infants are the heightened periods for children to become
attached. Evidence of a Tizard and Tizard study in 1972 seems conclusive that

attachments can develop up to two years of age, but beyond this there are no clear answers. The further question of whether later attachments, if they can be formed, are permanent and stable is also apparently unsolved. The answers to these questions may indeed have been found in our present longitudinal study where we have had an opportunity to watch children whose early life experiences had deprived them of both loving and stimulating relationships and who were later placed in foster and adopted homes. We have been able to evaluate their potential for affiliation and trust from the time of placement to eighteen years of age.

EFFECTS OF INSTITUTIONAL CARE

Studies on humans of the effects of deprivation have necessarily been in the context of institutional care. In view of the evidence that development has critical periods in infancy which determine later competencies, the effects of institutionalization would be expected to be most noticeable among those who had been exposed during this important period. Studies by Dennis and Najarian (1957) and Pringle and Bossio (1958) indicated that the longer the stay in an institution the greater was the cognitive deficit and the more extreme was the emotional and behavioural disturbance. Our own study of the security of infants in an institution reported in 1957 clearly demonstrated a decline in mental health status from three months of age through twenty-four months. The decline was accelerated after nine months of age and the conclusion was that mental health deficit was more marked the longer deprivation persisted. The effect of institutional care on mental health has been examined by Trasler (1960) in his study of foster care. He found that the breakdown of foster care was associated with previous prolonged institutional care and assumed it was related to 'bonding.'

The vulnerability of human infants to the deleterious effects of a barren environment has been established. However, their capacity to respond on a long-term basis to a reversal of adverse conditions has not been explored in any depth. White (1971) and Brossard and Décarie (1971), demonstrated that a rise in the developmental level of infants can take place as a result of relatively simple perceptual stimulation added to the infants' environment. However, animal studies have shown long-term detrimental effects when there was severe restriction to freedom of movement and exploration in their early environment. Studies of English and American children reared in culturally deprived areas indicate that short-term intervention such as Head Start programmes has little long-term effect. Verbal intelligence has been demonstrated to show greater impairment than does visuo-spatial abilities (Haywood, 1967, Tizzard, 1969). Thus severe restriction of sensory stimulation can impair overall development and different forms of stimulation can affect different intellectual skills. Recent findings indicate that probably the most important factor for the development of verbal intelligence is the quality of the child's language environment. The richness of the verbal interaction between a child and his environment is far more critical than the amount of talking that takes place. Thus the literature provides little to lead to firm conclusions about the long-term effect of depriving early experiences on intellectual skills. Our present study, in which the extreme poverty of stimuli in the early environment was relieved at a relatively late age, has shed some light on this position.

Growth deficits following privation have just begun to catch researchers' attention. The phenomenon of deprivation dwarfism has been investigated and the results seem to indicate that, when deprivation is relieved, compensation of growth is rapid but often not quite complete.

Evaluation of the outcome of this research project, designed to assist families in the development of healthy competent children, allows us to conclude that the intervention in the lives of these children from their early institutional rearing to age fifteen has produced salutary results.

The adjustment of the group as a whole can be described as healthy but immature. As a group, the children have demonstrated a remarkable capacity for in-depth affiliation with their parents and families. Whether this tie has contributed to the lag in social maturity or whether the lag is largely the result of the common severe deficit in social relationships observed in the conditions of their early rearing remains unclear. The intellectual function of the children showed marked improvement from their early life in the institution when they were largely untestable, to six years of age. From six, through fifteen years, there is evidence of increasing variability in performance among the group, but no significant change in the mean level of performance. The normal curve of distribution achieved by twelve and fifteen years of age would seem to indicate that the children were motivated to achieve up to their own unique potential. Evidence from the recorded comments of our psychologist indicates that the children were unusually highly motivated to do well during the tests. Such a conclusion is supported by the relatively high performance on sub-test items which are accepted as demonstrations of attention and persistence. The characteristic of the group as a whole to prefer performance over verbal tasks is marked, and may be a reflection of their early deprivation which held them aloof from the cadence of language as well as the acquisition of experiences and vocabulary with which to associate and describe events. Despite this, our group shows an advantage over other similarly deprived groups which are reported to show a deficit in language and abstract abilities. Neither of these aspects of their intellectual function shows particular disability.

An examination of the characteristics of concept formation of ten of the children has demonstrated no permanent damage to the quality of their function. We assume that this sample represents the group. There is, however, a consistent immaturity which remains evident still at fifteen years of age. Their needs indicate a heavy reliance on a structured environment, and they have not achieved much beyond the characteristics of a twelve-year level of function, according to an analysis of the Rorschach test. This immaturity in cognitive function has not precluded success in school, although only three of the children have yet shown outstanding academic potential. The group as a whole reflects strong preference for performance abilities as demonstrated on the WISC, but despite this they differ from other groups reported in their strength for verbal reasoning and acceptable level of definition of words on vocabulary items. This capacity for verbal reasoning and strength in performance tasks probably accounts for the adequate level of performance observed in school achievement. However, their lack of flexibility in defining words and apparent inability to develop enriched and colourful language probably are reflected in their preference for vocational training rather than academic. Furthermore, their strength in verbal reasoning tasks is thought to reflect a salutary capacity to adapt to the demands of both school and work life and make appropriate adjustments to community living.

Coinciding with the lag in concept formation is a lag in social maturity which is reflected in the life style of these children. Not one has become involved in group sports and most of them fail to participate in organized community activities. None has demonstrated an interest in or capacity for leadership in any particular aspect of living. Many of them have become solidly entrenched in extended families, the members of which enjoy each other and find social satisfaction in large family parties, picnics, and holidays. The children whose adjustment has been most satisfactory seem content with this 'in-group' kind of living. They have been less successful in peer relationships.

The parallel deficit in the levels of maturity in both social and concept formation leads to the speculation of its permanence. One asks the question, 'Will this immaturity be overcome as the children become more self-reliant and the demands of family and community place more social responsibility on them?' It is interesting to think back to the dearth of relationship among the children while they were in institutional care prior to treatment. Although this was relieved in large part by the therapeutic programme, there is no way of judging how much the children depended on each other for emotional support. Their disbursement to their various homes created a discontinuity of the human beings in their lives, a large part of which was their peer group. After placement, the research team encouraged the development of immature dependency on parents because of its apparently crucial nature in the mental health of each child. In so doing peer relationships suffered in the belief that a firm attachment to parents would eventually permit in-depth relationships with peers. At age fifteen it appears that this combined cognitive and social immaturity may be a deficit which will never be fully overcome. However, such a mode of function does not preclude them from a relatively successful and rewarding life. Their capacity for warm human relationships would allow them to acquire a partner and establish a family and their effortful approach to life will likely enable them to maintain a job. Furthermore, there is no reason to believe that social maturity has a developmental ceiling. Hypothetically it should continue for a lifetime.

There have been few exceptions to the successful development of dependence in these children, and the variety of factors in the children's lives which might have contributed to this failure defies any clear-cut explanation. Five of the twenty-five children have failed so far to find completely satisfactory relationships with family and community. Three of these children are girls who seemed from the beginning of the study to be particularly deficient in healthy personality assets. Of the two boys remaining, one child's disturbing behaviour could be attributed to the disappointment of circumstances beyond his own control which prevented his remaining in his adopted home; the last boy appears to have had opportunities to involve himself in family and community life but has rejected the values of both. Both of these boys have been delinquents. The three girls' main problems could be attributed to a lack of potential for in-depth relationships which has unfortunately been reinforced by intellectual capacities in the dull normal level. In the case of these three girls, we remain puzzled by an apparent inborn or constitutional factor which has defied responding to relatively supportive environments. In other words, the disabilities seem to be more in the children than in the environment.

The amount of intervention in these children's lives by the guidance and research worker has undoubtedly sponsored the healthy outcome for the group as a whole. The close, trusting relationship she was able to establish with the families allowed them to accept her advice regarding the children's development. The parents' dedication to the unique problems of their child provided a medium for the outcome. It is interesting that mental health has been accompanied by healthy physical growth which might not have been anticipated in view of the emaciated condition and slow motor development of the children at an early age. The fact noted earlier that 80% of the group are now average or above in height and weight is evidence of this. When we note also that no significant relationship is demonstrated between the length of time the children spent in the institution and any of the other variables investigated later (IQ, SQ, security rating, dependent trust, immature dependence, effort), it becomes apparent that events which took place after placement in homes were more powerful factors in the final outcome than were their earlier experiences. Healthy development has taken place even in children who spent their first five years in an institution.

We can conclude that the deficits of severe maternal and stimulus deprivation can be overcome to a considerable degree by a thoughtful approach to the long-term goals of growing healthy children in a family milieu.

The wider implications arising from this study have relevance to social policy, to the operation of a wide variety of kinds of residential care, to the case work practices of social agencies (particularly Children's Aid Societies) and to parenting practices designed to promote mental health.

The consequence of having a consistent developmental concept of mental health which was embodied in security theory has been laudible. Such theory, applicable from infancy through adolescence, lent continuity to the therapeutic programme within the institution and was extended through the period of contact with families after the children were placed in their homes. It has clearly demonstrated the usefulness of such theory to the successful operation of the institution. Because it could be described behaviourally, it was possible to transmit the implications of the behaviours to staff and later to parents. Such application could be extended to the operation of any residential or group home for both the child care staff and for the teachers (where large residences contain classrooms). It could be extended as a method of evaluation and guidance on discharge of children from institutions to the community. Staff of Children's Aid Societies could find it a satisfactory theory for evaluation of children in foster care. Parents could make use of such theory in the rearing of healthy children. Teachers in classrooms could find such a conceptual framework an aid to the assessment of children's feelings of competence which we know have direct bearing on academic performance.

Central to the success of the project described here was the role carried out by the child care worker. Her dedication to the children's future and her conviction that intervention could be effective presents an enviable model. Unfortunately it is far removed from the reality of most child care and case work service offered in agencies today. Continuity of contact and consistency of theory undoubtedly can prove effective in the supportive role adopted by workers who implement social policy designed to further the welfare of a child. The effectiveness of such continuous support is surely a demonstration of the need for continuity of service to welfare clients who need the security of a trustworthy figure on whom to rely. Such trust cannot be built readily nor can it be sustained from one worker to another without monumental setbacks as caseloads are shifted from worker to worker. Just as children lose faith in a discontinuous series of caretakers, so do families and children lose faith in the efficacy of changing case workers. The hostility and suspicion aroused in families by visiting case workers could be allayed if continuity could be maintained. As much concern should go into the change of a worker as is shown in changing a child from one home to another.

The ongoing guidance offered by the child care worker was a many-faceted service. No sitting behind a desk characterized her actions! She took initiative in alerting parents to potential problems, she baby-sat families to relieve pressured mothers to keep appointments, she responded to telephone calls at all times of the day, she accompanied mothers and children on visits to hospitals, schools, doctors, and clinics, she herself visited schools and teachers. Her guidance took the form of providing books about child-care, of giving direct advice about specific situations, of reflecting a generalized attitude of kindliness and a recognition of the limitations of development as well as encouragement to aim for the child's full potential. She spelled out in behavioural terms the kind of age-appropriate guidance procedures which would support each child's well-being at different points in time. She made regularly scheduled visits as well as many extra if the need were indicated. Should such service be even approximated by case workers, children and foster families would flourish and doners to Community Funds could believe that value was being received by recipients of service on which their donations were being spent.

Much is to be learned from the description of the children's institution 'before' the change. The efficiency, cleanliness, and sterility of the operation, with its total emphasis on accommodation to the requirements of the caretakers rather than a recognition of and accommodation to the needs of the children, spells out a story that needs constant repetition. Wherever one finds a group care situation in which too few adults care for too many helpless children or for too many helpless adults, much the same formula can be spelled out. Pressured caretakers, hurrying from one patient to another tend to the routine care of eating, washing, toileting, and bathing, and inevitably they lose their perspective on the human requirements which accompany such care. Patients no longer appear to be individuals with particular needs to be recognized. The personalized conversation, the recognition of an individual's pace of activity, the level of responsiveness and desire for social interaction go unrecognized. The patients glance towards the caretaker which is a plea for a kindly word or the nod of a head is deliberately avoided because the temporary respite in duties is regarded as a time to relax, to turn to a colleague for a few minutes conversation, or to leave for a coffee break. The patient is safe, he has no specialized relationship with his caregivers and as a result can make no real demand for human interaction. Observation of this common pattern is not confined only to children's institutions but can be seen in varying degrees in minimal quality infant and preschool day care centres, in understaffed hospitals, and in homes for the aged. The need to remind caregivers of the individualized needs of their charges is universal. It should be the responsibility of administrators of institutions not only to carry out the organizational duties of running such operations but also to remind their staff via personal contact, group discussion, and lectures that they are in charge of human beings who need human interactions on which to thrive.

The waste of human potential at either end of the human age spectrum is avoidable. Children can thrive, enjoy life, relate and learn given trustworthy supportive adults. Intact elderly people confined to institutional care can be productive, humorous, energetic, and interested in the world around them given an opportunity to relate to caretakers, given an opportunity to enter into some meaningful enterprise, and given the opportunity to feel the unique person he once was.

Personalized, individualized care can be given only when caregivers are convinced of its worth. It is enormously challenging and emotionally draining. It requires knowledge about human development and minimal recognition of the rules of mental health. Beyond these qualities, it can be given consistently only when the caregiver is a relatively mature self-disciplined person. Maturity takes time to grow. Its progress can be hastened by knowledge. Hence in-service staff training should be constant. The security theory could provide a means for such development.

One of the bitter observations which must be made about North American society is the recognition that despite its high regard for its children, there is low regard for its children's caretakers. Since the caretakers are the moulders of the children's character and can influence their development towards healthy or unhealthy outcomes, this surely is a conflicting set of values. The role of mother or group caretaker in North America is given very little status or financial reward. Salaries of day care workers and residential child care workers are close to minimum wage. Child care is considered anyone's field, yet it is one of the greatest challenges of a lifetime for individuals or for communities.

Why learn to drive a car but not learn something about rearing a child? High schools offer courses in driving skills and the rules of the road. Why the reluctance to offer courses in human development and an opportunity to interact with children in a day care facility housed in the high school? Each generation faces the challenge of preparing the next for life in home and community. This is surely as much the job of the high school as imparting an understanding of math and science. The study of human development is an ever unfolding science, still full of mystery and excitement. New discoveries abound each day to be fitted into the yet incomplete puzzle of our knowledge of the human person.

The excitement of discovery could be imparted to students in school while at the same time practice in a day care centre which is part of the school would allow the young adolescent the opportunity to test the reality of the theory. The one million single parents in Canada who struggle to find quality care for their children would reap the benefit as would their children. Surely this is good welfare policy as well as good education!

The recent decision in the Province of Ontario to remove mentally retarded children and adults from residential care to homes in the community is an attempt to humanize their care. For the individuals involved in such transfer there will be a long and difficult period of adjustment. Behaviours that have been appropriate while under residential care will no longer be appropriate for life in home and community. Families will be bewildered when expected behaviours do not appear. The compromise between what is expected and what is possible could be facilitated if some such procedure were adopted as the one described in this study. The ideas embodied in the need for regression during the period of adjustment, the need for immature dependence and later dependent trust to be established and the model of case work intervention and visiting could be a sound basis for such an operation.

Finally, a message of hope permeates this study. The faith that long-term planning and consistent intervention can ultimately bring about desired results shines through the years of work. The conviction that change can be effected by the application of knowledge to human problems has been confirmed.

Appendix

TABLE 1
Security scores on sixteen institutionalized infants*

Children	Age in months												
	1	2	3	4	5	6	7	8	9	10	11	12	13
A		32	33	21	15	12							
B			31	30	27	21	19						
C				45	34	29	22	20					
D				31	26	22	25	26					
E							49		40	44	21		
										29			
F							18		25	23	16		
										20			
G									-03	08		01	-04
H											39	11	18
I													24
J													
K													
L													
M													
N													
O													
P													
Total													
Average													
Median				+29					+21.5				

* Scores listed according to age of children with total scores for each child demonstrating a general decline with progressive age.

14	15	16	17	18	19	20	21	22	23	24	Total of scores of each child	Decrease from first test to fifth test
											113	20
											128	12
											150	25
											130	05
											183	28
											112	02
-03											-01	0
10	03										81	36
20	13	01									69	13
		11										
14	03	06	04	01							28	13
	28	30	19	19	06						102	22
		13	10	04	01	05					33	08
					22	21	21	21	13		98	09
						15	08	-01	05	07	34	08
							01	-21	-09	-01	-36	07
										-06		
							09	09	-01	08	32	01
												209
												13
	+10.5						+07					

TABLE 2
First and final scores of children listed according to age

Age in months	Average: first scores	Scores		Average: final scores	Difference between averages
		First	Final		
1		+.32	+.12		
2		+.31	+.19		
3	+.35	+.45	+.20	+.19	−.16
4		∸.31	+.26		
5					
6					
7		+.49	+.21		
8		+.18	+.16		
9		−.03	−.03		
10	+.26			+.09	−.17
11		+.39	+.03		
12					
13		+.24	+.11		
14		+.14	+.01		
15	+.20	+.28	+.06	+.06	−.14
16		+.13	+.05		
17					
18					
19		+.22	+.13		
20		+.15	+.07		
21	+.12	+.01	−.06	+.05	−.07
22		+.09	+.07		
23					
24					

TABLE 3
Security categories in percentage scores (stability through time, 6, 9, 12, & 15 years)

| No. | Age | Dependence | | | Effort | | Security rating | Diff. high & low scores |
		Imm. dep.	Dep. trust	Lack of	Self-worth & effort	Lack of		
2	6	33	43	24	44	56	60	
	9	61	31	8	57	43	74.5	
	12	20	50	30	60	40	65	14
	15	42	42	16	48	52	66	
19	6	23	61	16	67	33	75.5	
	9	55	45	0	75	25	87.5	
	12	0	75	25	82	18	78.5	12
	15	14	58	28	84	16	78	
20	6	54	15	31	52	48	60.5	
	9	37	37	26	58	42	66	
	12	10	36	54	72	28	59	7
	15	20	30	50	71	29	60.5	
18	6	58	42	0	83	17	91.5	
	9	58	25	17	63	37	73	
	12	30	50	20	80	20	80	23
	15	20	50	30	66	44	68	
17	6	33	21	46	54	46	54	
	9	22	33	45	42	58	48.5	
	12	33	25	42	48	52	53	7
	15	36	43	22	31	69	55	
16	6	67	8	25	44	56	59.5	
	9	50	0	50	44	56	47	
	12	8	67	25	62	38	68.5	21
	15	17	44	39	57	43	59	
13	6	23	31	46	32	68	43	
	9	50	25	25	26	74	50.5	
	12	35	24	41	15	85	37	13
	15	23	16	61	40	60	39.5	
8	6	42	21	37	34	66	48.5	
	9	29	0	71	47	53	37.5	
	12	30	46	24	47	53	61.5	24
	15	11	22	67	65	35	49.0	
26	6	27	55	18	66	34	74	
	9	50	33	17	84	16	83.5	
	12	0	40	60	77	23	58.5	25
	15	0	30	70	90	10	60	

TABLE 3
(continued)

| No. | Age | Dependence | | | Effort | | Security rating | Diff. high & low scores |
		Imm. dep.	Dep. trust	Lack of	Self-worth & effort	Lack of		
25	6	50	17	33	61	39	64	
	9	54	10	36	54	46	59.5	21
	12	25	0	75	62	38	43.5	
	15	33	9	58	50	50	46	
23	6	46	23	31	45	55	57	
	9	60	20	20	55	45	67.5	13
	12	20	40	40	70	30	65.5	
	15	33	42	25	65	35	70	
22	6	39	15	46	33	77	43.5	
	9	30	20	50	48	52	49	16
	12	20	40	40	37	63	48.5	
	15	33	33	34	52	48	59	
21	6	23	54	23	79	21	78	
	9	26	60	14	77	23	81.5	3
	12	30	50	20	82	28	81	
	15	26	42	32	87	13	77.5	
24	6	78	22	0	78	22	89	
	9	55	0	45	60	40	57.5	32
	12	23	31	46	65	35	59.5	
	15	10	63	27	90	10	81.5	
6	6	50	14	36	54	46	59	
	9	43	14	43	52	48	54	41
	12	27	27	45	35	65	44.5	
	15	8	17	75	12	88	18.5	
7	6	22	37	41	30	70	44.5	
	9	44	36	20	64	36	72	34
	12	23	54	23	75	25	76	
	15	71	21	8	64	36	78	
3	6	62	23	15	54	46	69.5	
	9	58	42	0	67	33	83.5	15
	12	13	87	0	53	47	76.5	
	15	46	36	18	55	45	68.5	

Mean, 19
Range (3–41)

TABLE 4
Vineland social maturity scores and intelligence scores at 9-12-15 years of age

Child	CA	SA	Soc. Quo.	IQ	Age (yrs.)	Child	CA	SA	Soc. Quo.	IQ
13	9.1	8.5	94	108	9	1	8.8	7.1	88	79
	11.8	8.8	74	104	12		12.4	9.3	75	81
	15.0	11.0	73	112	15		14.1	10.8	73	93
8	9.5	8.2	76	91	9	24	–	7.2	80	91
	11.5	10.0	88	104	12		12.1	10.0	83	90
	14.1	14.4	89	–	15		15.0	13.4	89	101
26	9.1	8.3	92	111	9	6	9.8	7.8	81	88
	12.6	12.3	98	104	12		12.9	9.0	71	84
	14.1	14.4	97	109	15		15.0	11.0	73	86
25	8.9	7.4	85	97	9	7	9.4	7.9	86	66
	12.3	10.3	84	98	12		11.4	9.3	82	67
	15.0	11.3	75	105	15		15.0	11.7	78	83
23	8.1	8.0	90	–	9	3	9.0	8.3	92	114
	12.0	11.0	92	95	12		13.0	9.7	74	103
	15.0	11.7	78	–	15		15.0	11.0	73	110
22	8.1	6.5	73	85	9	1	9.7	8.9	92	110
	11.8	8.8	74	–	12		12.2	11.0	90	117
	14.1	11.0	73	93	15		15.2	14.4	94	115
21	9.2	9.0	98	102	9	2	8.9	7.6	87	86
	11.1	11.3	102	102	12		12.3	9.4	76	86
	14.1	14.4	96	109	15		15.0	11.7	78	96
20	9.4	9.7	104	115	9	19	9.0	11.3	125	92
	11.1	12.0	101	101	12		11.1	12.0	108	92
	14.1	13.2	88	121	15		14.10	15.6	105	119
18	8.9	8.0	91	102	9	27	9.5	7.9	85	79
	12.3	10.0	82	112	12		13.0	10.3	79	87
	15.2	13.2	86	124	15		15.0	13.2	88	80
17	9.9	8.0	82	101	9	5	8.11	9.7	113	103
	12.8	10.0	79	101	12		11.10	11.7	99	113
	14.9	11.0	74	101	15		14.7	14.4	99	–
16	9.2	7.0	76	86	9	14	–	7.1	79	86
	12.6	9.0	72	100	12		11.6	8.4	72	–
	15.0	11.7	78	115	15		14.8	10.5	71	96
15	9.6	9.3	97	101	9	12	9.0	7.2	80	–
	12.6	11.0	88	–	12		12.6	9.7	77	76
	14.9	13.8	93	128	15		15.3	11.8	77	76
11	9.0	8.8	98	84	9					
	12.7	9.7	76	101	12					
	15.2	12.6	82	112	15					

Means at 9-12-15 yrs. of age

Age	SQ	IQ
9	89	94
12	83.5	95
15	83	103.5

TABLE 5
Spearman Rank Order Correlations between security variables, IQ, SQ, and variables related to time in the institution (15 years)

	Imm. depen.	Dep. trust	Effort	Security rating	IQ	SQ	IQ-SQ	Time in inst.	Time before therapy	Time in therapy	Age at discharge
Imm. dependence		-.31	-.52*	-.04	-.45*	-.54**	.01	.04	.16	.01	.08
Dependent trust			.54**	.71**	.23	.54**	-.01	-.12	-.01	-.17	0
Effort				.69**	.25	.88**	-.39*	-.18	0	-.33	-.09
										-.30†	
Security rating					-.07	.59**	-.47*	-.05	.21	-.14	.08
IQ						.40*	.71**	.11	-.10	.19	-.02
SQ							-.29	0	.02	-.07	.06
IQ-SQ								.06	.04	.16	.01
Time in inst.									.86	.74**	.98**
Time before therapy										.38*	.86**
Time in therapy											.66**
Age at discharge											

* .05 Level of significance.
** .01 Level of significance.
† Partialled correlation.

TABLE 6
Spearman Rank Order Correlations between security variables, IQ, SQ, and variables related to time in the institution (6 years)

	Imm. depen.	Dep. trust	Effort	Security rating	IQ	SQ	IQ-SQ	Time in inst.	Time before therapy	Time in therapy	Age at discharge
Imm. dependence								-.04	-.08	.16	-.06
Dependent trust	-.57**							.08	.14	-.22	.13
Effort	.18	.46*						-.27	-.18	-.42* / -.34†	-.20
Security rating	.24	.53**	.94**								
IQ								-.16	-.41*	.25	-.42
SQ											
IQ-SQ											
Time in inst.									.86**	.74**	.98**
Time before therapy										.38*	.86**
Time in therapy											.66**
Age at discharge											

* .05 Level of significance.
** .01 Level of significance.
† Partialled correlation.

TABLE 7
Spearman Rank Order Correlations between security variables,
IQ, SQ, and variables related to time in the institution (9 years)

	Imm. dep.	Dep. trust	Effort	Security rating	IQ	SQ
Imm. dependence		–.15	.18	.34*		
Dependent trust			.52*	.77*		
Effort				.83**		.45*
Security rating						
IQ						.56*
SQ						

  * .05 Level of significance.
 ** .01 Level of significance.

TABLE 8
Spearman Rank Order Correlations between security variables,
IQ, SQ, and variables related to time in the institution (12 years)

	Imm. dep.	Dep. trust	Effort	Security rating	IQ	SQ
Imm. dependence		–.57**	–.34	–.31		
Dependent trust			.36*	.80**		
Effort				.71**		.77**
Security rating						.33
IQ						.26
SQ						

  * .05 Level of significance.
 ** .01 Level of significance.
  † Partialled correlation.

TABLE 9
Rorschach analysis – mean percentage of location
and determinant scores: mean form level rating: mean IQ

	%	Age 6	9	12	15
Determinants	F	40	60	34	54
	FM	24	17	22	18
	M	11	7	14	12
	FC	14	1	11	5
	CF	9	8	5	2
	C	–	–	–	–
	C′	–	–	3	1
	c	–	–	4	3
	m	–	–	4	3
Location	W	34	50	35	39
	D	57	45	48	46
	d	10	4	9	9
	dr	–	–	5	2
	dd	–	–	–	.4
	di	–	–	–	.01
	de	–	–	.1	2
	S	–	–	.1	1
Form level rating		.62	1.5	1.6	1.1
Verbal IQ		–	–	–	104
Performance IQ		–	–	–	111
Full scale IQ		89	93	98	108

TABLE 10
Comparison of current fifteen year old results with
'typical' twelve and fifteen year old profiles on the Rorschach

%	'Typical' 15 profile	'Typical' 12 profile	Current 15 results
F	64	63	54
F+	94	93	90
W	51	42	39
D	43	48	46
d	0	4	9
dr	–	–	2
de	–	–	2
S	–	–	1
Form level rating			1.1
M	1.8	2.6	2.5
FM	1.6	2.2	3.5
m	.5	1.0	1.0
FC	.3	.3	.1
CF	.7	.8	.4
C	.1	.9	–

TABLE 11
Significant events during institutionalization

Children's symbols	Date of birth	Age at admission months	Pre-Intervention length of time yrs:mos	Age at intervention* yrs:mos	Time in therapy yrs:mos	Age at discharge yrs:mos	Time in institution yrs:mos
1	7/56	10	:9	1:7	1:0	2:7	1:9
21	11/54	9	2:6	3:3	1:0	4:3	3:6
17	2/57	7	:5	1:0	1:7	2:7	2:0
3	10/56	6	:10	1:4	1:1	2:5	1:11
2	3/55	3	2:8	2:11	2:0	4:11	4:8
7	6/54	2	3:6	3:8	2:4	6:0	5:10
19	12/54	2	3:0	3:2	1:5	4:7	4:5
16	10/54	1	3:3	3:4	3:2	6:6	6:5
13	3/55	1	2:10	2:11	1:6	4:5	4:4
9	7/57	2	:5	:7	1:3	1:10	1:8
23	10/54	1	3:3	3:4	2:1	5:5	5:4
27	10/54	3	3:1	3:4	1:3	4:7	4:4
11	3/55	1	2:10	2:11	1:11	4:10	4:9
24	4/57	5	:5	:10	1:2	2:0	1:7
20	6/56	Birth	1:8	1:8	2:0	3:8	3:8
18	2/57	Birth	1:0	1:0	1:9	2:9	2:9
25	1/55	Birth	3:1	3:1	1:1	4:2	4:2
6	9/55	Birth	2:5	2:5	2:3	4:8	4:8
12	9/54	Birth	3:5	3:5	2:1	5:6	5:6
14	9/55	Birth	2:5	2:5	:10	3:3	3:3
15	3/55	2	2:9	2:11	1:8	4:7	4:5
22	2/57	Birth	1:0	1:0	:7	1:7	1:7
8	4/57	1	:9	:10	3:3	4:1	4:0
26	4/57	Birth	:10	:10	1:2	2:0	2:0
Means			2:1	2:3	1:8	3:11	3:8
Median			2:5	2:8	1:6	4:3	4:1

* Therapy started February 1958.

Immature dependence
Has to be pushed into things
Dawdles in the bathroom
Needs firm controls
Made to do errands and look after clothing
Tell him over and over before doing anything
Needs tremendous encouragement re school
Father makes him do homework
I have to get him to read
Needs help
Needs to be told three times, procrastination
He will come for help before trying anything
Has to be told to take a bath
Still a little boy
TV supervised and rationed
Does regular chores
Accepts what mum says
Does what father says
Does what is expected

Dependent trust
Good common sense
Will listen to reason
Views adults as supportive – not try to manipulate
Knows parental limits
Has such trust in people
Figures if mother won't help, someone will
'Idolizes gym teacher – just like you, mum'
Is matter of fact about responsibilities
We do everything as a family
Matter of fact re adoption

Rejection of dependence and trust
Rejects mum's help
Prefers friend's help
Pouts
Doesn't like being helped
Defiant
Rejects restrictions related to TV, friends, and school
Adoptive parents may not have authority
Loses money – doesn't care
Refuses to do what dad asks
Blows up with interference from parents
Tries our patience to the end
Does it and then asks
Sly ways of getting attention
If he has problems, doesn't say much
Never tells us anything about friends
Doesn't like to lose and can't discuss it
Never mentions adoption

Shares feelings, argues and enjoys
Gets in a snit when father says something
If someone is bugging him he will come to me
When we are alone he puts his head on my shoulder
Questions adoption
Can discuss problems
Likes family to share hobbies
Child and father enjoy each others' company
Enjoys adoptive family
Dad and child are inseparable – child is treated as an equal
Loves to come shopping with us
Likes to do what dad does
Asks father's help in chess game
Loves to be helped
Enjoys family camping trips
Shares interests with family
Shares activities at the farm
Goes everywhere with mother

BEHAVIOURAL DESCRIPTIONS FOR SELF-WORTH AND EFFORT CATEGORIES

Self-worth – independent effort items
Conscious of styles and clothing
I have a girl friend
Has friends
Everyone likes him
Likes to go downtown by self
Does what others do
Thinks parents old fashioned
Usually settles own disputes
Gets along well with adults
Washes hair every morning
Conscious of body – does exercises

Lack of self-worth – lack of effort (DAs)
Shy (withdrawn)
Refuses to co-operate with tests
Must do things his way
Jealous
May be bossy
Bit of a loner – pushed
Dislikes being teased
Bugs him if he can't do something
Doesn't read
Doesn't concentrate
Feels inadequate mentally

Will confide in (adult) sister
Likes school – conscientious re homework
Has been in play (stage)
Worked hard planting trees
Usually willing to carry out chores
Man of the house
Does various jobs with father
Systematic about chores
Works at home for money
Takes care of lawn and garbage
Paints house for money
Good painter with Dad
Does chores for money
Caddies in summer
Has learned to drive truck
Can earn money
Saves in bank account
When on his own often draws
Ballroom dancing lessons
Carpentry and mechanics
Enjoys sports
Joins club; sports or interest
Y Club on Saturday a.m.
Loves music and singing
Skiing and skating, belongs to club
Chosen for crew in sailing cup race
Plays hockey on the street with kids
Likes geographic things
Likes to do things with hands
Can share
Matter-of-fact about responsibilities (chores)
Very relaxed with teacher – feels he has someone

Frustrated in school
Cannot wait to get out of school
Never sees anything to do
Easily diverted from chores
Gripes about chores
Careless with room
Never volunteers in shopping, has to be asked
Doesn't plan anything
Can't do this, can't do that
Discouraged, wants to give up when losing
Doesn't like to lose
Easily diverted from tasks
Needs a lot of approval

Figure 2
Trend lines of security scores from first to fifth tests for each infant in an institution

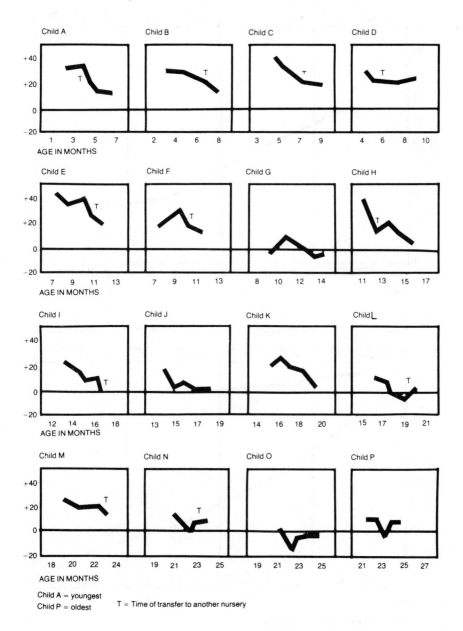

Child A = youngest
Child P = oldest   T = Time of transfer to another nursery

Figure 3
Trend of median scores for the total group.

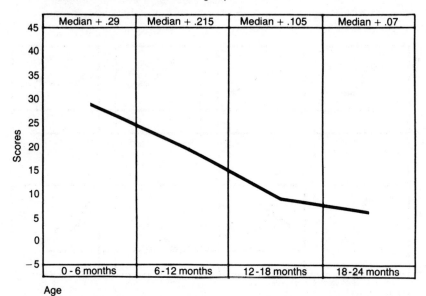

Age

Figure 4
Median scores of two different groups of children represented at six month intervals.

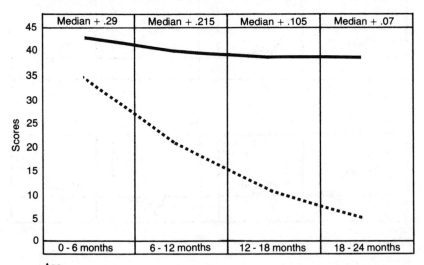

Age

well-adjusted group ▬▬▬
institutionalized group ▪▪▪▪▪▪▪

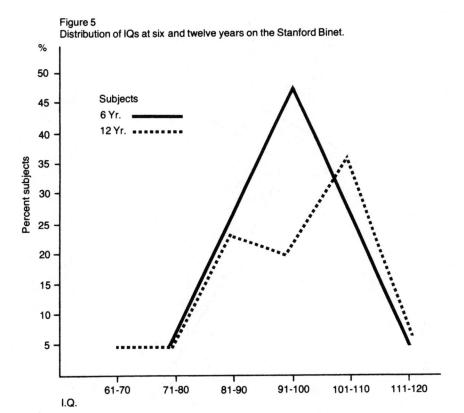

Figure 5
Distribution of IQs at six and twelve years on the Stanford Binet.

Figure 6
Distribution of IQs on the WISC at fifteen years (showing %s obtaining verbal, performance, full scale IQs).

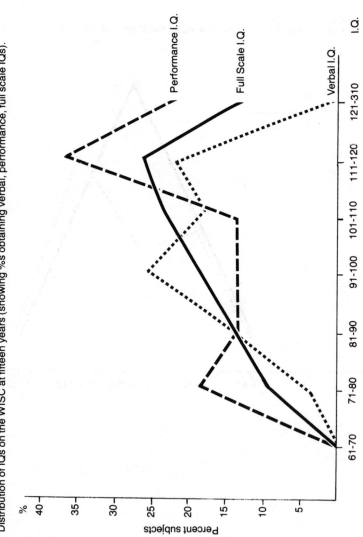

Figure 7
Group profile of WISC subtests (group mean–10.5).

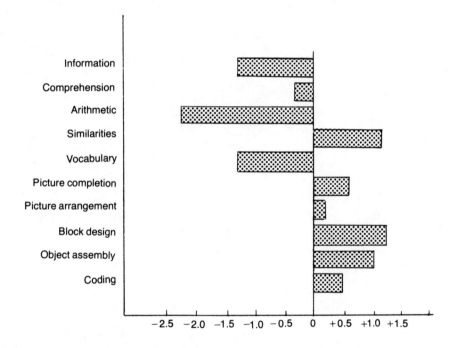

Scaled   score   Intervals   around   the   mean

Bibliography

Ackerman, N. (ed.) (1967) Expanding theory and practises in family therapy: New York: Family Service Association of America

Ainsworth, M.D. (1962) The effects of maternal deprivation A review of findings and controversy in the context of research strategy. Monogr. In *Deprivation of Maternal Care - A Reassessment of its Effects.* Geneva: World Health Organization

Ainsworth, M.D. (1963) The development of infant-mother interaction among the Ganda. In B.M. Foss (ed.), *Determinants of Infant Behaviour*, Vol. 2, London: Methuen

Ainsworth, M.D. (1964) Patterns of attachment behaviour shown by the infant in interaction with his mother. *Merrill-Palmer Quart.* Vol. 10, 51–8

Ainsworth, M.D. (1969) Object relations, dependency and attachment – A theoretical review of the infant-mother relationship, *Child Development*, Vol. 40, 969–1025

Ainsworth, M.D., and Bell, S.M. (1969) Some contemporary patterns of mother-infant interaction in the feeding situation. In A. Ambrose (ed.) *Stimulation in Early Infancy.* New York: Academic Press

Ainsworth, M.D., and Wittig, B.A. (1969) Attachment and exploratory behaviour of one year olds in a strange situation. In B.M. Foss (ed.), *Determinants of Infant Behaviour*, Vol. 4, London: Methuen

Ainsworth, M.D. (1972) Development of infant-mother attachment. B.M. Caldwell and H.N. Reccuiti (eds.), *Child Development Research* Vol. 3, Chicago: University of Chicago Press

Ambrose, J.A. (1961) The concept of a critical period for the development of social responsiveness. In B.M. Foss (ed.), *Determinants of Infant Behaviour*: Vol. 2, London: Methuen

Ambrose, J.A. (1961) Development of the sibling response in early infancy. In B.M. Foss (ed.), *Determinants of Infant Behaviour*, Vol. 1, London: Methuen

Ames, L.B., Metraux, R.W., and Walker, R.N. (1971) *Adolescent Rorschach Responses*: New York: Brunner/Mazel

Anastasi, A. (1968) *Psychological Testing.* New York: Macmillan

Bakwin, H. (1949) Emotional deprivation in infants, *J. Pediat.* Vol. 35, 512–21

Bender, L. (1947) Psychopathic behaviour disorders in children. In R.M. Lindner and R.V. Seliger (eds.), *Handbook of Correctional Psychology.* New York: Philosophical Library

Beres, D., and Obers, S. (1950) The effects of extreme deprivation in infancy on psychic structure in adolescence. *Psychoanal. Study of Child,* 5, 121–40

Blishen, B.R. (1958) The construction and use of an occupational class scale, *Can. J. Eco. Pol. Sci.* Vol. 24, Nov. 1958, 519–31

Bortner, M., and Birch, H.G. (1969) Patterns of intellectual ability in emotionally disturbed and brain damaged children. *J. Special Education,* 3 (4), 351–69

Boszormenyi-Nagy, I., and Framo, J.L. (eds.) (1966) *Intensive Family Therapy – Theoretical and Practical Aspects.* New York: Harper and Row

Bowlby, J. (1951) *Maternal Care and Mental Health.* Geneva: World Health Organization

Bowlby, J. (1958) The nature of the child's tie to his mother. *Int. J. Psychoanal.,* Vol. 39, 350–73

Bowlby, J. (1962) Childhood bereavement and psychiatric illness. In D. Richter, J.M. Tanner, Lord Taylor, and O.L. Zangwill (eds.), *Aspects of Psychiatric Research.* London: Oxford University Press

Bowlby, J. (1969) *Attachment and Loss.* Vol. 1 Attachment. London: Hogarth Press

Bowlby, J. (1973) *Attachment and Loss* Vol. 2 Attachment. New York: Basic Books

Brockman, L., Whitely, J., and Zubek, J. (1973) *Child Development: Selected Readings.* Toronto: McClelland and Stewart

Bronfenbrenner, U. (1968) Early deprivation in mammals A cross-species analysis. In G. Newton and S. Levine (eds.), *Early Experience and Behaviour.* Springfield, Ill.: C.C. Thomas

Bronfenbrenner, U. (1970) *Two Worlds of Childhood.* New York: Russell Sage Foundation

Brossard, M., and Decarie, T.G. (1971) The effects of three kinds of perceptual-social stimulation on the development of institutionalized infants Preliminary report of a longitudinal study, *Early Child Develop. Care,* Vol. 1, 211–30

Burlingham, D., and Freud, A. (1942) *Young Children in Wartime.* London: Allen and Unwin

Caldwell, B.M. (1962) Mother-infant interaction in monomatric and polmatric families, *Am. J. Orthopsychiat.,* Vol. 32, 340–41

Caldwell, B.M. (1964) The effects of infant care. In M.L. Hoffman and L.W. Hoffman (eds.), *Review of Child Development Research*, Vol. 1. New York: Russell Sage Foundation

Caldwell, B.M. (1968) The fourth dimension in early education. In R.D. Hess and R.M. Bear (eds.), *Early Education, Current Theory, Research and Action*. Chicago: Aldine Publishing Co.

Caldwell, B.M. (1970) The effects of psychosocial deprivation on human development in infancy, *Merrill-Palmer Quart.*, Vol. 16, 260–77

Caldwell, B.M., Wright, C.M., Honig, A.C., and Tannenbaum, J. (1970) Infant day care and attachment. *Am. J. Orthopsychiat.*, Vol. 40, 397–412

Casler, L. (1961) Maternal deprivation A critical review of the literature, *Monogr. Soc. Res. Child Devel.*, Vol. 26, No. 2

Casler, L. (1968) Perceptual deprivation in institutional settings. In G. Newton and S. Levine (eds.), *Early Experience and Behaviour*. Springfield, Ill.: C.C. Thomas

Clarke, A.D.B., and Clarke, A.M. (1960) Some recent advances in the study of early deprivation, *J. Child Psychol. Psychiat.*, Vol. 1, 26

Clarke-Stewart, K. Allison (1973) Interactions between mothers and their children: Characteristics and consequences. In *Monographs of the Society for Research on Child Development*, Vol. 38, 6–7

David, M., and Appell, G. (1961) A study of nursing care and nurse-infant interaction. A report on the first half of an investigation. In B.M. Foss (ed.), *Determinants of Infant Behaviour*, Vol. 1, London: Methuen

Davis, C. (1966) *Room to Grow: A Study of Parent-Child Relationships*. Toronto: University of Toronto Press

Dennis, W., and Najarian, P. (1957) Infant development under environmental handicap. *Psychol. Monogr.* Vol. 71, 1–13

Dennis, W. (1973) *Children of the Creche*. New York: Appleton Century Crofts

Deutsch, M., Katz, I., and Jensen, A. (eds.) (1968) *Social Class, Race and Psychological Development*. New York: Holt, Rinehart and Winston

Doll, E.A. (1953) *The Measurement of Social Competence*. Minneapolis: Educational Test Bureau

Flint, B.M. (1959) *Security of Infants*. Toronto: University of Toronto Press

Flint, B.M. (1966) *Child in the Institution: A Study of Deprivation and Recovery*. Toronto: University of Toronto Press

Flint, B.M. (1970) Need Kindergarten be Too Late? *Educational Theory*, Vol. 20, Fall, 1970, No. 4

Flint, B.M. (1974) Manual and scale: *The Flint Infant Security Scale*. Toronto: The Guidance Centre

Freeman, F. (1962) *Theory and Practise of Psychological Testing.* New York: Holt, Rinehart & Winston

Frost, J., and Hawkes, G.R. (eds.) (1970), *The Disadvantaged Child: Issues and Innovations.* 2nd ed., Boston: Houghton Mifflin

Furchner, C.S., and Harlow, H.F. (1969) Preference for various surrogate surfaces among infant rhesus monkeys, *Psychonom. Sci.,* Vol. 17, 279-80

Gardner, D.B., Hawkes, G.R., and Burchinal, L.G. (1961) Non-continuous mothering in infancy and development in later childhood, *Child Develop.,* Vol. 32, 225-34

Gardner, L.I. (1972) Deprivation dwarfism in the nature and nurture of behaviour: Readings from *Scientific American.* San Francisco: W.H. Freeman

Gesell, A., and Amatruda, T. (1941) *Developmental Diagnosis.* New York: P.B. Heeber

Gewirts, J.L. (1968) The role of stimulation in models for child development. In L.L. Dittman (ed.) *Early Child Care: The New Perspectives.* New York: Atherton Press

Glasser, W. (1965) *Reality Therapy.* New York: Harper & Row

Goldfarb, W. (1943) Effects of early institutional care on adolescent personality, *J. Exp. Educ.,* Vol. 12, 106

Goldfarb, W. (1945) Psychological privation in infancy and subsequent adjustment, *Am. J. Orthopsychiat.,* Vol. 15, 247-55

Goldfarb, W. (1945) Effects of psychological deprivation in infancy and subsequent stimulation, *Am. J. Psychiat.,* Vol. 102, 18-33

Goldfarb, W. (1947) Variations in adolescent adjustment of institutionally reared children, *Am. J. Orthopsychiat.,* Vol. 17, 449-57

Gordon, T. (1971) *Parent Effectiveness Training.* New York: P.H. Wyden

Gronlund, N.E. (1968) *Readings in Measurement and Evaluation.* New York: Macmillan

Harlow, H.F. (1958) The nature of love, *Am. Psychol.,* Vol. 13, 673-85

Harlow, H.F. (1961) The development of affectional patterns in infant monkeys. In B.M. Foss (ed.), *Determinants of Infant Behaviour,* Vol. 1, London: Methuen

Harlow, H.F. (1963) The maternal affectional system. In B.M. Foss (ed.) *Determinants of Infant Behaviour,* London: Methuen

Harlow, H.F., and Harlow, M.K. (1969) Effects of various mother-infant relationships on rhesus monkey behaviours. In B.M. Foss (ed.), *Determinants of Infant Behaviour,* Vol. 4, London: Methuen

Harlow, H.F., and Harlow, M.K. (1970) Developmental aspects of emotional behaviour. In P. Black, *Physiological Correlates of Emotion.* New York: Academic Press

Harlow, H.F., and Suomi, S.J. (1971) Social recovery by isolation reared monkeys, *Proc. Nat. Acad. Sci.*, Vol. 68, 1534–8

Harlow, H.F., and Zimmermann, R.R. (1959) Affectional responses in the infant monkey, *Science*, Vol. 130, 421–32

Harlow, H.F., Schlitz, K.A., and Harlow, M.K. (1969) Effects of social isolation on the learning performance of rhesus monkeys. In *Proc. Second Int. Cong. Primatol.*, Vol. 1: Atlanta, Georgia: S. Karger

Haywood, C. (1967) Experimental factors in intellectual development: The concept of dynamic intelligence. In T. Zubin and G.A. Jervis (eds.), *Psychopathology in Mental Development*. New York: Grune & Stratton

Hebb, D.O. (1949) *The Organization of Behaviour*. New York: Wiley

Hollingshead, A.W. (1949) *The Index of Social Position*. New Haven: Yale University Press

Howells, J.G. (ed.) (1971) *Modern Perspectives in International Child Psychiatry*. New York: Brunner/Mazel

Hunt, J. McV. (1972) Abstract early childhood education and social class, *The Canadian Psychologist*, Vol. 13, No. 4. Canadian Psychological Assoc., University of Calgary

Ilg, F.L., and Ames, L.B. (1971) *Adolescent Rorschach Responses*. New York: Brunner/Mazel

Jensen, A.R. (1969) How much can we boost IQ and scholastic achievement? *Harv. Educ. Rev.*, Vol. 39, 1–123

Jones, M.C., Bayley, N., MacFarlane, J.W., and Honzik, M.P. (eds.) (1971) *The Course of Human Development*. Waltham, MA.: Xerox College Publishing

Kagan, J., and Moss, H. (1962) *A Study in Psychological Development: A Prediction of Behavior from Birth to Maturity*. New York: Wiley

Kilgour, M. (1963) *The Jones Family*, available from Catholic Children's Aid Society of Metro Toronto

Klackenberg, G. (1956) Studies on maternal deprivation in infants' homes, *Acta Pediat.* 45, 1–12

Leifer, A.D., Leiderman, P.H., Barnet, C.R., and Williams, J.A. (1972) Effects of mother-infant separation on maternal attachment behavior, *Child Development*, Vol. 43, No. 4, University of Chicago Press

Lowney, L.G. (1940) Personality distortion and early institutional care. *Am. J. Ortho.*, Vol. 10, 576

Maas, H.S. (1963) The young adult adjustment of twenty wartime residential nursery children, *Child Welfare*, Vol. 42, 57–72

Maccoby, E., and Masters, J.C. (1970) Attachment and dependency. In P.H. Mussen (ed.), *Carmichael's Manual of Child Psychology*, 3rd edition. New York: Wiley

Mead, M. (1962) A cultural anthropologist's approach to maternal deprivation. In *Deprivation of Maternal Care: A Reassessment of its Effects.* Geneva: World Health Organization

Meeker, M.N. (1969) *The Structure of the Intellect.* Columbus, Ohio: Merrill

Moriarty, A.E. (1966) *Constancy and I.Q. Change.* Springfield, Ill.: C.C. Thomas

Newton, G. and Levine, S. (eds.) (1968) *Early Experience and Behaviour: The Psychobiology of Development.* Springfield, Ill.: C.C. Thomas

Patton, R.G., and Gardner, L.I. (1963) *Growth Failure in Maternal Deprivation.* Springfield, Ill.: C.C. Thomas

Piaget, J. (1952) *The Origins of Intelligence in Children.* New York: International Universities Press

Prechtl, H.F.R. (1963) The mother-child interaction in babies with minimal brain damage. In B.M. Foss (ed.), *Determinants of Infant Behaviour*, Vol. 2, London: Methuen

Pringle, M.L. (1966) *Social Learning and its Measurement.* London: Longmans

Pringle, M.L., and Bossio, V. (1958) Intellectual emotional and social development of deprived children, *Vita Humana*, Vol. 1, 66–92

Pringle, M.L., and Bossio V. (1960) Early prolonged separations and emotional adjustment. *J. Child Psychol. Psychiat.*, Vol. 1, 37–48

Provence, S., and Ritvo, S. (1961) Deprivation in institutionalized infants. *Psychoanal. Stud. Child*, Vol. 26, 189. New York: International Universities Press

Provence, S., and Lipton, R.C. (1962) *Infants in Institutions.* New York: International Universities Press

Rapaport, D. (1961) *Diagnostic psychological testing,* Vol. 1. Chicago: Year Book Pub. Inc.

Rheingold, H.L. (1956) The modification of social responsiveness in institutional babies. Monogr. *Soc. Res. Child Develop.* Vol. 21, Serial No. 63

Rheingold, H.L. (1961) The effect of environmental stimulation upon social and exploratory behaviour in the human infant. In B.M. Foss (ed.) *Determinants of Infant Behaviour*, Vol. 1. London: Methuen

Rheingold, H.L. (1969) The effect of a strange environment on the behaviour of infants. In B.M. Foss (ed.), *Determinants of Infant Behaviour*, Vol. 4. London: Methuen

Rheingold, H.L., and Bayley, N. (1959) The later effects of an experimental modification of mothering. *Child Devel.*, Vol. 30, 363–72

Rheingold, H.L., Gewirtz, J., and Ross, H. (1959) Social conditioning of vocalizations in the infant, *J. Comp. Physiol. Psychol.*, Vol. 52, 68–73

Ribble, M. (1944) *Infantile Experience in Relation to Personality Development: Personality and the Behavior Disorders.* J.McV. Hunt (ed.). New York: Columbia University Press

Riese, H. (1962) *Healing the Hurt Child*. Chicago: University of Chicago Press

Robertson, J. (1952) *A Two Year Old Goes to Hospital* (11 mm sound film with guidebook). Tavistock Child Development Research Unit

Robertson, J. (1958) *Going to Hospital with Mother* (16 mm sound film with guidebook). Tavistock Child Development Research Unit

Robertson, J., and Bowlby, J. (1952) Responses of young children to separation from their mothers, *Courr. Cent. Int. Enf.*, Vol. 2, 131–42

Robertson, J., and Robertson, J. (1967) *Young Children in Brief Separation: I. Kate, Aged Two Years Five Months in Fostercare for Twenty-seven Days.* Tavistock Child Development Research Unit

Robertson, J., and Robertson, J. (1968a) *Young Children in Brief Separation: II. Jane, Aged Seventeen Months in Fostercare for Ten Days.* Tavistock Child Development Research Unit

Robertson, J., and Robertson, J. (1968b) *Young Children in Brief Separation: III. John, Aged Seventeen Months Nine Days in a Residential Nursery.* Tavistock Child Development Research Unit

Robins, L.N. (1966) *Deviant Children Grown Up.* Baltimore: Williams & Wilkins

Rosenthal, R., and Jacobson, L.F. (1968) *Pygmalion in the Classroom: Teacher Expectation and Pupils' Intellectual Development.* New York: Holt, Rinehart & Winston

Roudinesco, J. (1952) Severe maternal deprivation and personality development in early childhood, *Understanding the Child*, Vol. 21, No. 4

Rutter, M. (1972) *Maternal Deprivation Reassessed.* Harmondsworth: Penguin Books

Ryan, T.J. (1972) *Poverty and the Child.* Toronto: McGraw Hill Ryerson

Schaffer, H.R. (ed.) (1969) *The Origins of Human Relations.* New York: Academic Press

Schaffer, H.R. (1971) *The Growth of Sociability.* Harmondsworth: Penguin Books

Schaffer, H.R. (1971) *The Origin of Human Social Relations.* Proceedings of Conference, London 1969. London and New York: Academic Press

Scott, J.P. (1968) *Early Experience and the Organization of Behavior.* Belmont: Brooks/Cole Publishing

Scrimshaw, N.D., and Gordon, J.E. (1968) *Malnutrition, Learning and Behavior.* Cambridge: M.I.T. Press

Siegal, Sidney (1956) *Non-parametric Statistics for the Behavioural Sciences.* New York: McGraw-Hill

Skeels, H.M. (1966) Adult status of children with contrasting early life experiences, Monogr. *Soc. Res. Child Devel.*, Vol. 31

Skodak, M., and Skeels, H.M. (1949) A final follow-up study of one hundred adopted children, *J. Genet. Psychol.*, Vol. 75, 85–125

Spitz, R.A. (1945) Hospitalism: An enquiry into the genesis of psychiatric conditions in early childhood. *Psychoanalytic Study of the Child*, Vol. 1, 53–74

Stone, L.J., Murphy, L.B., and Smith, H.T. (eds.) (1973) *The Competent Infant*. New Jersey: Basic Books

Taylor, A. (1968) Institutionalized infants' concept formation ability, *Am. J. Orthopsychiat.*, Vol. 38, 110

Taylor, A. (1968) Deprived infants: Potential for affective adjustment, *Am. J. Orthopsychiat.*, Vol. 38, No. 5

Taylor, A. (1970) Follow-up of institutionalized infants' concept formation ability at age 12, *Am. J. Orthopsychiat.*, Vol. 40, No. 3

Thomas, A., Chess, S., and Birch, H.G. (1968) *Temperament and Behavior Disorders in Children*. New York: New York University

Tizard, J. (1969) The role of social institutions in the causation, prevention, and alleviation of mental retardation. In C. Hayward (ed.) *Socio-Cultural Aspects of Mental Retardation*. New York: Academic Press

Tizard, J., and Tizard, B. (1971) The social development of two year old children in residential nurseries. In H.R. Schaffer (ed.) *The Origins of Human Social Relations*. New York: Academic Press

Tizard, J., and Tizard, B. (1972) The institution as an environment for development. In M.P. Richards (ed.) *The Integration of a Child into a Social World*. New York: Academic Press

Trasler, G. (1960) *In Place of Parents: A Study of Foster Care*. London: Routledge and Kegan Paul

Turner, F.J. (ed.) *Differential Diagnosis and Treatment in Social Work Part I. Stages of Human Development. Part II Psychosocial Pathology*. New York: The Free Press; London: Collier Macmillan

Warner, L., Havinghurst, R., and Loeb, M. (1944) *Who Shall Be Educated?* New York: Harper Bros.

White, B.L. (1971) *Human Infants: Experience and Psychological Development*. Englewood Cliffs, N.J.: Prentice-Hall

Wolkind, S. (1971) Children in care: A psychiatric study, M.D. Thesis, University of London

Yarrow, L.J. (1961) Maternal deprivation: Toward an empirical and conceptual re-evaluation, *Psychol. Bull.*, Vol. 58, 459–90

Yarrow, L.J. (1963) Research in dimensions of early maternal care, *Merrill-Palmer Quart.*, Vol. 9, 101–14

Yarrow, L.J. (1964) Separation from parents during early childhood. In M.L. Hoffman and L.W. Hoffman (eds.), *Review of Child Development Research*, Vol. 1. New York: Russell Sage Foundation